*The City and the Wilderness*

THE CALIFORNIA WORLD HISTORY LIBRARY

*Edited by Edmund Burke III, Kenneth Pomeranz, and Patricia Seed*

# The City and the Wilderness

## INDO-PERSIAN ENCOUNTERS
## IN SOUTHEAST ASIA

*Arash Khazeni*

UNIVERSITY OF CALIFORNIA PRESS

University of California Press
Oakland, California

© 2020 by Arash Khazeni

Library of Congress Cataloging-in-Publication Data

Names: Khazeni, Arash, author.
Title: The city and the wilderness : Indo-Persian encounters in Southeast Asia /
    Arash Khazeni.
Other titles: California world history library.
Description: Oakland, California : University of California Press, [2020] |
    Series: California world history library | Includes bibliographical references
    and index.
Identifiers: LCCN 2019045358 (print) | LCCN 2019045359 (ebook) |
    ISBN 9780520289680 (cloth) | ISBN 9780520289697 (paperback) |
    ISBN 9780520964266 (ebook)
Subjects: LCSH: Imperialism—Social aspects—Burma—History—18th
    century. | Burma—Description and travel. | India—Description and travel. |
    Iran—Description and travel.
Classification: LCC DS527.5 .K47 2020 (print) | LCC DS527.5 (ebook) |
    DDC 915.9104/3—dc23
LC record available at https://lccn.loc.gov/2019045358
LC ebook record available at https://lccn.loc.gov/2019045359

Manufactured in the United States of America

28  27  26  25  24  23  22  21  20
10  9  8  7  6  5  4  3  2  1

*For Noel Minus of Isfahan, Rangoon, Los Angeles*

# CONTENTS

# CONTENTS

# ILLUSTRATIONS

## MAPS

## FIGURES

# PREFACE

Through the morning mist of the surrounding hills, the devotees arrived to the temple Dukkanthein Paya with offerings in hand. The labyrinthine stone temple dates back to the late sixteenth century, its spiraling hallways lined with carved Buddha images leading to an inner gallery to reveal a sunlit golden Buddha in the Bhumiparsha *mudra,* or the earth-touching position. A crowd of blacksmiths were busy at work outside the walls of the temple, and fires were lit in the dawn to melt the ore for the casting of a new Buddha image. The gifts brought by the visitors as offerings to the temple were dented and bent scraps of old metal, discarded and placed in heaps at the blacksmiths' fires. That was the scene one morning in the old royal city of Mrauk U in Rakhine State of western Myanmar when I happened to travel there in the winter of 2014. I was visiting as a sort of pilgrimage to see what visible traces remained of the former Indo-Persian and Muslim subjects of the kingdom. But there were no signs of the old, destroyed Santikan Mosque or the residence of the Mughal prince Shah Shuja' and his Kaman archers. There were only ashes left. My guide Aung was left to navigate my wayward desire to break with the standard Mrauk U tour itinerary of famed Buddhist temples to seek out long-forgotten Muslim mosques and shrines. It was a tense time; most of the contested Muslim sites in Rakhine State were under "military guard" due to the violence committed against the Rohingya Muslims, and I had to receive special permission from the government to travel there in the first place. But that morning, Aung promised me, would be unique and allow me the chance to "make merit" by observing the casting of a golden image.

Standing above one of the heaps of metallic rubble on the ground to be sacrificed to the fire and image, I could see inscribed Persian letters from beneath the detritus of discarded and broken scraps of metal. Reaching down into the pile and brushing aside the dirt, I found a dozen trilingual Persian copper coins on the ground among the scraps to be melted down. The inscriptions on the coins—I was allowed to save and keep them for a donation— read in Persian, "*Shah 'Alam Badshah san-i jalus-i si u haft*"; they were minted in the thirty-seventh year of the reign of the Mughal emperor Shah 'Alam II (r. 1760–1806), circa 1796. The reverse side of the coins gave the denomination in Devanagari and Bengali script. Minted by the East India Company's Bengal Presidency in Calcutta, and exchanged beyond the Burmese frontier, the objects were relics from the end of a faded time of contacts and interconnections between the Indo-Persian world and Mrauk U. I had never planned to write a book about Burma, but after this encounter I set out to find everything I could in Persian about the Burmese and Arakanese kingdoms during the turn from the eighteenth to the nineteenth century.

Not long after, I realized that this search for an Indo-Persian Burma was also a search to understand a family. My wife Dana's grandfather, Noel Minus, a descendant of the Minassian family from the Armenian quarter of Julfa in Isfahan, whose ancestors had migrated from Iran to Burma to become envoys and merchants to Burmese kings in the eighteenth and nineteenth centuries, used to tell me stories back when I did not even know where Burma was. His tales of connections between Iran, India, and Burma once seemed distant to me, but standing amid the ruins of Dukkanthein, with Mughal coins in hand, those stories seemed closer. That is why this book is dedicated to the memory of the late Noel Minus—of Isfahan, Rangoon, and Los Angeles—and his beloved Nancy from the Shan Hills. This book is for the two of them, their descendants Christine, Dana, David—and Conrad. Family members still in Rangoon, Rachel and Richard, inspired my endeavors to salvage something of Indo-Persian Burmese history.

In Myanmar, I had the privilege of learning from friends who helped me in so many different ways. Sultan was an unforgettable friend and guide who shared his unmatched knowledge of the landscape of mosques and *dargahs* in Rakhine State. Soe was a brilliant companion in exploring the coastline and rivers of the Bay of Bengal and translating the Burmese inscriptions on the unusual tombs of saints we passed along the way. Other friends in Rakhine, often the keepers of shrines, welcomed me and shared their insights generously: 'Abd al-Hadi, 'Ali, Khin, Aung, and Saw Ran. In Rangoon, Than Htun welcomed me with warmth and hospitality, while sharing his knowledge of Burmese history and his wonderful collection of books.

Other friends and confidantes around the world helped immensely in the process of researching and writing this book. I am grateful to Annabel Gallop and San San May of the British Library for their gracious assistance in finding and deciphering rare Persian materials on Southeast Asia in the collection, such as the *farman* of Chandrawizaya Raja. I thank Kristina Münchow and other archivists at Staatsbibliothek zu Berlin for allowing me access to the Persian-Magh manuscripts in the John Murray MacGregor Collection. I had the opportunity to present versions of chapters of this book in various institutional settings, including Duke University, Princeton University, the University of California, Los Angeles, the University of Texas, and Yale University, where I received helpful feedback. I thank the European Research Council project, "Lawforms: Transactions and Documentation in the Persianate World," at the University of Exeter and its lead investigators Nandini Chatterjee, Fahad Bishara, and Christoph Werner for including my research in the project and its conversations. An earlier version of chapter 2 appeared in the journal *Past & Present,* and I thank Alexandra Walsham and the journal's editorial staff.

Various friends and colleagues offered essential feedback and suggestions that rendered this a better book, though all mistakes are mine to bear: Muzaffar Alam, Abbas Amanat, Assef Ashraf, Sebouh Aslanian, Fahad Bishara, Naindeep Chann, Nandini Chatterjee, John Demos, Thibaut d'Hubert, Emma Flatt, Annabel Gallop, Ali Gheissari, Dru Gladney, Nile Green, Mimi Hanaoka, Domenico Ingenito, Zayn Kassam, Ranin Kazemi, Mana Kia, Nabuoki Kondo, Susan McWilliams, Albert Park, Khodadad Rezakhani, James Scott, Sunil Sharma, Daniel Sheffield, Philip Stern, Sanjay Subrahmanyam, Ousmane Traoré, Farzin Vejdani, Alexandra Walsham, Christoph Werner, and Waleed Ziad. I thank the late Melford Spiro and Dennis Wills for all the Burma books. At Pomona College, this work has been sustained by the support of my colleagues and friends in the Department of History: Gina Brown-Pettay, Angelina Chin, Pey-Yi Chu, Gary Kates, Sidney Lemelle, April Mayes, Char Miller, Victor Silverman, Tomás Summers Sandoval, Miguel Tinker Salas, Ousmane Traoré, Helena Wall, Ken Wolf, and Sam Yamashita. During the course of writing this book, I have had the good fortune to have known and worked with brilliant students who have offered their time, help, and wisdom, and I should note the particular assistance of Anisha Bhat, Beshouy Botros, Jacinta Chen, Noor Dhingra, Sana Khan, Niyati Shenoy, and Ei Phyu Theint, who at some point connected with this project from Los Angeles to London to Rangoon. The support of the Hirsch Research Initiation Grant at Pomona College was essential to getting this project off the ground. A subvention from the Luce Foundation's EnviroLab Asia supported the production of the maps and index. My editor at the University of California Press, Niels Hooper, provided unstinting support from the beginning. I am grateful to Robin Manley, Kate Hoffman, Julie Van Pelt, and the editorial team at the press for all their patient and careful assistance in the book's production.

As ever, my deepest gratitude goes to my family, who have been with this project through many of its distant travels and its highs and lows. Farah, as always, nurtured and supported my research, even when it took me to unexpected terrains. To my beloved Dana, Layla, and Aiden, I am grateful for the journeys and the trekking to all those temples and mosques, times that I hope you will remember.

# NOTE ON TRANSLITERATION AND DATES

The Persian transliteration in this book follows the transliteration scheme of the *International Journal of Middle East Studies,* simplified without such diacritical marks as macrons and dots, while preserving the ayn and hamza. The standardized transliteration of Persian words and names is followed in all cases, except for words and names of people and places that have established renditions in English script. The ending *h* has been dropped for words such as *safarnama* but retained in instances where it is included in the standard English spelling for words such as *padishah* and *dargah.*

Dates are given in the Common Era calendar, except in cases where there is reason to include the Islamic lunar Hijri calendar.

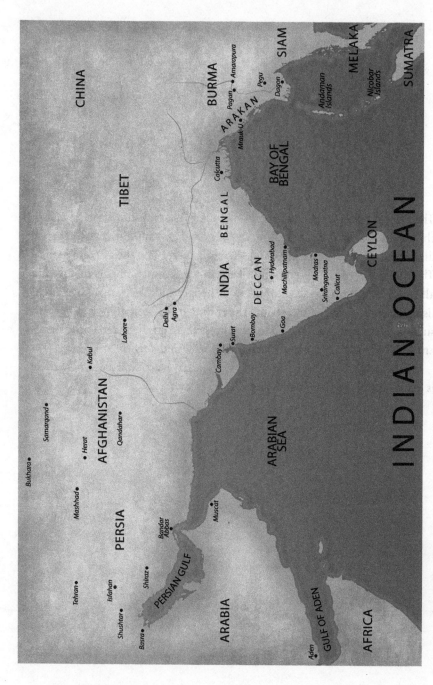

MAP 1.  Indian Ocean, from the Persian Gulf to the Bay of Bengal.

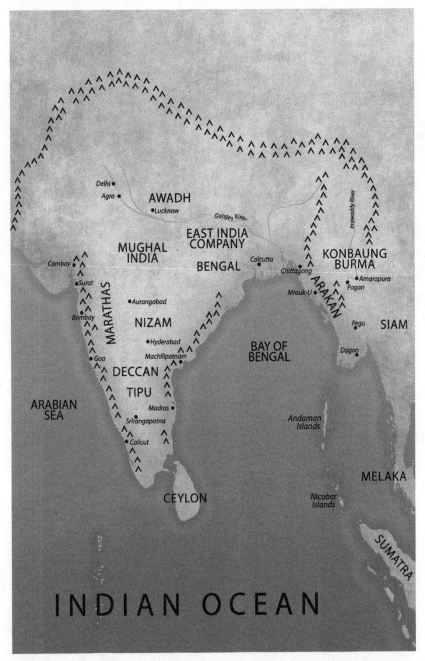

MAP 2. Bay of Bengal, detailing the main points of contact between Mughal India, Arakan, and the Burmese Konbaung Empire.

# *Introduction*

TUCKED AWAY DOWN A SIDE STREET on the northern fringes of
Rangoon, downhill from the golden spires and finials of Shwe Dagon Pagoda,
lies the grave of the last Mughal emperor of India, Bahadur Shah Zafar II
(1772–1862). There in a wooden house off U Wisara Road, the deposed king
lived the last four years of his life in exile, far from the majesty of Delhi's Red
Fort. The Mughal king was exiled to Rangoon along with his wife, Zinat
Begum Mahal, and family in 1858 following the defeat of the Sepoy Rebellion
against British rule in India. Kept under house arrest in a foreign land, without even a pen to write lines of his beloved Urdu poetry, Bahadur Shah Zafar
spent his last days in despair, etching verses on the walls of his prison with
burned pieces of wood. When he died in 1862, his body was placed in a
shroud and hastily buried without ceremony in an unmarked grave in the
garden of the enclosure. There was to be no trace of the resting place of the
last Mughal. In time, the site became hallowed as a dargah, the tomb of a Sufi
saint and a place of pilgrimage, visited by Indian and Burmese Muslims to
gain blessings, or *baraka*. The location of the grave remained a mystery until
1991, when workers unearthed it while digging at the site, and the tomb has
since been enshrined by a green gilt-edged silk cloth, in a space with a memorial and verses attributed to the king engraved on the walls.

Bahadur Shah Zafar was among the last of a trail of "Mughal" travelers
from India to the Burmese Kingdom. Since the early modern period, Indo-
Persian traders, soldiers, slaves, refugees, and royal intermediaries from India
and Iran had established a presence in the Southeast Asian mainland, with
Persian becoming established as a language of inter-Asian trade, diplomacy,
and literature. These crossings and connections persisted to the turn of
the nineteenth century and became transformed as Indo-Persian travelers,

scholars, diplomats, artists, and scribes in Mughal India with connections to the East India Company came into closer contact with the Burmese Empire and its littoral in Southeast Asia. As Persian peaked as a language of exchange and correspondence during times of transition from Mughal sovereignty to colonial rule, inter-Asian travels and encounters yielded new descriptions and mappings of the Southeast Asian frontiers of India. This wave of colonial Persian accounts of Southeast Asia merged Indo-Persian knowledge and its perceptions of the wondrous edges of the Indian Ocean with the Orientalist pursuits of the East India Company and its scientific wing, the Asiatic Society, in surveying Indic environments, economies, empires, languages, and religions. Indo-Persian travel writers inscribed the Burmese Empire as a sovereign ecological and cultural space, a forest landscape and Buddhist kingdom on the margins of the Mughal world.[1]

In this transitional period between Indo-Persian Mughal and European colonial empires, the Burmese borderland of India came to be defined. As the Mughal Empire disintegrated, Indo-Persian travelers found in the Burmese Konbaung Empire a still-lasting Indic imperial space, writing graphic new accounts of the Southeast Asian kingdom and its littoral marked by the empiricism and estrangement of new travels and contacts. Early modern views of the Burmese borderland as a liminal and wondrous forest region at the ends of the world, a place both close-by and faraway, were recast as a distinct geo-cultural space. In this way, late eighteenth– and early nineteenth-century Indo-Persian connections to the Burmese Empire also fostered disconnections and the construction of a hardening sense of difference.[2] The place of the Burmese Kingdom as the frontier of the Indo-Persian world, and an earlier inter-Asian context, has been obscured and almost forgotten in times of colonial and postcolonial belonging.

## OF THE INDO-PERSIAN PERIPHERY

The history of Indo-Persian contact with Southeast Asia remains obscure, but for centuries a global system of interimperial trade linked Mughal India to the Southeast Asian mainland and archipelago. By the fifteenth century, Islam had become established through trade and pilgrimage in the Indonesian Archipelago, while on the Southeast Asian mainland Buddhist empires blending Islamic and Indo-Persian influences rose to power. Although most of the kingdoms of mainland Southeast Asia did not convert to Islam, unlike in the archipelago, the growth and spread of Theravada Buddhism stimulated trade and interaction with Islamic, Indo-Persian societies.

The "Persianate world" refers to the early modern geographical continuum where Persian once had a presence as a spoken or written language of courtly literature and correspondence. During the period from 1400 to 1800, it encompassed Safavid Iran, Timurid Central Asia, Mughal India, and parts of the Ottoman Empire. The genealogy of the concept of the Persianate is traceable to Marshall Hodgson's *The Venture of Islam*. Hodgson defined it as a linguistic and cultural space created through the shared Persian language "within Islamdom."[3] Hodgson's main project was to conceive of Islamic history as world history through the notion of the "Islamicate," a wide Afro-Eurasian ecumene extending from the "Nile to Oxus" river regions, and its subdivision of the "Persianate zone," east of the Euphrates valley in West, South, and Central Asia.[4] Hodgson's concept of the Persianate attempted to capture an alternate cultural and linguistic "zone" of Islam, a world connected not by Arabic and sharia-minded Islam but rather by Persian, its vernacular literature, and heterodoxical and antinomian religious practices. This Persianate ecumene, identified with the "bloom of Persian literary culture," cohered after the "classical age of Islam" and Arabic and roughly coincided with the age of the medieval Turko-Mongol empires and their early modern successors of the Timurid, Safavid, Mughal, and Ottoman empires in times that Hodgson called "the expansion of Islam in the Middle Periods."[5]

From the beginning, Hodgson's Persianate view held the promise of breaking free from certain geographically bound and traditional conceptions of Islamic, Near or Middle Eastern, and Iranian and Indian history. But perhaps due in part to Hodgson's enigmatic nomenclature, the concept of Persianate, similar to its counterpart Islamicate, did not take off at first. The idea of the Persianate simmered in its first decades but has flowered since the late 1990s, particularly in the context of the revival of world and global history and discontent with the paradigms of nationalist historiography. There has been a lively return to Hodgson's concept in what could be identified as a historiographical movement in the field, a "Persianate turn," disrupting the enclosed framings of Iranian and Indian nationalist historiography.[6] Meanwhile, two recent edited collections have surveyed the emerging field of Persianate studies and attempted to define its scope and contours.[7]

While concerned with parallel processes of interconnection, this book by contrast does not use the frame of the Persianate world. Rather than explicitly setting out to define the boundaries and limits of an intertwined geographical and shared cultural formation that was Persianate, this project adopts the concept of encounters to trace Indo-Persian contacts and exchanges with a specific ecological and cultural space, the Southeast Asian frontier of the Mughal world. The perspective of Indo-Persian encounters permits a more close-up view and consideration of not only connections and exchanges but also the construction of difference and alterity.[8] What is more, this was an Indo-Persian world, as opposed to the often Iran-centric notion of the Persianate world, in the sense that while the language of writing and cultural exchange was indeed Persian, a vast corpus of Persian literature, especially works on Southeast Asia, was produced within a Mughal and South Asian context, with its audience composed predominantly of South Asian readers. It was through India that Persian reached the Southeast Asian mainland.

Southeast Asia represented the farthest limits of Indo-Persian geographical and cultural space—the fringes of the Indian subcontinent. Hodgson referred to Southeast Asia as "the most distant parts" of the Islamicate world and "Perso-Arabic culture," but he noted the role of the Indian Ocean, "the Southern Seas, those from the South China Sea to the Red Sea, which carried the goods of the land from Nile to Indus, of China, and of the Indic lands in between, and of East Africa and Malaysia," in spreading "Irano-Semitic" culture via "commercial life" and blending it with the "Indic" cultural landscape of the Southeast Asian mainland and archipelago.[9] In this new ocean world of Islam, "every merchant was a missionary, and even sayyids, sometimes from the older centres from Nile to Oxus . . . were wont to tour the remoter outposts to gather honours and perhaps also souls." Islam in Southeast Asia was "strongly Sufi-minded," and conversion occurred through "the development of Sufism as a matrix of a faith of the masses" and its "itinerant preachers," whose spiritual message of revival "was accessible to people of any background."[10] Thus, Hodgson claimed, "the Muslims in all these southeastern areas brought their traditional culture from the lands from Nile to Oxus."[11]

Hodgson's passage on Islamicate Southeast Asia was preliminary and schematic, but it contained some key observations. Hodgson noted the connective role of India and "South Indian merchant groups" in spreading Islamicate culture "along the Malay peninsula and the north Sumatra coast."[12] He also alluded to important contrasts between the mainland and archipelago, "between the great mainland river valleys and the island archipelago." Whereas along the inland river valleys of Southeast Asia, such as the Irrawaddy Delta, there grew "large kingdoms" that "remained Buddhist" but maintained contacts with Muslims on their "coastlands," in the Southeast Asian archipelago, such as Malaya and Sumatra, "agrarian rice growing kingdoms" steeped in the "Indic tradition" were "everywhere near to the sea" and thus converted to Islam.[13]

Although the Islamic Southeast Asian archipelago, where the Arabic script Jawi used for writing the Malay and Acehnese languages prevailed, has been the subject of a flourishing field of scholarship, the Buddhist Southeast Asian mainland, where the presence of Islamicate connections lay more hidden and where Persian was a lingua franca of trade, diplomacy, and literature, has been overlooked.[14] Held back by ingrained constructions of regional and cultural boundaries, studies of the Indo-Persian and Mughal worlds have only rarely explored interactions with Southeast Asia.[15] A pioneering early foray into the subject was written by the French Orientalist Gabriel Ferrand, whose *Relations de voyages et textes géographiques arabes, persans et turks relatifs à l'Extrême-Orient,* published in 1913, included a compilation of Persian accounts of Southeast and East Asia from the eighth to the eighteenth century. During the 1960s, the Italian Orientalist of Persian literature Alessandro Bausani examined the influence of the Persian language in Southeast Asia in such works as *Malesia: Poesie e leggende* and *Le letterature del sud-est asiatico.*[16] It was only in the 1980s, within the nascent field of the history of the Indian Ocean world, with its focus on transregional economic and cultural exchanges, that a body of work on Indo-Persian and Mughal Southeast Asia began to take shape. The publications of the French scholar Jean Aubin, including his seminal essay "Les Persans au Siam sous le règne de Narai, 1656–1688" and his book *Marchands et hommes d'affaires asiatiques dans l'Océan Indien et la Mer de Chine,* coedited with Denys Lombard, revealed an early modern world of the Indian Ocean that embraced the kingdoms of Southeast Asia within the sphere of the Mughal realm, connected by the Persian language and its literary and imperial culture.[17]

Most recently, Sanjay Subrahmanyam has brought to light the importance of Persian as a language of trade, literature, and diplomatic contact between South and Southeast Asia, in particular among the kingdoms of Ayutthaya in Thailand and Mrauk U in Arakan (now Rakhine State), in a range of essays that have appeared in such works as the two-volume *Explorations in Connected History* and *Indo-Persian Travels in the Age of Discoveries,* the latter coauthored with Muzaffar Alam.[18] Complementing studies of Islam in the Malay world and the Indonesian Archipelago based on the Arabic script Jawi, the emphasis in this sparser strand of the literature has been on Persianization in early modern Southeast Asian courts and the role of Persian as a language of imperial culture and exchange between the kingdoms of Burma (Myanmar) and Thailand into the seventeenth century.[19] Richard Eaton has likewise conveyed the porous nature of the borderlands between the Indian subcontinent and the Bay of Bengal region in late medieval and early modern times through an examination of the "frontiers of Islam" in the forests and tidal marshes of Bengal, and more recently from the perspective of the wide Indo-Persian cultural complex of the "Persian cosmopolis" in the Deccan.[20]

What remains to be discovered, however, is how Indo-Persian connections with Southeast Asia persisted and were altered during the late Mughal and early East India Company period through the production of colonial Persian texts and narratives. The prevailing impression has been that the early modern Indo-Persianate world had "ruptured" during the crises of the eighteenth century and been "eclipsed" by the nineteenth century as the Mughal Empire disintegrated and waned. But this process of unraveling was punctuated by elements of continuity as the spell of the Persian language lasted and spread still farther in the late eighteenth and early nineteenth centuries, reaching new places in new ways before its eventual decline in the 1830s. During this time of transition from the Mughal to the colonial era, Persian reached the Southeast Asian littoral of the Indian Ocean as a medium of contact, correspondence, and translation. In the aftermath of the East India Company's conquest of Bengal and the establishment of the Asiatic Society in the late eighteenth century, Persian was the language through which the company came to know the Burmese Empire, and until the First Anglo-Burmese War (1824–26) it remained the diplomatic lingua franca between the East India Company and the Konbaung dynasty, the rulers of Burma.

## INDO-PERSIAN TRAVEL WRITING

Indo-Persian contacts and exchanges with Southeast Asia came to be recorded in forms of travel literature. The genre of the *safarnama* (travel book) chronicles the trails of travelers across the frontiers of the Indo-Persian world. The safarnama was an enduring genre in an Indo-Persian empire of letters, a genre that flourished from the eleventh through the nineteenth centuries and drew elements from Persian and Arabic geographies, road books, and wonder tales. In recent decades, scholarship on Persian travel writing has developed, exploring such themes as ethnographic descriptions and representations and the construction of cultural difference through readings of the rich archive of Persian travel literature.[21] With some notable exceptions, the existing studies have most often focused on travelers who were "westward bound," most often en route to "Farang," or Europe.[22] Still, thus far there have been only schematic explorations of Indo-Persian travel writing at its liminal edges on the oceanic frontiers of Southeast Asia.

One of these points of Indo-Persian reckoning with the Southeast Asian littoral occurred during the last decades of the eighteenth century, as the nascent Burmese dynasty and British Indian Empire converged in the tidal and forested marshes of the Bay of Bengal. By the late eighteenth century, the Burmese Konbaung dynasty (1752–1885) had consolidated its rule over the Irrawaddy River delta and the adjacent coast of the Bay of Bengal, which had splintered into various overlapping Buddhist kingdoms since the fall of the Pagan Empire in the thirteenth century. In 1752, the Konbaung dynasty ousted the Mon, or Hanthawaddy Kingdom (1287–1539; 1740–57) of Lower Burma from the capital of Ava on the upper Irrawaddy River and in 1757 took the Mon city of Pegu, continuing its southern expansion to the Thai Kingdom of Ayutthaya in 1767. In 1784, with the conquest of the Arakanese Kingdom of Mrauk U (1430–1784) on the eastern shores of the Bay of Bengal, the boundaries of the Konbaung dynasty reached the edges of colonial Bengal under the rule of the East India Company. The East India Company had become established in the port city of Surat in 1601 and over the next century and a half evolved into a company-state in Bengal, with sway over the Mughal throne in Delhi and gradually reaching out into the princely states and outer kingdoms of India. Through their expansion, the Burmese Empire and the East India Company both became immersed within the prevailing Mughal imperial order that preceded them, adapting the language and repertoire of Indo-Persian courts. Within this context, the Burmese Empire and the East India Company in Bengal entered a wider Indo-Persian Mughal imperium and imperial constellation that ranged from the Middle East to South Asia, from Qajar Persia and Durrani Afghanistan to Mughal India and the princely states of Tipu Sultan and the Nizam of Hyderabad in the Deccan. The Burmese Kingdom comprised the liminal periphery, the eastern oceanic limits, of this Indo-Persian imperial and cultural space.

Due to this Indo-Persian empire of letters and the persistence of Persian as a language of trade, diplomacy, and correspondence, agents of the East India Company and the Indo-Persian intermediaries in their service in colonial Bengal began to study the land, culture, and customs of the hidden and little-known Burmese Kingdom. Indo-Persian writers and travelers, treading trails that linked the Mughal world and Southeast Asia, mediated the company's encounter with the Burmese Empire and left behind accounts of the kingdom's terrains and customs. From the late eighteenth century, they conducted surveys of the Southeast Asian empire's landscape and environment, translated the kingdom's Buddhist texts into Persian, and described the nature of its sovereignty. Long-established Indo-Persian and Mughal contacts with Southeast Asia, and their literary methods of description, were transformed in the early period of company rule and came to be recorded in colonial Persian accounts.

Indo-Persian and European travel literature shared a mutual concern for themes of mapping and representing "otherness," but these genres were often written from different perspectives. Indo-Persian travel books of the times blurred the lines between the peculiarities and differences in Persian and European genres of travel writing. They combined ethical narratives of journeys to idealized kingdoms with narratives of discovery. Following enduring themes in Indo-Persian travel literature, travelers wrote of Southeast Asia in the form of journeys through cities and wilderness to reach a wondrous realm at the far reaches of the Indian Ocean. But these Indo-Persian texts mapped the Burmese Kingdom in new ways and became tinged by contact with the East India Company, the Asiatic Society, and the colonial sciences of geography, botany, and archaeology, while becoming imbued with a sense of the Oriental sublime that reveled in the remoteness of vast, untouched natural landscapes. Merging elements from these different sciences and modes of travel, the authors of colonial Persian narratives mapped the Burmese Empire as a forest kingdom at the crossroads of South and Southeast Asia. In their visions of the "East," Indo-Persian intermediaries were merchants of a viable Mughal meridian that still reached the edges of Southeast Asia.

Persian is usually taken to be only the language of Iran, with its ardently nationalist historiography that time and again emphasizes the country's resistance to colonial occupation, its independence, and its emergence as a nation. While this is true on its face, there remain other, more global threads to trace in the trajectory of Persian and its contact with the colonial. In the field of South Asian historiography, such well-worn protonationalist characterizations of European colonial expansion and conquest, and of indigenous societies and vernacular cultures doomed to resist or be eclipsed and disappear, have given way to subtler explanations of the interactive, negotiated emergence of the colonial world during the late eighteenth and early nineteenth centuries. Initiated by works such as the late C. A. Bayly's *Empire and Information*, which appeared in 1996 and has had a key influence on this book, a series of studies have revealed the ways in which the colonial modern was shaped by the Indian context, and how it was that Indo-Persian and Mughal cultural practices lasted into the first decades of the nineteenth century.[23] These studies have brought nuance to postcolonial analyses of imperial expansion and cultural domination, including those spurred by Edward Said's groundbreaking *Orientalism* (1978) and works in the subaltern strand of South Asian historiography, which, despite offering radical critiques of colonialism, have tended to cast Asian societies as reacting to European empires and their knowledge systems.[24]

By contrast, newer literature on colonial encounters in South Asian history has detailed the lasting influence of Mughal imperial customs and cultural practices, including Indo-Persian and Mughal statecraft, language, and power, into the first decades of the nineteenth century, mediating and shaping the colonial experience in ways that disrupt the conventional binaries in narratives of colonialism. The emphasis in these works has remained mostly on the European encounter and its English-language archive, while taking account of the degree to which vernacular knowledge entered into the colonial "information order" and served the East India Company in "knowing the country" and expanding the frontiers of its Indian empire.[25] To date, the prevalent focus has remained on the ways in which indigenous knowledge shaped colonial expansion and ultimately the formation of a global "Imperial Meridian," which saw the dominion of the British Empire overseas in South Asia and the Middle East during the French Revolutionary and Napoleonic era.[26] Accordingly, the literature on munshis (scribes), native information gatherers, and scribal cultures under company rule has focused exclusively on the question of the colonial reception of the knowledge they gathered and its operation in colonial rule.[27] But this vernacular knowledge was also part of the persistence of a "Mughal Meridian," a still-lasting imperial repertoire; an Indo-Persian imperium and cultural world, which though in the years of its twilight, continued to shape inter-Asian connections and exchanges in the early colonial period.[28]

The question of how this was an interconnected Indo-Persian world, one that reached from Iran and India to the littoral of Southeast Asia, may be answered through the notebook of Qazi Ghulam Qasim Mihri, a traveler adrift on the Indian Ocean at the close of the eighteenth century. The journal, a manuscript in the British Library, contains poems and fragments in the form of *qasidas, ghazals,* and *masnavis* written in the Persian script of *shi-kasta amiz.*[29] The author, who assumes the *takhallus* (pen name) Qasim, begins his notebook with the heading "Verses of the Poor, Humble, and Lowly Qazi Ghulam Qasim Mihri."[30] In his poems, Qasim gradually reveals the fragments of his life and identity, and the ways his journeys crossed an entwined Indo-Persian world that reached the eastern edges of the Indian Ocean. In some of his poems, he identifies himself as "the son of Qazi Husayn, the learned of the age" (*fazil-i 'asr*) and "a native of Bombay" (*balada-yi Bombay mutivatin*).[31] While he does not give his occupation, he was possibly a mariner or itinerant lascar (soldier) of some sort, unmoored across the Indian Ocean. In certain poems, he identifies himself as a Sufi affiliated with the Naqshbandi and Qadiri orders, praising the founding saints of these *tariqa* and thus suggesting his immersion within Indo-Persian Sufi networks originating from Bukhara and Baghdad.[32]

Qasim's travels took him far from home and the main cores of the Indo-Persian world, however, and his venturesome path reached the eastern boundaries of the Indian Ocean in maritime Southeast Asia. A fragmentary poem on the truth and essence of God, written "in the time before sunrise on the night of the twenty-second of Jamada al-Awwal in the year 1205 [1791] off the port city of Bandar Aceh" on the island of Sumatra, conveys Qasim's far-flung passages.[33] Another poem, a long qasida, was composed the same year "in [the] end of the month of Dhu al-Hijjah off the coast of Ceylon during a voyage to the Nicobar Islands and Pegu."[34] The qasida is one of several in the notebook written in praise of Tipu Sultan (1750–99), ruler of the Kingdom of Mysore in the Deccan, famed for his resistance to British colonial expansion from his fortressed city of Seringapatam. In the course of his travels, Qasim does not so much long for home as he seeks to reach the court of Tipu Sultan, casting the prince as a heroic universal sovereign, an ethical king and Indo-Persian world ruler. In the qasida titled "Verses in Praise of Tipu Sultan Ghazi," he lauds the prince as a "warrior of the faith" (*ghazi*) and "the second coming of Alexander the Great" (*Sikandar-i thani*); "the shadow of truth" (*sayih-i haqq*) was found in his "glorious court" (*dargah-i jalalat*).[35] Qasim's journeys across the Indian Ocean and the travel notebook of verses he left behind are a record of an Indo-Persian traveler between South and Southeast Asia. What is more, his enigmatic verses offer views of the networked trails of the Persian language and its poetics, Sufi religious beliefs, and Persianate political mentalities and ethics on the Southeast Asian frontiers of the Indo-Persian world. Through the reading of travel and encounter literature, the following pages attempt to recover and piece together the fragments of the Indo-Persian encounter with Southeast Asia.

## SPACE AND SOVEREIGNTY

Indo-Persian travel writings on Southeast Asia inscribed the encounter with ecological space and the physical environment. In the late Mughal and early colonial period, such narratives were framed as travels to forest landscapes and kingdoms of the Indian Ocean. The forest worlds of Southeast Asia were a foreign terrain and unfamiliar ecology that came into focus through Indo-Persian conceptions of space and sovereignty. Indo-Persian travelers envisioned the forest landscape through narratives of the ideal ruler, the perfect sovereign, preserving natural and cosmological balance in the kingdom. Journeys to forest landscapes on the margins of the Indian Ocean cast as encounters with an ethical realm. In the Burmese Empire, Indo-Persian travelers and scribes depicted the land of a universal sovereign, lord of a forest kingdom and its manifold rarities. In narratives of kingship and sovereignty over the city and the wilderness, the Burmese Kingdom became rendered within an Indo-Persian and Mughal view of the world.

The theme of the city and the wilderness—in Persian, *abad u biyaban*—is a long-standing spatial motif in Persian literature. From legendary epics of crossing the frontier between the steppe and the sown, to the verses of Sufi poets on mystic wandering in the wilderness, to the chronicles of Islamic empires founded by pastoral peoples, the juxtaposition of the alternate spaces of cities and wilderness, the built environment of architecture and cultivated gardens within and the untamed abode of wildness beyond the city walls, have been recurring literary landscapes. The interface between inhabited and uninhabited places—between sedentary and pastoral spaces—defined Indo-Persian conceptions of nature and environment. Above all, the city and the wilderness were interconnected spaces, marked by a degree of symbiosis and crossed by those who wandered between the urban and the wilds. The landscape of cities and wilderness were interlinked and together formed a spatial conception of the balance of the world. In their accounts of the Burmese Empire, Indo-Persian writers described the kingdom's forest landscape in all its different manifestations. The forest was a landscape of refuge and sanctuary, the realm of a universal sovereign, the habitat of exotic flora and fauna, and a place of Buddhist wandering and enlightenment.

These narratives were premised upon certain views of space and sovereignty that do not mesh with the literature on the environmental history of South Asia, with its prevailing emphasis on British colonial transformations of environments and knowledge systems of the natural world. The predominant focus in the field has been on the ways in which the colonial experience altered South Asian environments through a repertoire of developmental measures that led to the "conquest" of environments and the rupture of the ecological practices of precolonial Asian empires.[36]

On the construction of built and natural environments in precolonial Asian empires we need to look to other strands of historiography. In the field of Mughal history, a body of work has evolved on the agrarian encroachment of South Asian empires and the built environment of cities onto the frontiers of wild, unsettled lands. Such works include Richard Eaton's *The Rise of Islam and the Bengal Frontier, 1204–1760,* on the Islamic conversion of the landscape in eastern India, and more recently his book written with Phillip Wagoner, *Power, Memory, Architecture,* on the material culture of fortresses in the Deccan.[37] In addition to studies of the agrarian transformations of frontier environments, a body of work in medieval and early modern South Asian history has turned to examine the subject of the nature of Indian empires, including the political ecology of the hunt, the domestication and imperial usage of elephants, and the spatial history of gardens.[38]

Quite separate from these studies of the physical and built environment of the Mughal world are works in the history of science that have examined South Asian knowledge systems about the natural world and their transfer into colonial scientific projects and paradigms. Beginning with Richard Grove's *Green Imperialism: Colonial Expansion, Tropical Island Edens and the Origins of Environmentalism, 1600–1860,* historians of European imperial science have acknowledged the influence of local environmental knowledge and practices in shaping new colonial attitudes about nature and its limits, noting the "pervasive and creative impact of the tropical and colonial experience on European natural science" and the "diffusion of indigenous environmental philosophy and knowledge into western thought." Still, the emphasis in *Green Imperialism* remains the synthesis of knowledge from the Indies within the expansive system of European Enlightenment, science, and environmentalism. Since then, the place of Indo-Persian knowledge in the history of science has been more explicitly detailed, even "relocated," becoming detached from notions of a vernacular influence on what remained essentially a European conception of the natural world and shifting to the view that knowledge of environments was mutually constructed and forged through encounters between European and Asian societies. This perspective on scientific knowledge as being built up through the "contact zone" of global interactions was introduced by Kapil Raj in *Relocating Modern Science: Circulation and the Construction of Knowledge in South Asia and Europe, 1650–1900*, and other works have subsequently explored the ways in which Indian intermediaries and their knowledge systems became transmitted and embedded into European colonial scientific practices.[39] Building on these strands of work that recognize the incorporation of local knowledge in the canon of European science, it now seems worthwhile to delve more deeply into the archive of vernacular representations of spaces and environments, not within the context of the European encounter but rather within the missing terrain of inter-Asian contacts and exchanges.

## THE CITY AND THE WILDERNESS

*The City and the Wilderness* explores microhistories of Indo-Persian connections with Southeast Asia in the late Mughal and early colonial periods of the late eighteenth and early nineteenth centuries. Through an archive of Indo-Persian travel writing and encounter narratives about the margins of the Indian Ocean in Southeast Asia, the book explores inter-Asian contacts and crossings on the Burmese frontier. It argues that Indo-Persian travelers, munshis, translators, scholars, and artists with ties to the East India Company and its Orientalist wing, the Asiatic Society, surveyed the Burmese Empire and its environment, sovereignty, and Buddhist customs as intermediaries and gobetweens, mapping the Southeast Asian kingdom as a sublime forest world stewarded by an ideal universal sovereign, a Buddhist landscape of marvels at the far ends of Mughal India.

Finding the traces of a lost world of inter-Asian encounters, *The City and the Wilderness* recounts the life journeys and microhistories of Indo-Persian travelers across the Indian Ocean and their experience of the Burmese Kingdom and its littoral.[40] Through fading histories of unknown or overlooked traverses recorded in late eighteenth- and early nineteenth-century Persian accounts of travel and encounter in Buddhist Southeast Asia, some found in manuscript at the British Library in London and the Staatsbibliothek in Berlin, it reveals the mobile and malleable geographies of Indo-Persian travelers who crossed the Indian Ocean and reached its edge. The following pages trace the paths of Indo-Persian contacts with the Burmese Empire, its forest landscape and Indian Ocean littoral, its royal court and Buddhist culture, to recover a lost trail of almost forgotten and now fading interconnections. These are the microhistories of an inter-Asian encounter.

Part 1, including the first two chapters, explores perceptions of Southeast Asia in travel literature in the Indo-Persian tradition of the safarnama, written as journeys across landscapes of city and wilderness to reveal distant foreign kingdoms. Part 2, consisting of the final three chapters, turns to Indo-Persian accounts more immersed in the colonial measures of the East India Company to survey and map the worlds of the Burmese Empire.

Chapter 1, "Offshore," follows the trail of two Persian drifters across the Indian Ocean. In 1766, Mirza Shaykh I'tisam al-Din, an Indian munshi from Bengal in the service of the East India Company, voyaged across the Indian Ocean from India to Europe. Following his return to India nearly three years later in 1769, he wrote a Persian account of his travels titled *Shigarfnama-yi vilayat*, or the "Wonder book of provinces." In it he described the wondrous places across land and sea that he encountered, including an overlooked detour through the islands, archipelagos, and kingdoms of Southeast Asia. The *Shigarfnama* became the prototype for subsequent late eighteenth-century Indo-Persian travel writing about the Indian Ocean that detailed inter-Asian contacts within a colonial context and merged Persianate and colonial knowledge about Southeast Asia.

Mirza I'tisam al-Din's *Shigarfnama* found echoes in the writings of Mirza Abu Talib Khan Isfahani, "a wanderer over the face of the earth," who set sail from Calcutta in March 1799 across the Indian Ocean on an East India Company ship bound for London. Offshore in the Bay of Bengal, Abu Talib Khan also had an eastern detour, to the Nicobar, a chain of islands extending from the littoral of the Burmese Empire to the Malay Archipelago. He was swept into the island world of the Indies, long seen by Muslim geographers as the far side of Asia, a mythical islanded region known as the lands "below the winds" of the Indian Ocean monsoons. In his book of travels, *Kitab-i masir-i Talibi*, Abu Talib Khan wrote of the Indian Ocean and its islands as the maritime edges of the Mughal world. Published in English in 1810 as *Travels of Mirza Abu Taleb Khan in Asia, Africa, and Europe*, his travelogue detailed the incomprehensible wonders and oddities of the sea, while also seeking to identify the natural history of the ocean, its submarine reefs and sea life, its island archipelagos, flora and fauna, and societies. It was a narrative of travel that mapped fragments of Indian Ocean geography and natural history. Abu Talib Khan's *Masir-i Talibi* brought together Indo-Persian and Orientalist knowledge to create a new account of the pelagic borderlands of Mughal India circa 1800. Through a reading of Mirza I'tisam al-Din and Abu Talib Khan's writings, chapter 1 examines the construction of Indo-Persian knowledge of the edges of the Indian Ocean and views of the Mughal Empire offshore during the late eighteenth century.

Chapter 2, "Of Elephants, Rubies, and Teak," explores the travels of Mir 'Abd al-Latif Khan Shushtari, an itinerant scholar and merchant from Iran, across the Indian Ocean from Basra in the Persian Gulf to Calcutta in the Bay of Bengal in 1788, during the waning of the Mughal Empire and the onset of East India Company rule in India. In his book of travels, *Tuhfat al-'alam* (Rarity of the world), written in Hyderabad in 1801, 'Abd al-Latif draws upon long-standing Mughal views of the wondrous nature of Southeast Asia, tinged by colonial notions of the sublime wildness of nature, to cast the Burmese Empire and its forest landscapes as the edges of the Mughal world. Through the narrative of a journey to the realm of a universal sovereign and ideal Indo-Persian king, a raja and a padishah, reigning over the city and the wilderness, 'Abd al-Latif surveyed the Burmese Empire as a vast forest kingdom, a land of dense jungles of teak, herds of wild elephants, and rich mines of precious stones, a mythical littoral region of exotics and strange customs, a distant half-known world on the frontiers of Islam.

Chapter 3, "Immortal City," examines the first official East India Company mission to the Burmese court, led by the Irish envoy Michael Symes in 1795. The embassy was dispatched at the height of Anglo-French imperial rivalries and the anticolonial resistance of Tipu Sultan in Southern India, at a time when the Burmese Konbaung dynasty had expanded and consolidated its rule on the Southeast Asian mainland. Symes's mission was to establish diplomatic contact with the Burmese Kingdom and to open up trade with its ports, the route to accessing the vast teak reserves of the interior. Fluent in Persian, Symes was accompanied by a crew of Orientalists, scientists, *pundits* (scholars), and munshis into an unknown imperial realm of outer India. Symes navigated the Southeast Asian kingdom and its foreign customs through his knowledge of Persian, corresponding with the Burmese sovereign and his representatives in Persian and following Indo-Persian, Mughal codes of conduct in interactions with the court in order to find common ground and complete his embassy. A narrative of the mission was recorded in Symes's extraordinary book of travels, *An Account of an Embassy to the Kingdom of*

*Ava* (1800). In content and style, Symes's travel account of a mission to the Indic forest realm of a Buddhist sovereign in the Indian Ocean reveals the immersion of European agents of the East India Company versed in Persian within the stream of contacts between Mughal India and Southeast Asia.

Chapter 4, "Forest Worlds," recovers the microhistory of an unknown Bengali botanical artist and the visual traces of Mughal encounters with Southeast Asia and the forest landscapes of the Burmese Kingdom. It follows the East India Company artist Singey Bey on a botanical expedition through the Burmese Empire. Singey Bey's botanical and landscape drawings were sketched during the 1795 East India Company embassy to the Burmese court and engraved and signed as lithographs in the printed narrative of the mission, *An Account of an Embassy to the Kingdom of Ava,* written by the envoy Michael Symes, the visual artifacts of a lost encounter in the Burmese forest. The embassy sought to open up access to the monsoon forests of the Burmese upland interior, which held three-quarters of the world's teak reserves, and came into contact with a forest landscape teeming with wildness and plant and animal life. As the mission journeyed up the Irrawaddy River into the upland forests of the interior and to the royal capital, Singey Bey strived to draw the environs encountered along the journey, most notably botanical drawings, which conveyed the abundant flora and fauna of the region's forests in the late eighteenth century. But there was more that he saw. Looking through the forest landscape, he perceived an archaeological terrain bearing signs of the material culture, relics, and idols of Theravada Buddhism and its cycles of the birth, destruction, and rebirth of the natural world: hieroglyphic footprints of the Buddha pressed in stone, bronze images of Gautama in the state of nirvana, cosmic temples and their gilded spires, and ornately carved monuments made of teak.

Chapter 5, "In the Wilderness of Pali," turns to examine the Indo-Persian Buddhist Kingdom of Mrauk U in Arakan. Based in the densely forested tidal backwaters of the Bay of Bengal, Mrauk U (1430–1784) was once a hub of Indian Ocean trade and the monumental capital of a syncretic Buddhist dynasty steeped in the Indo-Persian and Islamic court culture of Bengal and the Mughal Empire. In the aftermath of the conquest of Mrauk U in 1784 by the Burmese Konbaung dynasty (1752–1885), Buddhist Arakanese—in contact with Mughal India, and known as the "Magh"—fled across the Burmese borderlands into colonial Bengal. Due to the persistence of Persian as a language of mutual encounter and exchange between Mughal India and Burma, the East India Company came to rely on Indo-Persian intermediaries, travelers, and munshis tied to long-standing networks of exchange with Southeast Asia to survey and gather knowledge about the fallen Magh Kingdom of Mrauk U, in particular its syncretic Theravada Buddhist imaginary and culture. Through a body of rare late eighteenth-century Persian manuscripts produced by munshis for the Asiatic Society of Bengal—including ethnographic descriptions, botanies, and Buddhist cosmographies and variations of *jataka* tales translated from Pali into Persian—the hybrid Buddhist Indo-Persian world of Mrauk U comes to light. Playing a prominent role in this process of translation was Shah ʿAzizallah Bukhari Qalandar, a munshi in the service of East India Company Orientalist John Murray MacGregor (1745–1822) who ventured into the Bengal borderland and the ruins of Mrauk U to translate Theravada Buddhist texts from Pali into Persian. Through translation of its Buddhist cosmographical texts, he recast the kingdom within an Indo-Persian and Sufi imaginary.

The epilogue offers a retrospective on Indo-Persian contacts with the Burmese frontier detailed in the book through an archaeology of ruins. It turns from textual sources to the fading material culture and architectural traces of Indo-Persian connections to Myanmar. Based on travels and fieldwork in Myanmar between 2014 and 2016, it reads the material remains of Islamic sacred spaces—mosques, tombs, shrines, and their inscriptions—to close the book with a discussion of the lasting physical signs that mark the spaces of Indo-Persian encounters with the early modern Buddhist kingdoms of Myanmar. The cross-cultural connections between the Islamic Mughal world and Buddhist Southeast Asia found expression in the remarkably varied and cosmopolitan Muslim societies of the Burmese empires and the weathered temple-like stone mosques and dargah (tombs of Sufi saints) that still mark the urban and forest landscape of Myanmar. These ruins and remains of multiconfessional, syncretic Buddhist empires are now fast disappearing, lost to natural disasters, destroyed by human violence, and ravaged by the passing of time. These broken places are the vanishing remnants of a lost world of Indo-Persian connections, endangered by the hardening divide between Buddhist and Muslim identities and the intercommunal violence and climate of persecution that has decimated and displaced long-standing Muslim societies in Myanmar.

PART ONE

_____

*Indian Ocean Wonders*

# ONE

# *Offshore*

## MIRZA I'TISAM AL-DIN AND
## MIRZA ABU TALIB KHAN

IN MARCH 1799, THE INDO-PERSIAN TRAVELER Mirza Abu Talib
Khan Isfahani boarded an East India Company ship from Calcutta bound
across the Indian Ocean to London. The voyage would take him from the
Bay of Bengal along the edges of the Indian Ocean archipelago to the Arabian
Sea, around the cape of Africa, and ultimately to Europe, or "Farangistan."
Offshore in the Bay of Bengal, the ship was blown off course and, in need of
provisions, detoured in the Nicobar Islands, an archipelagic island chain at
the southeastern edge of the Bay of Bengal, extending from the coast of the
Burmese Empire to Sumatra. Enchanted by the forest environment and seascape of the Indian Ocean archipelago—its bountiful, sylvan seascapesand
idyllic, free societies—Mirza Abu Talib Khan and the Indian sepoys aboard
the ship found it an earthly paradise and sought to leave behind the burdens
of their seafaring lives and take refuge on the islands.

In his Persian book of travels, *Kitab-i masir-i Talibi* (Book of travels for
learning), published in English in 1810 as *Travels of Mirza Abu Taleb Khan
in Asia, Africa, and Europe,* Abu Talib Khan journeyed the span of the
Indian Ocean, from the maritime edges of the Mughal world in the East
Indies to the African littoral, before reaching Europe. His travelogue detailed
the incomprehensible wonders and oddities of the Indian Ocean and its
island archipelagos, describing the natural history and societies he encountered. Abu Talib framed his travel narrative as an Indo-Persian journey
*sayr va safar,* spanning the geography of the Indian Ocean but also incorporated Orientalist knowledge to create a hybrid colonial Mughal text.[1]
YKitab-i Masir-i Talibi was a text between worlds but has been seen only
through one side of the journey, its endpoint in Europe and the encounter
with London society, with its oceanic drift in Southeast Asia and its littoral

circa 1800 hardly being remembered.[2] Through a reading of Abu Talib Khan's writings juxtaposed with an earlier colonial Mughal narrative, *Shigarfnama-yi vilayat* (Wonder book of provinces) by Mirza I'tisam al-Din, this chapter examines the construction of Indo-Persian knowledge of the edges of the Indian Ocean and the Southeast Asian frontiers of the Mughal Empire in the late eighteenth century .

## THE STRANGE AND THE WONDERFUL:
## SOUTHEAST ASIA IN THE MUGHAL IMAGINATION

For Indo-Persian travelers, Southeast Asia was the geographical and cultural limit of the Indian Ocean world. In early modern Indo-Persian geographies, Southeast Asia was known as the *zirbad,* the "lands below the winds" of the Indian Ocean monsoons. An almost mythical forested realm of marvelous landscapes on the fringes of the Mughal world, its kingdoms belonged to the wonderful and enchanting oddities at the ends of the Indian Ocean. These perceptions of distance and difference came to be produced through contacts with Southeast Asia and were recorded in the accounts of sea captains, sailors, and mariners in such texts as Buzurg ibn Shahriyar's tenth-century *'Aja'ib al-Hind* (The wonders of India) and Zakariya Qazvini's thirteenth-century text on marvels, *'Aja'ib al-makhluqat wa ghara'ib al-mawjudat* (The wonders of creation and the strange things existing).[3] These perceptions of distance and difference were by the early modern period combined with more empirical and graphic descriptions formed through contacts with Southeast Asia, as new and distinct narratives of difference in the "lands below the winds" came to be produced.[4]

Long-standing notions of the "wonders" of the Indian Ocean, derived from stories of magic on oceans (*bahr*) and islands (*jazira*) told by Persian and Arab sea captains, sailors, and mariners, persisted into the late Mughal period.[5] These ocean tales were recounted in such texts as Qazvini's *'Aja'ib al-makhluqat wa ghara'ib al-mawjudat* on "the wonders of creation," variations of which continued to be reproduced in the workshops and libraries of Indo-Persian dynasties and princely states. An eighteenth-century Persian manuscript of Qazvini's *'Aja'ib* from India recounts marvelous voyages across the Indian Ocean (Bahr al-Hind), alternately called the China Sea (Bahr al-Sin), to mysterious foreign islands and kingdoms, and encounters with wondrous landscapes, unusual flora and fauna, and strange customs and practices.

In it are descriptions of the enigmatic and almost incomprehensible islands of Waq Waq, corresponding to the margins of the known world, somewhere in the chains of islands between India and China.[6] On the islands of Waq Waq could be found the wondrous Waq Waq tree, which bore fruit resembling young women, attached to the tree by their hair. When the fruit was ripe, the leaves of the tree emitted the enchanting sound *waq waq*. According to the eighteenth-century manuscript of Qazvini's text, "it is said that Waq Waq is comprised of a chain of seventeen hundred islands and ruled by a *padishah* who is a woman."[7] The manuscript refers to the tenth-century traveler from the Persian Gulf to China and India, Abu Zayd al-Hasan al-Sirafi, and his tales of travel *Akhbar al-Sin wa`l Hind,* which recounted meeting the queen of the Waq Waq islands, "Arjun," sitting in the nude upon the throne and wearing only a crown, surrounded by her similarly attired four thousand attendants.[8] In a variation on the legend of Waq Waq, the manuscript depicts the magical trees on the islands as bearing the heads of animals as fruit.[9] The geographical descriptions of the oceans and islands between India and China, and the edges of the knowable world, continued with accounts of the islands of Ramni and Zabaj, corresponding to Sumatra and Java, and the wondrous flora and fauna and oddities of existence to be found there—from forest-dwelling societies and their strange customs to mines of precious stones and metals to the unfamiliar species of rare trees, plants, and animals.[10]

These schematic and fantastical accounts of the wonders of Southeast Asia and the margins of the known regions of the Indian Ocean changed over time to adapt to new knowledge of the sea and its distant shores. Trade, diplomacy, and the prevalence of Persian as a literary and courtly language linked early modern empires across South and Southeast Asia. In the Kingdom of Ayutthaya in Thailand during the reign of King Narai (1656–88), a thriving community of Persian merchants from Safavid Iran attained influence and prestige in the Thai court. Likewise, the syncretic Buddhist Kingdom of Mrauk U in Arakan was steeped in the culture and trappings of Islamic kingship, with its kings adopting Persian names and minting their titles as "shahs" onto coins bearing the *kalima,* the profession of the Islamic creed.

This familiarity between the Indo-Persian world and Southeast Asia did not merely nourish connections; conversely, it also led to disconnections and the construction of difference in the writing of more empirical and observational tales of wonder and enchantment. The presence of Iranians and the influence of Persian in the court at Ayutthaya, as well as along the southern littoral of Burma in Pegu, were vividly detailed in Muhammad Ibrahim Rabi's seventeenth-century travel account of an embassy to Thailand, *Safina-yi Sulaymani* (The ship of Sulayman).[11] *Safina-yi Sulaymani*, like other early modern Persian travel literature about Southeast Asia, depicts the region as part of the *'aja'ib*, the distant awe-inspiring places of the sublunar world often associated with the farthest edges of the Indian Ocean, while incorporating a graphic description of the court of the Ayutthaya Kingdom in Thailand. Similarly, in the travel book *Rawzat al-tahirin* (The garden of the immaculate), written in 1607, Tahir Muhammad Sabzavari describes the Mrauk U Kingdom of Arakan and the Mon Hanthawaddy Kingdom of Pegu as places neither Muslim nor Hindu that were part of "the marvels and wonders of the islands and ports" near Bengal (*'aja'ib u ghara'ib dar banadir u jaza'ir*).[12] Likewise, Tawfiq Shirazi's *Tazkirat al-muluk*, a history of the Adilshahis of Bijapur completed in 1611, draws upon the account of a certain Munjan Khan to describe the royal city of Pegu in a chapter on Bengal and the Indian Ocean. And in the widely read Persian chronicle *Tarikh-i Firishta*, also known as *Gulshan-i Ibrahimi*, written circa 1612, the Iranian chronicler Muhammad Qasim Hindushah "Firishta" refers to Pegu as among the "distant islands" (*jazira-yi dur*) ruled by a raja who "has always two white elephants, and that when one dies, orders are issued to search the woods for another to supply his place."[13]

These early modern accounts and narratives of Southeast Asia were comprised of often-told and long-standing legends surrounding mysterious "Indian" voyages, islands, and kingdoms, mixed with new graphic observations of Southeast Asian empires, cities, and environs. Pegu was seen as a fabulous realm, a terra incognita reached by a journey of many days through a country of uninhabited forests abounding with elephants, rhinoceros, and exotic flora and fauna. Its cities were studded with magnificent, often gilded temples, worshipped by idolaters with their own customs and languages.[14]

The dual tones in early modern Indo-Persian travel writing on the Indian Ocean and its Southeast Asian littoral, combining elements from the *'aja'ib* genre and more observational forms of description, persisted and were further honed in the late Mughal and early colonial period. By the late eighteenth century, the long-standing interconnections through Persian across the Indian Ocean to the "lands below the winds" had entered new times and were being redefined in the context of new contacts during the early colonial period. Indo-Persian travel narratives continued to cast Southeast Asia and its forest kingdoms as realms of wonders. Echoes of the *'aja'ib* still lasted, but they also became tinged by contact with the East India Company and its Orientalist wing, the Asiatic Society, as well as the colonial sciences of geography, archaeology, and botany. New narratives of the wondrous Indian Ocean surveyed Southeast Asia in its physical and natural environment and became imbued with a sense of the Oriental sublime that reveled in the wildness of natural landscapes. At the same time, these colonial Persian histories, travel accounts, and narratives more categorically and precisely mapped Indian Ocean environments and spaces on the Southeast Asian edges of the Mughal world.

## DRIFTER

In 1767, Mirza I'tisam al-Din, an Indian munshi from Bengal in the service of the East India Company, traveled across the Indian Ocean on a voyage from India to Europe. Following his return to India nearly three years later in 1769, he wrote an account of his travels in Persian titled *Shigarfnama-yi vilayat*, or the "Wonder book of provinces." In it he described the wondrous places across land and sea that he encountered on his journey. The Persian text of I'tisam al-Din's travel account survives in the British Library, dated in the month of Muharram in 1227 Hijri Qamari during the sixth regnal year of the Mughal emperor Akbar II, corresponding to 1812.[15] An abridged Urdu version and English translation, excluding many early passages on the Indian Ocean and Southeast Asia, were later published in 1827 as *Shigurf Namah-I-Velaët; or, Excellent Intelligence Concerning Europe: Being the Travels of Mirza Itesa Modeen in Great Britain and France.*[16] By returning to the original Persian manuscript, the *Shigarfnama* may be approached in its total context, and I'tisam al-Din's detours in and perceptions of the Indian Ocean and maritime Southeast Asia, preceding the European leg of his journey, may be more fully recovered.

In the opening of the *Shigarfnama,* Mirza I'tisam al-Din recounts his humble origins, his wandering travels from India to Europe and back, and his writing of a book on his experiences and the various "wonders" he had seen:

> To the travelers of the times and those who have seen the world [*sayyahan-i ruzgar va jahandidagan*], it will be written that this lowliest of men traveled to the English Vilyayat due to destiny and the necessities of life. The rare facts and features I saw and heard on land and sea comprise strange tales and allegories full of wonders [*dastani ast gharib va hikayat-i bas shigarf*]. In the year 1199 Hijri [1775], after returning to the sacred land of Bengal, as my mind drifted to the farthest places [*aqsa-yi maratib*] and I suffered distress from the turn of my fate, and the chaos and upheaval of the times, that I turned to the beneficial effects of the pen [*khama*] and the story [*dastan*]. It was at

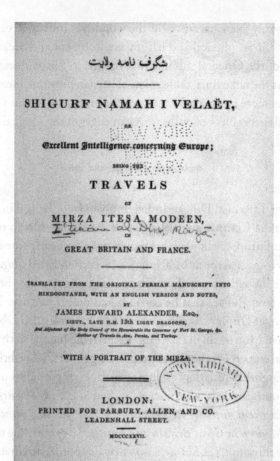

شگرف نامه ولايت

SHIGURF NAMAH I VELAËT,

OR

Excellent Intelligence concerning Europe;

BEING THE

TRAVELS

OF

MIRZA ITESA MODEEN,

IN

GREAT BRITAIN AND FRANCE.

TRANSLATED FROM THE ORIGINAL PERSIAN MANUSCRIPT INTO
HINDOOSTANEE, WITH AN ENGLISH VERSION AND NOTES,

BY

JAMES EDWARD ALEXANDER, Esq.,

LIEUT., LATE H.M. 13th LIGHT DRAGOONS,

And Adjutant of the Body Guard of the Honourable the Governor of Fort St. George, &c.
Author of Travels in Ava, Persia, and Turkey.

WITH A PORTRAIT OF THE MIRZA.

LONDON:
PRINTED FOR PARBURY, ALLEN, AND CO.
LEADENHALL STREET.

MDCCCXXVII.

FIGURE 1. *Shigurf Namah I Velaët; or, Excellent Intelligence concerning Europe: Being the Travels of Mirza Itesa Modeen in Great Britain and France,* English and Urdu translation by James Edward Alexander and his munshi "Shumsher Khan" (London, 1827).

the insistence of friends that this most guilty of sinners, I'tisam al-Din, the son of the late Shaykh Taj al-Din, an inhabitant of the village of Tajpur, put pen to paper [*khama ra bih mashatigi-yi chihria-yi matlab biyarast*] to write an account of the wondrous journey [*dar tarqim-i halat-i shigarf*]. Because the purpose of the book is to inform and be useful to the reader, and since I lack literary talents, I have refrained from ornamenting it with complex language and colorful phrasing. I have gathered these stories in a collection and called it *Shirgarfnama-yi vilayat* [Wonder book of provinces] so that it may be remembered in the pages of our times [*bar safah-i ruzgar yadgar nigasht*].[17]

FIGURE 2. Mirza I'tisam al-Din in *Shigurf Namah I Velaët,* front plate (London, 1827).

Mirza I'tisam al-Din learned to read and write in Persian from Mirza Qasim, the *mir munshi,* or head scribe, in the Bengal court of Nawab Mir Ja'far 'Ali Khan (r. 1757–60; 1763–65), and through his skills in Persian he came into the service of the East India Company. In 1765, I'tisam al-Din was honored with an audience in the presence of the Mughal emperor Shah 'Alam II (r. 1760–1806), who gave him the title of "Mirza" and appointed him as munshi in his court. In the same year, Shah 'Alam II selected I'tisam al-Din as his representative and as the Persian munshi of Captain Archibald

Swinton on an East India Company mission entrusted to dispatch a royal letter, along with a gift of a lakh of rupees, from the beleaguered Mughal emperor to the king of England, George III (r. 1760–1820).[18] "Being then in the days of my youth [*ayyam-i javani*]," I'tisam al-Din recalled, "the pull of fate led me to travel, and resting content with God's intentions, I embarked with Captain Swinton on a journey to vilayat."[19]

Mirza I'tisam al-Din's times were marked by the waning of Mughal power and the emerging ascendancy of the British East India Company. The East India Company had been in South Asia since the reign of the Mughal emperor Jahangir in the early seventeenth century. As Mughal power declined during the eighteenth century, the company evolved from an association of merchants pursuing commercial trade in India into a colonial state in Bengal with dominion over the Mughal emperor in Delhi. By 1765, the year I'tisam al-Din set out on his journey, the East India Company had established indirect imperial rule over the *nawab,* or regional governors, of Bengal and gained the right to administer and collect revenue throughout the province, thus compromising the sovereignty of the Mughal throne in Delhi. I'tisam al-Din was well apprised of the political circumstances of his times and that surrounded his journey, recalling how the mission was ultimately betrayed by the maneuvers of Major General Robert Clive, who withheld the Persian letter from Shah 'Alam II and presented the Mughal emperor's diplomatic gifts in his own name. After "the hardships of an arduous six month voyage at sea" (*shadayid-i safar va la'b-i jahaz bar kavayir-i ab ba'd az shish mah*) and "waiting in England for a year and a half for the emperor's letter to arrive," I'tisam al-Din came to realize that "no benefit would come of the journey; the mission was lost and out of my hands like an arrow shot from the bow" (*kar az dast raft va tir az shast rahha shuda bud*).[20] Being so far away from India, he became homesick and lamented, "Love of the homeland is better than the throne of Solomon / The thorns of home are sweeter than hyacinths" (*Hubb al-vatan az Takht-i Sulayman bihtar / Khar-i vatan az sunbul khushtar*). [21] He returned to Bengal three years later to witness the anarchy of his times, amid the disintegration of the Mughal Empire and the expansion of British colonialism in India.

But *Shigarfnama-yi vilayat* is more than simply a tale of Europe and the global ascendancy of the East India Company. Indeed, it presented a sense of the global in other ways. Mirza I'tisam al-Din's sea journey to vilayat in the nascent age of British colonialism in India brought him into contact with different worlds, including the Indian Ocean and the littorals and islands of the East Indies—Pegu, Java, Sumatra, Sri Lanka, and the Maldives. The most marvelous of all things he described was the sea (*darya, bahr*) itself, and the encounter with the ocean framed his narrative. In his travel book's first lines, he uses the sea as a metaphor for the infiniteness of God's creation:

> My pen breaks on paper [*qalam bar kaghaz shikasta*] and is not capable of writing about the creation of God. In an endless sea with distant shores [*darya-yi napayda kinar*], the ship of essence sailed through the storm of wonder [*tufan-i hayrat*] and was left silent upon anchoring on land.

I'tisam al-Din juxtaposed the boundless abyss of the ocean with the minutiae of its smallest organisms—from the sea and horizon to islands to seashells—in order to depict the all-encompassing presence of the divine in nature. He wrote, "Even the celestial sky is like an island in the sea of his power [*jazira ist dar miyan-i bahr-i qudrat-i u*], for the secrets of the divine are vaster than the sea and more infinite than seashells [*na darya gunjad asrar-i ilahi, na darya-yi gush mahi*]."[22]

Mirza I'tisam al-Din bid farewell to friends and, with the dread of loneliness, began his long journey in January 1767, boarding a ship on the Hugli River in Calcutta.

> On the 9th of Shaban, in the Hijri lunar year 1180, trusting in the mercy of God, I boarded [the] ship and ventured into the salt sea [*darya-yi shur*] with the grace and wisdom of the true protector [*hafiz-i haqiqi*] and this poem:
>
> In this endless ocean, in this worsening storm,
> We headed out to sea, praying "in the name of Allah, for its sailing and its
> anchorage" to reach another shore.[23]

Journeying "the salt sea, characterized by its black water" (*ab-i siyah 'alamat-i an ast*) and "its vast shores" (*kinar-i darya-yi shur vasat bisiyar darad*), he was overcome by a mood of loneliness due to "the separation from native land and sense of isolation" (*az firqat-i vatan va judayi*).[24] So he drowned his sorrows in a contemplation of what seemed a boundless Indian Ocean and the extant knowledge about it.

Mirza I'tisam al-Din's travel narrative was woven around the long-standing Indo-Persian idea of the wonders of creation, as indicated by the title of his account, *Shigarfnama*, or "Book of the wondrous." And thus, in describing the sea, he wrote of the ocean's marvelous features that he saw and experienced firsthand or heard of during his travels. The sight of the sea and its colors astounded his vision and spurred his sense of enchantment:

Near the seashore, the ocean is shallow and its color is white [*rangin-i safid ast*] like its sandy floor, but upon passing that and reaching the desert of the open sea [*sarhadd-i darya*] . . . it turns a deep sky blue [*nilgun*]. At night, the foaming waves glow like lights [*mawj-i ab-i darya durust bih rang-i chiraghan midarakhshid*]. It is the opinion of sages that an emerald mountain encircles the earth [*kuh-i muhit-i dunya ast az sang-i zumurrud*] and it is so lofty that they call it the Mountain of Qaf. The blueness of the sky is a reflection of the emerald mountain and the blueness of the ocean is a reflection of the sky [*nili-yi ab-i darya az aks-i asiman ast*]. This is the reason seawater is clear when held in the palm of the hand.[25]

Physically immersing his body in the sea, he came to know it further and praised the healing powers of its salt water: "European doctors are of the opinion that seawater and air are healthy and advantageous. This I myself experienced, and by bathing in saltwater, I did not become sick during the voyage."[26] The experience of being at sea altered Mirza I'tisam al-Din's perceptions and bodily senses, washing away his homesickness for India as he sailed the expanse of the Indian Ocean, seaborne on the route to vilayat.

The sea was an infinite expanse to Mirza I'tisam al-Din, a vast and fathomless marvel of divine creation that could never be fully known. Its span and depths were immeasurable. In a section on "the vastness and endless depths of the salt ocean" (*zikr-i fushat u vas'at-i darya-yi shur va 'adam-i intiha-yi 'amiq*), he wrote of the sea as inconceivable and boundless:

It must be known that the vast limits of the salt ocean's shores and the fathomless depths to the sea's bottom are not known to anyone other than the Creator and are beyond human comprehension [*ma'lum nist va 'aql bar an kar nimikunad*]. On board the ship [*dar halat-i jahaz nishini*], whenever I contemplated the vast horizons of the sea and sky [*fashhat-i darya u asiman*], the power of the divine Creator became apparent [*qudrat-i kamal-i khudayi zahir mishavad*].[27]

His firsthand experience of the salt sea, the *darya-yi shur*, left him awestruck by its incomprehensible vastness.

Mirza I'tisam al-Din was reminded of tales of the legendary maritime exploits of Alexander the Great in the Indian Ocean. In Persian literary romances, such as Nizami's *Iskandarnama* and Amir Khusraw's *Ayni-yi Iskandari,* the figure of Alexander was recast as Iskandar Dhu al-Qarnayn, a philosopher and sage who searched for the eternal "Water of Life" accompanied by the mystic seafaring Sufi saint Khwaja Khizr.[28] In Amir Khusraw's rendering of the legend, Iskandar is further transformed into an adventurer-saint and scientist who embarks on a long sea voyage to explore the secrets and measure the depths of the Indian Ocean, accompanied Khizr, Ilyas, Aristotle, and Plato. Iskandar descends into the depths of the sea in a glass diving vessel and, guided by an angel underwater, he sees the wondrous mysteries of the ocean. While beneath the sea, the angel foretells Iskandar's imminent death and limited time on Earth, and he returns to land to die as an old man.[29] These Indo-Persian legends of the oceanic exploits of Alexander the Great reached as far as the Malay Archipelago. The seafaring adventures and oceanographic knowledge of the Malay Alexander were recorded in the epic *Hikayat Iskandar Zulkarnain,* while the preeminent court chronicle and genealogical history of the fifteenth-century Melaka Sultanate, *Sejarah Melayu* (Malay annals), claims the kingdom's rulers came from the line of a descendant of Alexander who had made an underwater journey from India to Sumatra.[30]

But the traveler Mirza I'tisam al-Din was reluctant to concede too much to the ancient Macedonian turned Indo-Persian hero when it came to knowledge of the sea. "People who have never seen the sea [*mardum kih ru-yi darya gahi nadida and*], suppose that Iskandar Dhu al-Qarnayn dared to venture all the seas, but this is impossible [*hich surat imkan nadarad*]," he wrote, "since the depth of the ocean is endless [*'amiq-i darya payani nist*] and the span of the sea is unseen [*tul va 'arz-i darya nadida ast*]." He questioned, "How could it be possible for Alexander and the sages of his time, who were only human, to have measured the ends of the sea [*nahayat-i darya paymayish kunand*] and dropped anchor in its fathomless depths?"[31] I'tisam al-Din concluded that the "shaykhs" who had recounted Alexander's knowledge of the ocean must have been referring to his sailing of the seashores and coastlines (*kinara-yi darya*), casting doubt on the truth of old Persian and Arabic histories of kings and prophets that were based on legendary oral accounts.[32]

Adrift on the Indian Ocean, Mirza I'tisam al-Din came to know the sea's different conditions and moods, from its raging storms to its calm and restless solitude. After some days at sea, he began to realize that the ocean was unpredictable. The ocean's wind patterns were always changing, which contributed to the tempestuous nature of the sea. The wind and sea could be rough and treacherous, or there could be quiet periods when the winds disappeared altogether and the ocean's skin was becalmed, leaving the ship's passengers suspended and immobile in the vast expanse. During such times I'tisam al-Din, whose preference for the shore was never in doubt, became restless and pondered whether he would ever leave the ship and see his country again.

Through the long sea voyage, Mirza I'tisam al-Din immersed himself in the knowledge and experience of the Indian Ocean and its shores. It was not just the ocean itself that captivated him but also the previously hidden mysteries and aquatic life-forms it contained, as he classified the fish, mollusks, and cetaceans he encountered. "The ocean is full of wonders ['aja'ib u ghara'ib-i darya bisiyar ast]," he wrote, "such a multitude of wonders that it was impossible to write of them all."[33] He described the curiosities of the ocean across different scales, from the smallest minutiae of nature to the grandest marvels of existence.

In his observations, Mirza I'tisam al-Din detailed sea's most small and subtle life-forms. Among the wonders of the Indian Ocean that caught his eye were its manifold world of seashells to be found on its islands, in particular the cowrie shell of the Maldives. In a passage in the *Shigarfnama* on the "way of rounding up cowries" (*tariq-i gard kardan-i kawri*), he described how the islanders collected the shells, a valued form of currency and exchange in Indian Ocean trade:

> During the low tide [*bi vaqt-i jaz-i laghi-yi bahar*], on behalf of the *padishah*, fleets of boats manned by fifteen hundred mariners sail to isolated places along the shoreline and dig holes in the sand. And when the sea rises, the flow [*saylab*] of the high tide and the breaking waves [*mawj*] fill the pits with live cowries, and when the tide recedes the cowries are left behind in the holes. The boatmen pull quietly and quickly to the hollowed spots, load the shells into their boats, and take them away. The collected cowries are then left in a ditch for a few days, where they soon die, and their flesh rots away. When the insides of the shells dry up, they are gathered in heaps, placed in storage, and sold to merchants from Bengal [*sawdagaran-i Bengal*] and other places.[34]

The description of cowrie shells in the *Shigarfnama* conveys a conchology of the local practice and culture of shell collecting in the Maldives and its ties to the maritime economy and commerce of the Indian Ocean world.

At the other end of the spectrum of scale, Mirza I'tisam al-Din encountered the most charismatic megafauna of the sea:

> I had heard stories about the whale of the sea [*nahang-i darya-yi*]. The people of India call it *nahang* but this is incorrect and in the English language it is called whale. In size, it is equal to two large elephants [*barabar-i du fil-i kalan*], and even larger: its head and jaws are also like those of an elephant. On the crown of its head is a spout [*surakh-i bini bala-yi sar darad*], and in the act of breathing [*har gahi ki nafas birun kunad*] when water gets into

its throat, the water is thrown out from it, rising like a fountain in height equal to a tall tree [*favara miqdar-i dirakht-i buland*], and with a loud noise that can be heard at a distance. During the journey, one appeared on the surface of the ocean. Seeking something to eat, and in order to see the ship, the whale approached us. It swam to the left and the right of the ship, and at one time it dived and sounded, and at another rose above the surface. If it had happened to strike the ship in its movements, even slightly, the vessel might have broken and sunk. The sight of the giant whale and its near approach was a cause of great fear and alarm [*az didan-i an harasi bih khatir ayad*]. The captain [*jahazban*] related that in the early days of sailing the seas [*dar ava'il-i ayyam-i daryagahi*], whales had little fear of humans and approached close to ships, at times capsizing them. In those times, whales were frequently seen. But since the arrival of ships with guns and cannons that hunted and wounded whales, their sightings became rare.[35]

Although this meeting with the leviathan astounded I'tisam al-Din, he did not consider the species an unfathomable and colossal sea monster, a view that proliferated in previous works in the style of the *aja'ib* genre, but rather as classifiable sea life. While the sense of wonder remained, his description of the whale, its behavior, and the ecology of its ocean habitat had echoes of cetology.

This mixture of the wondrous and the empirical, a blending of tones with roots in early modern texts, also framed the geographical accounts of the Southeast Asian littoral in the *Shigarfnama*. The theme of wonders, following the template of an existing Indo-Persian stock of conventional tales about the Indian Ocean and its strange and mysterious islands, persisted amid Mirza I'tisam al-Din's more graphic and detailed mappings of Southeast Asian kingdoms and landscapes. He brought these different elements together in a section of the *Shigarfnama* titled "Bayan-i hal-i jaziraha" (A description of the situation of islands), which presented a new cartographic account of Southeast Asia, identifying the islands of the *zirbad* more graphically as Pegu, Melaka, and Java. Through narratives of the coming of Islam and trade to the islands of the Indian Ocean, I'tisam al-Din delineated Southeast Asia as the frontiers of the Islamicate Indo-Persian world.

In offering this account of the Indian Ocean littoral, Mirza I'tisam al-Din related the extraordinary and strange recollections of Southeast Asia found in Tahir Muhammad Sabzavari's early seventeenth-century travel book *Rawzat al-Tahirin* (Garden of the Immaculate). I'tisam al-Din cited Tahir Muhammad and his text as the source of his knowledge on the lands and kingdoms of Southeast Asia:

Shaykh Tahir Jamal al-Din Husyan Unjook, one of the commanders and ministers of the Mughal emperor Akbar, traveled as ambassador to the court of Adil Shah, the king of Bijapur, and remained for a length of time in the Deccan. He gave a description of the Deccan and other countries, in a book that he compiled, called *Rawzat al-Tahirin*. It is also entitled *Muntakhab al-Tawarikh*.[36]

He then went on to recount Tahir Muhammad's descriptions of the marvelous environs and strange peoples and customs of the island of Pegu (*jazira-yi Pegu*) and how it was brought within the fold of Islam by a mysterious Muslim saint known as "Sayyid Pak":

> In former times, the people of this island had no religion [*marduman-i jazira hich dini nadashtand*] and did not know the difference between the unlawful and the lawful [*haram u halal farq nimikard*]. It happened that a *sayyid* arrived in Pegu aboard a merchant ship [*jahaz-i sawdagaran*]. He instructed the people in the mode of praying and fasting [*ayin-i namaz va rawza*], and reading the Qur'an, and calling to prayers according to the custom of Islam. Seeing the way of Islam [*tariq-i Islam*] and hearing Sayyid Pak reading the words [*kalam-i zabani*] of the Qur'an, the people gathered around him in order to learn the rituals and practices of the religion. Until it came that the leaders of the island recognized Sayyid Pak as their saint [*imam*] and king [*padishah*], and followed his sway. Until this day, the descendants of the sayyid are nobles among the community and still follow the practices and customs of Islam [*sha'ar-i Islam*].[37]

These were fables of the liminal spaces and frontiers of Islam in the Indian Ocean, tales of conversion from places deemed distant from Indo-Persian and Muslim lands and customs. In concluding the parable of Sayyid Pak in the Kingdom of Pegu, Mirza I'tisam al-Din cast the Muslim saint as being swayed by the taboos the of the island and being carried to the edges of belief and the margins of Islam. Recounting a *hikayat*, or story, from *Rawzat al-Tahirin*, I'tisam al-Din wrote, "It was said that the saint had tamed a fairy [*bari*], who lived with him for seven years and gave birth to their children, until at last the fairy became faithless, abandoned her children, and returned to the world she came from [*bih vatan-i 'asli-yi khud shitaft*]." The magical tale of Sayyid Pak and the fairy in the kingdom of Pegu, claimed I'tisam al-Din, "was well known in Bengal as a wondrous occurrence in the world [*dar Bangala ham az jumla-yi ghara'ibat-i mashhur ast*]."[38]

Following the model of the story of Sayyid Pak in Pegu, Mirza I'tisam al-Din recounted other parables of Sufi saints who had brought Islam to the forested islands of the Malay Archipelago. Reaching the island of Melaka (*jazira-yi Malaka*), he found its lands fertile and "well cultivated" (*bisiyar abadi darad*), with rice, varieties of grains, and mangoes and other fruits of the tropics (*shali, aqsam-i ghala, va amba*). He described the inhabitants of the archipelago as being "black like the Abyssinians" (Habashi) and surmised that some of the Malay islanders were "the descendants of black Africans" (*nasl-i siyah Afriki*).[39] The shores of Southeast Asia came into focus and, I'tisam al-Din could glimpse the land-form of Melaka, writing that "during the journey to Vilayat the black shadow of the island could be seen in the distance" (*az dur siyahi minamud*).[40]

Mirza I'tisam al-Din recounted the geographical description of the Malay Archipelago through an apocryphal narrative of how Islam had reached the distant islands in the first years following the advent of Islam in the seventh century. When it came to the culture and customs of Melaka he deemed, "They know nothing of religion and custom" (*az din va ayin khabari nadarand*). More specifically, of the inhabitants of the Malay islands, "some were Muslim, some were half Muslim, but most were lost and pathless" (*ba'zi musalman, ba'zi nim Musalman, va aksar gumrah*).[41]

Despite his dismissiveness of non-monotheistic local religions, I'tisam al-Din related the apocryphal story of the intrepid Muslim disciple who sailed the seas from Basra in the Persian Gulf to bring the faith to the Malay Archipelago. In the times of the early caliphs, I'tisam al-Din recounted, a respected saint committed himself to the path of "divine love and travel" (*'ishq-i ilahi va siyahat*) and "journeyed the world" (*jahan paymayi namud*), seeking "to carry the message of the religion of Islam to the universe of the unknowing."[42] Reaching the island of the Melaka, the saint "instructed the people in ways of prayer, fasting, reading the noble Qur'an, and the calling to prayers." He imparted "the laws and pillars rituals of Islam and the customs of religion" (*sha'ar va arkan-i Islam va ayin-i din dari*).[43] In turn, "the people of the island, seeing the ways, customs, and rituals of Islam, became drawn to his path and the worship of the true God" (*'ibadat-i ma'bud-i haqiqi*). "Every day they gathered around the saint," Mirza I'tisam al-Din detailed, "to discover the customs of the religion and the true divine path" (*tariq-i haqq al-yaqin*). The saint "brought the belief in God and the prophets [*zikr-i khuda va rasul*] to the islanders who knew nothing about religion." Being unbelievers, "they asked 'what is God' and 'who are the prophets'" (*guftand khuda kist, rasul kudamast*)? So "he revealed to them the nature [*zat*] and attributes [*sifat*] of God and instilled the memory of the prophets and saints who recognized the signs of the exalted words of God." And so it came to pass that "some of the people of the country became converted to the religion of Islam [*nisf-i marduman-i mulk bih dini Islam iman avurda*] and others were only halfway Muslim [*nisf-i digar nim Musalman mandand*], while those people on the margins of society continued to follow the ways of old [*marduman-i atraf va janib bar halat-i qadim*]."[44]

The saint came to "favor the island" (*az anja khush amad*) and "its people held him dear" (*marduman-i anja u ra jan-i ʿaziz dashtand*) in return; some "would not separate from him for a moment" (*yak lahza az u juda-yi nimi namudand*). They insisted that he stay and take residence on the island and pleaded with him not to leave, but he insisted on going back to the caliph in the Hijaz and sharing the news of his travels in the name of Islam. The saint then sailed on a merchant ship to Basra and traveled from there to Medina, appearing before the caliph and describing the distant island and how he had spread the religion of Islam there. With the permission of the caliph, he returned to Melaka and settled there, as the Malay people of the island elevated him to the status of their own leader and saint.[45]

Iʿtisam al-Din's tales of mobile Muslim pilgrims and wandering holy men and their conversion of the peoples of Pegu and Melaka to Islam were premised on enduring views of the Southeast Asian shores of the Indian Ocean as strange and almost incomprehensible. Such accounts of itinerant shaykhs bringing the message of Islam to remote Indian Ocean islands, converting and cultivating a forest terrain and foreign cultural world into the Islamic community of the *umma,* connected the Southeast Asian periphery to the Indo-Persian world. Mirza Iʿtisam al-Din's *Shigarfnama* was a formative text in between different traditions of travel writing that blurred together. In describing Pegu and Melaka as places of extraordinary rarities and astonishing customs, he borrowed from the existing repertoire of tales of wonder and difference in early modern Mughal travel literature about Southeast Asia, but he did so by way of a sea journey to Farang tinted by European knowledge. In this way, the *Shigarfnama* became passed on as the template for subsequent late eighteenth- and early nineteenth-century works containing narratives of Southeast Asia that bridged Indo-Persian and colonial knowledge.

### INDIAN OCEAN ARCHIPELAGO

The encounter with Indian Ocean seascapes and environments is an experience recounted in the well-known travel book of Mirza Abu Talib Khan.

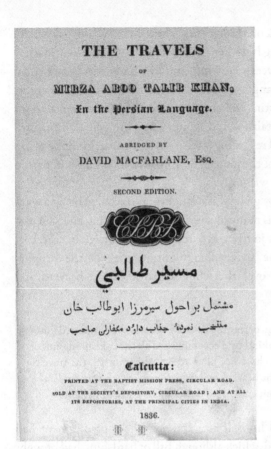

THE TRAVELS

OF

MIRZA ABOO TALIB KHAN,

In the Persian Language.

ABRIDGED BY

DAVID MACFARLANE, Esq.

SECOND EDITION.

مسير طالبي

مشتمل بر احول سيرمرزا ابوطالب خان
ملتخب نمودهٔ جناب داوّد مكفارلن صاحب

Calcutta:

PRINTED AT THE BAPTIST MISSION PRESS, CIRCULAR ROAD.
SOLD AT THE SOCIETY'S DEPOSITORY, CIRCULAR ROAD; AND AT ALL
ITS DEPOSITORIES, AT THE PRINCIPAL CITIES IN INDIA.

1836.

FIGURE 3. *The Travels of Mirza Aboo Talib Khan,* the printed Persian text of *Masir-i Talibi* (Calcutta, 1836).

Fully titled *Kitab-i masir-i Talibi fi bilad-i Afranji bih tasnif Abu Talib bin Muhammad Isfahani* (Book of travels for learning in the lands of the Franks as told by Mirza Abu Talib son of Muhammad Isfahani), the work was written in 1803 upon completion of Abu Talib Khan's journeys, and the oldest manuscript is dated 1806.[46] An English translation by the East India Company Orientalist Charles Stewart was published in 1810, and Persian editions were printed in 1812 and 1827.[47] The work found relatively wide readership at the time of its publication in the early nineteenth century as an Indo-Persian account of England, and it has been frequently cited and analyzed by scholars as a Persian encounter narrative of Europe. This is quite understandable for a self-proclaimed book of "travels to the lands of the Franks," written by an author known among friends as Mirza Abu Talib Khan of London ("Landani"). Europe was the destination and its description certainly comprised the bulk of *Masir-i Talibi*. Still, in the worldview of Abu Talib Khan and his seafaring Indo-Persian contemporaries, the long journey was framed as an Indian Ocean crossing, and like his predecessor I'tisam al-Din, his journey to Farang took certain inter-Asian detours along its routes. Building on the existing literature about Abu Talib's travel account as an example of "Occidentalism" and "counterflows to colonialism," still more remains to be explored regarding inter-Asian encounters and the places in between the end points of the journey, as *Masir-i Talibi* is also in parts a text of travel and encounter within Asia.[48]

Abu Talib Khan began by giving his thoughts on traveling, being a wanderer, and the reasons for his many journeys. Seeking blessing and safe passage, Abu Talib framed his journey as a religious pilgrimage in search of knowledge, referencing the apocryphal night journey of the Prophet Muhammad, "the traveler over the whole expanse of the heavens and firmament":

> After giving praise to the God of the universe, the one who has conferred innumerable blessings on humankind, and accomplished all the laudable desires of his creatures. Praise to the chosen of all worlds [Muhammad], the traveler over the whole expanse of the heavens and firmament [*sayyah-i faza-yi falak-i 'azam*], and blessings without end on his descendants and companions.[49]

Abu Talib Khan identified himself as a traveler whose predicament had forced him to take to the road, which although full of hardships, had brought him knowledge of the world:

> The wanderer over the lands and seas of the universe [*masir-i bar u bahr-i 'alam*], Abu Talib the son of Muhammad of Isfahan, begs to inform the curious in biography, that, owing to several adverse circumstances, finding it inconvenient to remain at home, he was compelled to undertake many eventful journeys [*safarha-yi bisiyar ittifaq*] during which he saw the wonders of seas and the strangeness of lands [*'aja'ib-i bahr va ghara'ib-i bar*] and associated with all peoples [*ba har tayifa*] he met along the way.[50]

The wonders he saw encompassed the land as well as the sea—the Indian Ocean—that was a "middle ground" of encounters between the end points of his journey from India across Asia and Africa to Europe.

Abu Talib Khan continued to frame his observations and experiences during his travels as a tale of "wonders," revealing a new world of the *'aja'ib* that introduced new geographical and cultural knowledge to Muslims:

FIGURE 4. The Indo-Persian traveler "Aboo Taleb Khan" in white turban, illustration by William Ridley after Samuel Drummond, frontispiece in *European Magazine* (1801). Prints and Drawings, British Library, London.

It therefore occurred to me, that if I were to write down all the circumstances of my journey to Farang, to describe the wonders and marvels [*aja'ib u ghara'ib*] which I saw, and to give some account of the customs of the various nations visited, all of which are little known to Muslims [*ahl-i Islam*], it would be instructive for them. I was also of the opinion that these new reports of the customs, crafts, and sciences would cause a sense of joy and lead to the progress of those who search for knowledge [*harakat-i talibin*].[51]

The knowledge gained from the tales told in his book promised to contain elements that were foreign to Persian readers but would ultimately yield a different worldview. This knowledge entailed not only that of Farang but also of unfamiliar and lesser-written-of places in the Asian expanse and the Indian Ocean world.

Promising tales of "new discoveries and inventions," Mirza Abu Talib Khan warned that his readers may be estranged by "a book that contains a number of foreign names [ism-i ghariba], treats on uncommon subjects, and alludes to other matters that cannot be understood at the first glance, but require a little time for consideration." Collecting his scattered notes of travel together upon his return to India in 1803, he called the work Book of Travels for Learning:

> Thus, on first setting out to travel, I began to keep a journal recording the events that occurred and the reflections that came to mind. When that long journey came safely to an end in Calcutta in the year 1218 Hijri [1803], I collected my notes, arranged the pages in the present book, and gave it the title *Kitab-i masir-i Talibi fi bilad-i Afranji* (Book of travels for learning in the land of the Franks).[52]

In his *Book of Travels,* Abu Talib Khan detailed his family's migration from Iran to India, his career with the Mughal Empire and the East India Company, and his travels to Asia, Africa, and Europe via the Indian Ocean.

Early in *Kitab-i masir-i Talibi,* Abu Talib Khan recounts the story of his life and the origins of his family. His father, Hajji Muhammad Bayg Khan, was of Turkish descent and had been born in the village of Abbasabad in Isfahan but fled from Iran to India during the chaos and upheavals that occurred in the reign of Nadir Shah Afshar (r. 1736–47). Hajji Muhammad Bayg Khan settled with his wife and family in the city of Lucknow and entered into the service of Nawab Safdar Jang of Awadh. Abu Talib Khan was born in Lucknow in 1752, but in 1766 he moved with his family to Bengal, traveling to Murshidabad by boat. At age fourteen, this was his first journey, but being "accompanied by [his] mother, it was free from anxiety." When his father died in 1768, "the whole charge of his affairs, both public and private, devolved upon" Abu Talib Khan at the tender age of sixteen. Still in his teens, he was wed to a daughter of Khan Baba Khan, a relative of the nawab of Bengal, Bahadur Muzaffar Jang, "remaining several years happy and contented" while in the service of the nawab.[53]

In 1775, on the invitation of Mukhtar al-Dawla, the prime minister (*nayib al-mulk, vazir*) of the nawab Assaf al-Dawla of Awadh, Abu

Talib Khan returned to Lucknow and was appointed tax collector (*'amaldar*) for "several districts between the rivers Jumnah and Ganges," living on the move and in tents (*bih harakat va dar khayma*) for two years while collecting revenues and roaming the countryside. Following the death of Mukhtar al-Dawla and his replacement by Haydar Bayg Khan Kabuli as prime minister, he was removed from his post and returned to Lucknow, where he resided for one year without employment. He became an assistant to Colonel Alexander Hannay, collector of revenues in the district of Gorakhpur, and returned to the work of collecting taxes while living on the road in tents and temporary dwellings of reed mats and bamboo (*khana-yi chub u nay*) for three years.[54]

Moving back to Lucknow, Abu Talib Khan became mired in rising tensions between the nawab of Awadh and the East India Company, making his life in India increasingly difficult. He fell out of favor in the court of Awadh due to his close contacts with officers in the British company. Caught between a waning Mughal imperium and an uncertain colonial order, in 1787 he left Lucknow, traveling on the Ganges River until he reached Calcutta, but he struggled to find work there. At great expense, he sent for his family to join him in Calcutta and built a house and garden for them on the outskirts the city. But this ended in distress and misfortune. Still without work after four years, Abu Talib Khan was left in debt. Tragedy entered his life when his beloved fourteen-year-old son, unaccustomed to the climate of Bengal, fell ill and passed away. With a broken heart, Abu Talib Khan traveled between Calcutta and Lucknow in search of appointments but remained unsuccessful in his quest. Abandoned by his friends and family members, including some of his children, he was left down and out in Calcutta and fell into a state of desolation and loneliness.[55]

It was at this lowest point in Abu Talib Khan's life when an old Scottish friend of his, Captain David Richardson, paid him a visit. Richardson was fluent in Persian, through which the two conversed on various subjects. He invited Abu Talib Khan to join him on his impending journey to Europe, offering to teach him English and be his guide. The voyage would give Abu Talib Khan something to do with his time, Richardson added, and the change of scene, along with the "wonders and curiosities"(*'aja'ib u ghara'ib*) encountered, would relieve him from his sense of loneliness (*diltangi*).[56] Abu Talib Khan considered the proposal for some time, and seeing that it was a long journey full of dangers (*safar-i pur khatar-i daraz*), by sea and through different countries, that could cause his death and save him from the anxieties and oppression of the earthly world, he resolved to travel across the Indian Ocean aboard an East India Company ship.[57]

In his journal, Abu Talib Khan wrote verses that described the loneliness that led him to make the journey across the "Indian Ocean" (Bahr-i Hind) to the "Lands and Islands of the South" (Arz-i Junub):

If in the beginning love gave me happiness once or twice,
It left me only half drunk and languished,
With a broken intellect and a wounded step,
Crushed and suffering.

Suffering from the defeat of knowledge by my own ignorance,
Ashamed of seeing the crimes of humanity,
Oppressed by the harassment and schemes of the envious,
And by the departure of friends that left my soul in a state of loss.

I took to travels across land and sea,
In the east and west and south and north.
First through India, where I found contentment in no place,
And then across the Indian Ocean to the lands and islands of the south.[58]

Abu Talib Khan's verses hint at the predicaments that led late eighteenth-century Indo-Persian travelers adrift on the Indian Ocean. They took to the sea under various circumstances, as mariners, traders, lascars, and drifters. But despite their varying lot, they were all unmoored, treading across the currents of the Indian Ocean during new and uncertain times.

Abu Talib Khan and Richardson booked passage on the *Charlotte,* an East India Company ship, but a few days afterward the vessel caught fire, forcing them to find passage on another ship, the *Christiana.* On February 7, 1799, they departed Calcutta by barge on the Hugli River. Boarding the ship three days later at anchor, they found it to be disordered and poorly built, with "cramped, dark, and stinking" cabins. The crew was comprised of Bengali soldiers, without much experience of sailing the sea.[59]

The departure of the ship was delayed due to naval engagements between the British and French East India Companies on the Bay of Bengal. It was the age of Tipu Sultan, ruler of the southern Indian Kingdom of Mysore, who rivaled the British East India Company and forged an alliance with revolutionary France, which under Napoleon Bonaparte had conquered Egypt and threatened the British position in India. Only months before the defeat of Tipu Sultan at his capital of Seringapatam, Abu Talib Khan conveyed the tense mood of the times, recounting how his ship was forced to remain at anchor at the river mouth to avoid being captured by the French frigate *La Forte* as it roamed the coastal sandbanks of Bengal. In early March, Abu Talib Khan and his fellow passengers looked on as the battle-scarred English ship *La Sibylle* towed the vanquished wreck of the much larger *La Forte*, with all its masts blown off, up the river.[60]

With permission granted for ships to head out to sea, on March 9, 1799, the pilot came aboard the *Christiana* and, according to Abu Talib Khan, "carried us into the deep black water, called by the English the 'Bay of Bengal.'"[61] In his journal, he recalled the verses of Hafiz as he considered the precariousness of his existence in the deep ocean and its waves:

We entrusted our hearts and lives to the storm of misfortune [*tufan-i bala*].
It said, "Come to the flood of sorrow [*sayl-i gham*] and cut your ties from home."[62]

Again recalling Hafiz, he wrote:

The darkness of night, the danger of waves, and terrible cyclones,
What do they know of the lives of us insignificant passengers from the shores [*sabkbaran-i sahilha*]?[63]

The vulnerable predicament of the passengers at sea was compounded by the uncertainties of the route that lay ahead. They had only sailed southward on the Bay of Bengal for a few days when the captain steered the ship eastward to a chain of islands off the coasts of Burma and Thailand. Abu Talib Khan called the archipelago Jazira-yi Malaka, or the Melaka Islands, in reference to the realm of the Malay Archipelago that marked the eastern maritime edges of the Mughal world.[64]

In fact, Mirza Abu Talib Khan considered the Burmese Empire and its offshore islands to be a part of India, or Hindustan. As he wrote earlier in a 1793 Persian manuscript, a universal history titled *Lubb al-siyar va jahan numa* (The edge of travel and the book of the world), the world of India "comprised the countries" (*mulk*) to the southeast such as Melaka, Siam, Pegu, Assam, and Ava, by which he was clearly referring to Burma, Thailand, and the Malay Archipelago and their connections to the Indian subcontinent.[65] He was also familiar with the colonial literature on India and Southeast Asia. In London and Calcutta, Abu Talib Khan would form a close friendship with Michael Symes, East India Company envoy to the Burmese court in 1795, and had read Symes's definitive travelogue, *An*

*Account of an Embassy to the Kingdom of Ava.* According to Abu Talib, Symes's experiences and work in the East had made him well known among "the great men of London" (*akabir-i Landan*):

> Colonel Symes was a man of honor and integrity [*mard-i abirudar*] and had passed some time in India [*muddati dar Hind bud*]. He was sent on an ambassadorial mission [*sifarat*] to Pegu and Ava, and wrote a book, describing all the characteristics of that country [*khususiyat-i an mulk*], and the customs of its inhabitants, which until written in his book had remained veiled [*dar parda-yi hijab bud*]. As an envoy, he conducted himself such that he was accepted by both nobles and common people [*maqbul-i khas u 'amm uftad*] in the Burmese Kingdom. I saw much kindness from him and in London he was like a brother to me.[66]

Abu Talib Khan and Symes formed such a close friendship in London that they made plans to sail back to India together, until their plans fell through and Symes traveled alone back to India en route to a second mission to the Burmese Empire in 1802.

Back in Calcutta in 1803, upon return from his own journeys, Abu Talib Khan "lost no time in visiting" Symes and was for several months a frequent guest at his table, where he and the English translator of his travel book, Charles Stewart, would listen to Symes "relate a number of anecdotes respecting his travels."[67] Thus, Abu Talib Khan had heard and read much about the geographical and cultural worlds of the Burmese Empire and its littoral. This knowledge informed his representations of Southeast Asia and the archipelago of islands he encountered offshore from the Burmese Empire.

The islands appeared to Mirza Abu Talib Khan as a "wonder"—'ajuba—barely visible on the horizon of the seascape. He was perplexed by the vision of the islands:

> In our approach to these islands, a circumstance occurred which was quite novel to me. When we came in sight of the islands, I wished to behold them more distinctly, and for that purpose borrowed a telescope. But looking through the instrument I could not distinguish the land. Being astonished [*ta'ajub kardam*] at this circumstance, I requested one of the most intelligent officers to explain to me the cause of it. He replied: "These islands are, in fact, still below the horizon, being concealed from our view by the spherical body of water between us and them; and what we now behold is caused by the power of refraction, which, in a dense atmosphere, apparently raises all bodies considerably above their real altitude, reflecting the image of the island on the surface of the water.[68]

Abu Talib Khan regarded the islands and seascapes of the Indian Ocean as wonders while learning to read the ocean's horizon and distances scientifically.

Striving to classify the islands more definitively than the broad category of "Malay Archipelago," he identified the islands he reached off the coast of the Burmese Empire as the "Nicobar." He characterized them as a chain of exposed islands shaped by the elements of wind and sea:

> These islands [*jazira*] are called the "Nicobar" and are seventeen in number. We attempted to reach the largest and most inhabited of the islands, "Car Nicobar," but were blown past it by the winds. The ship then attempted to reach a second island but sailed past it as well, until finally anchoring [*langar kardan*] off the coast of a third island after midnight.[69]

Arriving to the islands at the beginning of the monsoon season, and incessant wind and rain, the ship was "blown off" the island of "Car Nicobar" but managed, after some difficulty, to land on the island of "Teressa" in sight of two neighboring isles named "Chowrie" and "Bampukaha."[70] Abu Talib Khan wrote of the wet, rainy, and tropical climate of the Melaka islands of Teressa, Chowrie, and Bampukaha during the monsoon season:

> These islands are situated below the equatorial line [*istiva*], and for seasons they have two springs and two autumns. As the sun had passed to the north of the equator, and it was the beginning of *barshkal,* the season of the monsoon, we had incessant showers of rain [*baran*].[71]

Abu Talib Khan sketched the seascapes and monsoon climate of the Malay Archipelago in *Masir-i Talibi.*

Having surveyed the islands from the vantage of the ocean, Abu Talib Khan turned to an account of their local terrain, inhabitants, and customs. He sketched an ethnographic description of the islanders, describing their physical characteristics, material culture, and beliefs:

> The people of the islands are strong and lively; their faces resemble the inhabitants of Pegu, but they are tall and their skin is of a wheat color. Their clothing consists merely of a *languta,* a narrow strip of cloth wrapped around the waist. Going on shore for the purpose of hunting, we had frequent encounters with their children, whom I thought to be handsome and of a sweet character [*shirin shama'il*]. Their circular houses are built of wood and bamboos, with roofs of thatched straw, and built to store grains. The larger ones, however, consist of two or three stories, made of wood, with the ground floor for the

animals, the second level for the men, and the third for the women. Their religion is Islam, and their women remain hidden behind the curtain of the *hijab*, and never interact with strangers. They build excellent small boats in the style of Bengal, and even possess two or three ships built like those of Europe on the island.[72]

The inhabitants of the islands seemed to Abu Talib Khan to be marooned societies from the domains of Southeast Asian empires—"resembling the inhabitants of Pegu"—who had taken flight from the mainland to the sea, deriving sustenance from the resources of the islands and the ocean, at safe distance from the reach of the revenue-seeking Mon and Burmese kingdoms of the river deltas.[73] In Abu Talib Khan's account of the islands, imperial presence and authority was seemingly nowhere to be found there. The islanders' way of life and value systems were likewise different than on the mainland, shaped by the closeness of their existence to the sea. The economy on the islands was based on subsistence agriculture and the cultivation of coconut trees in the rich tropical soil, as well as the trade of the Indian Ocean:

> The people of all three islands came and went to the ship, bringing with them an abundance of delicate coconuts [*narjil*] and pineapple [*ananas*], wild berries [*zalzalak*], and the best varieties of juicy limes [*limu*], along with betel nut [*pan*] and spices, and ducks and fowls, all of which they readily traded [*mu'amala*] for cloth [*parcha*], tobacco [*tanbaku*], and metal tools [*alat-i ahan*] like swords and knives. And there is such an abundance of coconuts on the islands, that ten large, delicate, and fresh coconuts are exchanged for one tobacco cheroot, which costs next to nothing in Bengal.[74]

Abu Talib Khan remarked on the islanders' quite different value systems and modes of exchange, noting that economic transactions on the island were not monetized, with little value placed on precious metals such as gold: "In exchange they offer many objects for trade, since gold [*zar*] has no value or use in their country, unless gold coins are worn in bracelets around their hands."[75] Here, Abu Talib Khan's description of the islands' resources and the values of their inhabitants, including his observation that gold possessed little worth among the islanders, hinted at a cultural and economic world that placed value upon different objects of nature. Indeed, his identification of the name of the island "Chowrie" alluded to the abundance of seashells and their role in the economy and culture of the islands and littorals of the Indian Ocean.

By the late eighteenth century, the names of the "cowrie" islands of the Nicobar, such as "Chowrie" recorded by Abu Talib Khan, had come to connote the world of seashells and the shell trade in the Indian Ocean. To travelers, the Nicobars seem to have been known in Sanskrit as Nakkavar, or the Land of the Naked, and this is the origin of "Nicobar," from which the Arabic name "Lankhabalus" was derived.[76] The geographical names for the different islands, such as Chowrie and Nancowrie, however, seem to have been derived from the cowrie shell found in abundance on the islands. By the 1760s, the names Nancowrie and Souri were used in European maps and reports compiled by European travelers to the islands.[77] A report in the East India Company journal *Asiatick Researches* in 1794 claimed, "The largest of those islands is called *Nancaveri* or *Nancowry*. . . . The second is called *Soury* or *Chowry*" after the seashells scattered on the islands. The report detailed that the sea surrounding the islands "abounds with exquisite fish, shell fish, as cockles and turtles; and a most splendid display of beautiful shells of the rarest sort are to be met with on the shore."[78] In 1756, the Dutch East India Company established a factory on "*Soury* Island" for naturalists to collect "shells and other natural curiosities, which they send annually" to Dutch colonies in southern India.[79] Travelers were awestruck by the variety of "shell-fish, which are found in great abundance and beauty on most of the islands," with some led "to perceive the blessing of God resting upon these exertions" of nature.[80]

The Indo-Malay islands were awash in seashells, the shores teeming with numerous varieties. Disembarking from the ship and setting foot on the sand, Abu Talib Khan saw and walked over these seashells, medals of creation from the ocean tide. Scattered through the sands of the Nicobars, following the receding tide, were a myriad of seashells. The beautiful genus of shell called the *Tellina*, known for its circular shape and the radiance of its colors, inhabited the isles in great variety and number.[81] The *Cardium*, commonly known as the "cockle or heart shell," and named for its resemblance to a heart, could be found on the shores of the islands.[82] The islands were a habitat for the *Venus*, highly regarded for its exceptional beauty, with its various species being "of almost every possible shade; and sometimes of the most beautiful and lively tints."[83] The beaches of the Nicobars were also home to the iconic scallop shell, classified as the genus *Ostrea*, its surface elegantly adorned with ridges of diverse colors and intricately marbled patterns. Sometimes worn by pilgrims, such shells were held "as a mark of . . . . having crossed the sea."[84] Smooth-surfaced cone shells, known under the genus *Conus*, washed up on the shores of the Nicobars, displaying a range of colors in stripes, bands, clouds, veins, and marbled markings.[85] The turban shell, or *Turbo*, an iridescent, spiral-shaped cone with gibbous whorls gradually decreasing from the base to the apex, inhabited the Nicobar Islands.[86] The cowrie, classified as the genus *Cypraea*, thrived in the Indian Ocean and could be found on the islands; smooth, glossy shells of "great brilliancy of color," marked with lines, stripes, and dots of remarkable variety—one species being known as *arabica* because its marks were thought to resemble the letters of the Arabic alphabet.[87] The cowries of the "Indian Islands," classified by Linnaeus as *Cypraea moneta*, or "money cowry," became known as "a shell of the Indian Islands . . . transported into Bengal, Siam, and Africa; where it is used in commerce, as a substitute for money."[88]

Writing of the natural history of the islands and sea, Abu Talib Khan recorded his detailed observations about the horizon, the sky, and its constellations, which were important signs for navigation. During calm seas, drifting off the shores of the Nicobar Islands, near the equinoctial line (*khatt-i istiva*), he surveyed and described "the sun in the vertical" (*muhazat-i aftab*). On clear nights, he stayed up until "half the night" (*nisf-i shab*) to view and consider the position of the Polar Star (Sitara-yi Jidi/Sitara-yi Qutb) at "the end of the horizon" (*taha-yi afaq*), with Ursa Major and Minor, the Big and Little Dipper (Banat al-Na'ash va Farqadayn), suspended above it.[89] At other times, he was amazed by the wondrous fauna of the sea and described the strange fish (*mahiyan*) and birds (*parandagan*) he encountered.[90]

The remoteness of the islands, far away at sea and at a distance from the Indian and Burmese Empires, made it seem to Abu Talib Khan like an idyllic paradise in the wilds of the Indian Ocean. He wrote of the Nicobar Islands fondly:

> I was so much captivated by the beauty of the climate [*hava*], environs [*faza*], streams [*anhar*], and the way of life and freedom of those people [*zindagi u azadi-yi an mardum*], that I had nearly resolved in my heart to settle down and take my abode on that land [*sarzamin*].[91]

Most of the sepoys and sailors on the ship agreed and shared similar thoughts about the appeal of the islands. Like Abu Talib Khan, the sailors, sepoys, and mariners aboard the *Christiana* were drawn to the freedom and the way of life in the Indo-Malay Archipelago. One morning, it was discovered that sixteen of the most skilled Indian sailors and crewmembers had deserted the ship, disappearing onto one of islands and taking refuge (*panah*) in the forest. Rumors were prevalent on the ship that the rest of the crew were only awaiting the darkness of night to follow. The people of the island (*mardum-i jazayir*), fearful of reprisals for any perceived collusion with the deserters (*farariyan*), volunteered to bring them back and in return for their troubles, the ship captain promised them pieces of cloth, which was a rare commodity on the island. Being well acquainted with the forests and mountains of the island, the inhabitants found the deserters in little time, bringing them aboard the ship at night. The captain promised to open the hold and reward the islanders with the promised cloth in the morning, but when daylight broke, he weighed anchor and sailed southward, leaving the islanders behind.[92] Abu Talib Khan's brush with the islands of the Indo-Malay world had lasted for barely three weeks. From there, the ship sailed across the Arabian Sea to Africa and around the Cape of Good Hope on the route to London, where Abu Talib Khan would live for three years before returning to India in 1803.

. . .

The wonders of the Indian Ocean were a recurring theme in the genre of Indo-Persian travel writing. Stories of wondrous encounters at sea recounted by mariners and sea captains conjured enchanted environs and natural phenomena, foreign kingdoms and island littorals, distant climes on the far side of Hind. This repertoire of tales and legends of the strange and the wonderful in the Indian Ocean world were schematic and conceptual narratives retold into the eighteenth century and beyond. The stock of accepted and received knowledge about the far ends of the Indian Ocean took on new, more graphic perspectives in the early modern period due to increasing contacts between South and Southeast Asia. This empiricism reached further during the late eighteenth century as Indo-Persian travelers and migrants increasingly journeyed to the Southeast Asian borderlands of Mughal India across the Indian Ocean and wrote narratives of their encounters. Some were sepoys and munshis in the service of the East India Company, while others were travelers and journeymen who voyaged on company ships sailing the Indian Ocean and its routes. Due to the long-standing connections between South and Southeast Asia via the Indian Ocean, Indo-Persian travelers came to serve the East India Company as intermediaries, interpreters, and translators of environments, kingdoms, and cultures on the edges of Mughal India. Eighteenth-century Persian travel narratives about the Indian Ocean and Southeast Asia came to reflect and bear the signs of this new colonial age of inter-Asian crossings and exchanges. Indo-Persian travelers journeyed to the margins of the Mughal Empire offshore, encountering the

Indian Ocean and its island archipelagos. Recording their observations of places they encountered in the Indian Ocean itinerants like Mirza I'tisam al-Din and Mirza Abu Talib Khan brought Southeast Asia into view as it had never been seen before in the genre of Indo-Persian travel writing.

It was in this context of late eighteenth-century Indo-Persian travel writing and descriptions of the Southeast Asian margins of Mughal India that a panorama of the Burmese Empire beyond the Ganges and across the Bay of Bengal cohered. The closest Southeast Asian kingdom to Mughal India, the Burmese Empire—often identified in Persian sources as "Pegu" after the Mon Hanthawaddy Kingdom—came to be surveyed in its physical and cultural environment, etched at once as nearby and faraway, a sovereign Buddhist kingdom and forest landscape on the margins of the Mughal world.

# TWO

# Of Elephants, Rubies, and Teak

## MIR ʿABD AL-LATIF KHAN

AT THE TURN OF THE NINETEENTH CENTURY, Indo-Persian travelers crossing the Indian Ocean encountered the Burmese Empire in Southeast Asia, depicting it in Persian travel narratives as forest world beyond the borderlands of Mughal India. These inter-Asian contacts came about during a time of transition from Mughal to colonial rule and merged Indo-Persian knowledge with the Orientalist pursuits of the East India Company and its scientific wing, the Asiatic Society. In the Burmese Kingdom, where South and Southeast Asia meet, Indo-Persian travel writers found a wondrous ecological and cultural frontier. By portraying the Burmese Empire as a verdant forest landscape ruled by an all-powerful, universal sovereign with the mandate of guardianship over the city and the wilderness, Indo-Persian authors and their encounter narratives inscribed the Southeast Asian kingdom as the limits of the Mughal world.[1]

This view of the Indo-Burmese frontier is recorded in the travels of Mir ʿAbd al-Latif Khan Shushtari, a scholar and merchant from Iran. Written in Hyderabad in 1801, *Tuhfat al-ʿalam* (Rarity of the world) chronicles his voyage across the Indian Ocean from Basra to Calcutta in 1788 and his experiences in India during the waning of the Mughal Empire and the onset of East India Company rule in Bengal.[2] Drawing upon enduring Mughal views of the wondrous nature of Southeast Asia, colored by colonial notions of the transcendent wildness of the natural world, ʿAbd al-Latif casts the Burmese Empire as a land of dense teak jungles, herds of wild elephants, and mines rich in precious stones, a mythical coastal region: the "lands below the winds" of the Indian Ocean monsoons. The Burmese Empire was an unfamiliar region of exotics and strange customs, a Buddhist land on the frontiers of Islam, a distant, half-known world. Through the tale of a journey to the realm of an ideal Persianate sovereign, a *padishah* (king among kings) and raja reigning over the city and the wilderness, 'Abd al-Latif casts the Burmese Empire as a forest realm at the ends of Mughal India.

## TUHFAT AL-'ALAM (RARITY OF THE WORLD)

Mir 'Abd al-Latif Khan (1757–1806) was an itinerant Muslim scholar, merchant, and *sayyid* (claimed descendant of the Prophet Muhammad) from the city of Shushtar in southern Iran. He was a scion of the Shushtari clan, a learned family of Shi'i divines and scholars originally from Basra who had risen to prominence in Iran during the Safavid period. His grandfather Sayyid Nimatallah Jazayiri (1640–1700) was a renowned scholar who had moved to Iran during the reign of Shah Sulayman I (1664–94); he was appointed Shaykh al-Islam (the outstanding scholar of Islamic law in the empire) and leader of Friday Prayers, and he assisted Muhammad Baqir Majlisi in the compilation of his compendium of hadith traditions, *Bihar al-anwar*.[3] For generations, merchants in the Shushtari family had spread their intellectual and mercantile networks as far as India. In 1730, in the wake of the fall of the Safavid Empire and the ensuing dynastic instability and uncertainty in Iran, 'Abd al-Latif's uncle Sayyid Riza Shushtari (d. 1780) looked toward India and migrated from Iran to the Deccan, where he was given land and patronage by the Nizam of Hyderabad. Following the path of his relatives, in 1788 'Abd al-Latif crossed the Indian Ocean from the port city of Basra in the Persian Gulf to Calcutta in the Bay of Bengal and, in 1801, wrote the record of his life and journeys titled *Tuhfat al-'alam*.[4]

'Abd al-Latif dedicated *Tuhfat al-'alam* to his paternal cousin Sayyid Abu'l Qasim Bahadur Mir 'Alam, the representative of the nizam of Hyderabad to the British government in Bengal, after whom the work was named. A lithograph edition was published in Bombay in 1847 by the printer Mirza Zinal Abideen Kermany. Its main audience was Persian readers in Bengal and the Deccan, particularly in Hyderabad. Its readership in Hyderabad seems likely to have been due to the prominence of the Deccani city in the text, and its circulation there is attested by the imprint of the seal of the "Imperial School of Sciences in Hyderabad the Auspicious Foundation of the Deccan" (Madrassa-yi Dar al-'Ulum-i Hyderabad Farkhanda Bunyad-i Deccan) in surviving copies of the lithographed edition. Apart from this, it might be suggested that the audience for *Tuhfat al-'alam* and similar texts of

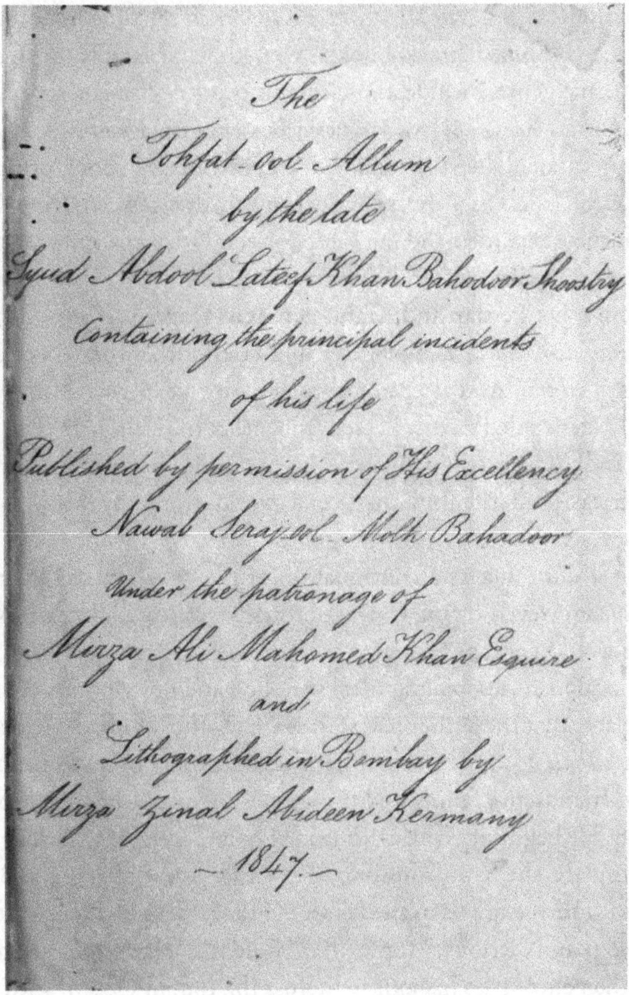

The
Tohfat-ool-Allum
by the late
Syud Abdool Lateef Khan Bahodoor Shoostry
Containing the principal incidents
of his life
Published by permission of His Excellency
Nawab Serajool Molk Bahadoor
Under the patronage of
Mirza Ali Mahomed Khan Esquire
and
Lithographed in Bombay by
Mirza Zinal Abideen Kermany
—1847.—

FIGURE 5. English-title transcript of *Tuhfat al-ʿalam,* printed in Bombay by Mirza Zinal Abideen Kermany (1847).

the time, such as the more widely circulated and translated travel account of Mirza Abu Talib Khan, consisted of Indo-Persian readers as well as European scholars and Orientalists of the Asiatic Society in Bengal who were familiar with the Persian language.[5] Thus, *Tuhfat al-ʿalam* was an Indo-Persian text in the sense that it was written in the Persian language within a Mughal context and closely concerned with South Asia.[6]

Drawing upon the author's journeys from the Persian Gulf across the Arabian Sea to the Bay of Bengal and India, and borrowing from diverse sources of information, *Tuhfat al-'alam* is a work in the time-honored Persian genre of the *safarnama* (travel book).[7] Well-known examples of this ornate, poetic literary genre include the eleventh-century Persian *Safarnama* by Nasir-i Khusraw (1004–88), which describes a pilgrimage to Mecca, continuing on to Jerusalem and Cairo; and the *Seyahatname* (Book of travels) by Evliya Çelebi (1611–82), the seventeenth-century traveler from Istanbul whose journeys spanned the far limits of the Ottoman Empire.[8] In their constructions of distance and difference, these travelogues borrowed elements from other Persian and Arabic genres of geography (*jughrafiya*), road books (*kitab al-masalik al-mamalik*), and tales of the wonders of creation. In *Tuhfat al-'alam,* 'Abd al-Latif recorded his own experiences and observations but also included tales collected from other travelers, including descriptions of India (especially Calcutta, Hyderabad, and Bombay), England, the Americas, and the Indian Ocean world from the Middle East to Southeast Asia.

*Tuhfat al-'alam* marks a continuation of the wide-ranging genre of the *safarnama.* However, owing to the unusually eclectic nature of its subject matter, it would perhaps be better classified as a miscellany (*jung*), since it includes local histories, biographical sketches, and descriptions of travels to faraway places that the author had seen as well as those he had heard and read about. In *Tuhfat al-'alam,* 'Abd al-Latif tells the story of his life and travels, and of his friends and family and the people and places he has encountered on the way. He begins with a description of home, sketching the local history of his birthplace, the city of Shushtar, the nearby cities of Basra and Baghdad, and the Shi'i shrine towns in the Persian Gulf. He also includes a biographical anthology and dictionary (*tazkira*) of the local *sayyids* from the Shi'i Nuri sect. He then chronicles his journey across the Indian Ocean, with a narrative titled "'Aja'ib-i jazayir va gharayib-i bahar" (On the wonders of islands and the strangeness of seas), before describing the lands of "Hindustan." He details the geography and customs of India, while incorporating material on "Farang" (Europe), the affairs of the East India Company in Bengal, and news of discoveries in the New World.[9]

In some aspects, *Tuhfat al-'alam* also falls into the category of *andarz* writings, the wisdom literature that includes the "mirrors for princes" genre of Persian prose, since it offers glimpses into other kingdoms and advice for rulers. Thus, an abridged edition of the text appeared under the title *Qava'id al-muluk* (Axioms for kings), written on the orders of Fath 'Ali Shah Qajar of Iran (r. 1797–1834) by his court historian Mirza Muhammad Sadiq Vaqa'i' Nigar.[10]

In addition to 'Abd al-Latif's own travel experiences, *Tuhfat al-'alam* was also largely based upon a diverse corpus of existing travel literature. 'Abd al-Latif drew heavily upon other Persian travel accounts, including those of Muhammad 'Ali Hazin Lahiji, Sayyid 'Abdallah Shushtari, and Mirza 'Abu Talib Khan.[11] But while *Tuhfat al-'alam* owes much to early modern Persian knowledge of Southeast Asia and its repertoire of encounter narratives of exotic lands, it also reflects the experience of colonialism and the projects of the East India Company. It bears the imprint of 'Abd al-Latif's contacts with scholars in the Asiatic Society of Bengal, including its founder, Sir William Jones (1746–1794), and Sir Robert Chambers (1737–1803), chief judge of the East India Company in Calcutta, to whose vast collection of Persian and Sanskrit manuscripts the Persian traveler was given access.[12] From the material on the Burmese Empire and its relations with the East India Company that appears in *Tuhfat al-'alam*, it seems clear that its author was also familiar with Michael Symes's *Account of an Embassy to the Kingdom of Ava* (1800), based on the first official company mission to the Burmese court. 'Abd al-Latif likely first heard about Symes's description of Burma from Mirza Abu Talib Khan, a close friend of Symes whom 'Abd al-Latif frequently met in Calcutta and later Bombay. During his mission, Symes corresponded with the Burmese court in Persian, while the mission employed Indo-Persian munshis as liaisons, as well as translators, collectors, artists, and botanists.[13] From the late eighteenth century, they conducted surveys of the empire's densely forested landscape, translated its Theravada Buddhist texts into Persian, and portrayed the nature of its sovereignty. Although not officially part of these circles of colonial science and reconnaissance, 'Abd al-Latif was loosely affiliated with them, and thus his *Tuhfat al-'alam*, while rooted within a Persian literary genre, also had links with colonial knowledge of India and the Indian Ocean world.

One of the underlying themes in the text is the emergence of colonial rule under the East India Company, expanding from Bengal, and the ways in which colonial power was navigated by the empires and princely states of India. 'Abd al-Latif traced this theme through various episodes. He related the tale of the decaying Mughal Empire in India, which was "in truth, a country without a master," dismantled by competing princely states and the encroachment of the East India Company. He outlined the different paths taken in facing the increasing power of the company in India, from the anticolonial resistance of Tipu Sultan, the nawab of Mysore, defeated at the gates of his southern Indian capital of Seringapatam in 1799, to the co-opted state of the Nizam of Hyderabad, which entered into alliance with the British in order to preserve its independence. 'Abd al-Latif brought the Burmese Empire into view, a kingdom in the nascent stages of contact with the East India Company that still held on to its sovereignty.[14]

## FROM BASRA TO BENGAL

*Tuhfat al-'alam* begins with its author traveling as a drifter and pilgrim in the borderlands of southern Iran and Iraq. During the early 1780s, while still in his mid twenties, Mir 'Abd al-Latif Khan traveled by ship to the port city of Basra on the Persian Gulf and from there to Bushire, a port in the southern Iranian province of Fars south of the city of Shiraz. Here he settled for "a period of time," falling in with Iranian merchants and hajjis resident in the city and hearing stories of their travels. In 1784 he returned to Basra, from where he made pilgrimages to the Shi'i shrine cities of Iraq—Najaf, Karbala, Kazemayn, and Samarra. However, he was overtaken by a recurring sense of loneliness and alienation (*bigana*) and again turned to wandering (*sargardani*). In 1786 he left Basra for Baghdad, continuing to make pilgrimages to the sacred tombs and cities (*'atabat*) of Shi'i saints and imams, but after two years in Baghdad he returned to Basra. There, in the Persian Gulf, "the air of Hindustan came over him" (*hava-yi Hindustan bar sar amad*), and he decided to hitch his fortunes to family connections with the nizam of Hyderabad.[15]

In July 1788 he boarded an English ship bound for the Bay of Bengal and the east coast of India. His family and friends accompanied him to the docks and prayed for his safe journey, while his elder brother, who had traveled with him around the Persian Gulf, recited a verse beloved by mariners from the eleventh Sura of the Qur'an, on Noah's Ark, and bid him farewell from the shore. As the ship weighed anchor and hoisted its sails, heading out to sea, 'Abd al-Latif had mixed emotions about the voyage in view of the ship's uncertain destiny and wrote the following lines, incorporating the verse his brother had recited from the Qur'an:

In this endless ocean, in this worsening storm,
We headed out to sea praying "in the name of Allah, for its sailing and its
    anchorage" to reach another shore.
Unless the endless sea turns to rival the broken heart,

FIGURE 6. Sayyid 'Abd al-Latif Khan Bahadur-i Nizam 'Ali Khan in the year 1794 (as written on the seal), wearing Indian cloth. *Tuhfat al-'alam* (Bombay, 1847).

And, like an ocean of fire, drowns us in its swell, frenzied and distraught.
Full of sorrow, my heart craves the sea journey like the whale.[16]

With this poem on the uncertainties of leaving home and embarking on a sea voyage, 'Abd al-Latif commenced his journey across the Indian Ocean.

The Indian Ocean, or Darya-yi Hindustan, was conceived by 'Abd al-Latif as among the marvels of existence, delineated in a chapter titled *"Dar durr afshani-yi qalam-i bada'i' nigar bi zikr-i ba'z az 'aja'ib-i jazayir va ghara'ib-i bahar"* (On the pearls spread from the brush of the painter of rarities on some of the wonders of islands and the strangeness of the sea). As this elaborate title suggests, the notion of the strange wonders of creation as the divine source of all existence frames the discussion of the sea in *Tuhfat al-'alam*. The vast realm of the sea was strange and marvelous, and it contained phenomena that were beyond human understanding. Citing the tradition of Zakariya Qazvini's *'Aja'ib al-makhluqat wa ghara'ib al-mawjudat* (The wonders of creation and the strange things existing), 'Abd al-Latif recounts tales of an almost incomprehensible ocean nature, including fierce, tempestuous storms and the sighting of mermaids and fish inscribed with the name of Allah.[17]

Despite the framing device of the strange and wondrous, 'Abd al-Latif seeks to uncover the natural history of the sea, revealing an openness to modern European knowledge in the process. He begins by examining "the causes of the existence of oceans and the movement of the sea waves" (*'illat-i vujud-i daryaha va tikun-i bahar*), rejecting the traditional religious explanation that the sea was created in the aftermath of Noah's Flood (Tufan-i Nuh). Rather, he provides a scientific and evolutionary perspective, claiming that the "globe of water [*kurra-yi ab*] exists independently of the Flood and through its great power the prosperity of the existence of plants and animals came to be created." In describing "the true cause of the rising and falling of the tides of the ocean" (*haqiqat-i madd u jazr-i bahar*), he relays the view of the English (*jama'at-i Inglisiha*) that planetary bodies (*kura*) gravitate toward one another and that high and low tides result from the gravitational pull (*khud kishad*) of the moon (*kurra-yi qamar*).[18] Similarly, his far-ranging sketch of the geographical boundaries of the Indian Ocean includes references to the New World:

The Ocean of Hindustan is the greatest ocean in the universe and it is said there is no wider sea. Its extent is from the west [*maghrib*] to the east [*mashriq*], from the ends of East Africa [*iqsay-i Habsha*] to the ends of India [*iqsay-i Hind*], and includes within its sphere Rome, China, Europe and the Americas, which is the name of the "new land" [*arz-i jadid*]. It was this ocean that took on the name of every country it reached.[19]

'Abd al-Latif's voyage traversed the Indian Ocean from the Persian Gulf to the Bay of Bengal. After some days sailing through the Persian Gulf, the ship passed through the Strait of Hormuz to reach the port of Muscat in Oman, under the rule of the Abu Sa'idi dynasty, before setting sail eastward on the Arabian Sea. 'Abd al-Latif wrote of the changes that occurred on the open sea:

> Until that time, the ship had sailed the Gulf of Persia and Oman, and the sea was not so vast and rough. But upon entering the Indian Ocean, there was turbulence as mountains upon mountains of waves constantly rolled by until I was certain I should drown. There was so much tumult and rage in the endless ocean [*darya-yi bipayan*] that, in truth, its overwhelming power was apparent at every moment.[20]

'Abd al-Latif was helpless amid the fury of the Indian Ocean and its colossal waves:

> A sea without borders, with waves that strike the sky
> Its breaking peaks collide with the constellations
> The crests of its waves reach the axis, like fish upon a hook
> Every drop from that rising sea sprays the stars. . . .
> At times it seemed to me that the horizon, was covered by the ocean waves.[21]

Near the island of Ceylon, which 'Abd al-Latif knew by its Persian name "Sarandib," off the southern coast of India, the ship encountered gale winds and stormy weather. The relentless rains of the summer southwestern monsoons poured down with thunder and lightning, as the rough sea spilled onto the deck of the ship, threatening to capsize it. As 'Abd al-Latif recalled, the passengers on the ship became lost and disoriented, like strangers to one another, with every person on their own, desperately fearing for the loss of their life and crying out in languages foreign to one another. After three long days, the storm abated and the sea became calm again.[22] The ocean was a wilderness to 'Abd al-Latif and he longed to reach an inhabited place (*ma'mura*). He hoped to make it across the vast darya and reach another shore, somewhere where there was cultivation. After more than a month at sea, the ship dropped anchor at Machilipatnam, the main port city of Hyderabad on the east coast of the Deccan. This was the first time 'Abd al-Latif had experienced India. Nearly a week later, the ship sailed for the city of Calcutta, where the weary traveler recovered from the travails of the Indian Ocean. He was thirty years old.[23]

Settling in Calcutta, 'Abd al-Latif entered into the service of his influential paternal cousin Sayyid Abu'l Qasim Bahadur Mir 'Alam, the representative of the nizam of Hyderabad to the East India Company. Mir 'Alam would later lead the nizam's army in the decisive campaign against Tipu Sultan's forces at Seringapatam in the service of the British in 1799. Many details about 'Abd al-Latif time in India come from the writings of his friend Mirza Abu Talib Khan, the subject of the previous chapter, who knew him well in Calcutta and Bombay.[24]

'Abd al-Latif drew upon his connections in Basra to make substantial profits as a gold merchant in India, importing the valuable metal to make Indian goods that were then reexported to the Persian Gulf. He married Mir 'Alam's sister and in 1800 was appointed Mir 'Alam's representative (*sarkar*) to the governor-general and colonial government of Bengal. As a consequence, 'Abd al-Latif became a wealthy and prominent man. He lived in Calcutta and Hyderabad for nearly two decades, traveling extensively through the cities of Bengal and the Deccan, collecting information about these regions, as well as making two journeys to the city of Lucknow in Awadh.

'Abd al-Latif was in Hyderabad when he wrote and compiled the *Tuhfat al-'alam,* confined to the city following a family scandal owing to the marriage between his cousin Khayr un-Nissa Begum and James Achilles Kirkpatrick, the British resident at the court of Hyderabad.[25] However, 'Abd al-Latif's constant journeys in the tropical climate of India led to prolonged illness, and he resolved to set off for the western coast of the Deccan and take a ship home to Basra. But his plans were frustrated when the governor-general assigned him to a position in Bombay serving as host to Persian ambassadors (*ilchi*) from Qajar Iran, and he took up residence in that city. This is the last we hear of him until his death back in Hyderabad in 1806.

## LORD OF THE WHITE ELEPHANT

After nearly two decades in Bengal, during which he had "seen most of the surrounding country" and collected information that he had "heard from reliable sources," 'Abd al-Latif turned to describing the forest world of imperial Burma. In the course of his survey of the environs of Bengal and its outer reaches in *Tuhfat al-'alam,* he included a graphic description of the Burmese Empire, writing about it in the form of a journey to the land of a universal sovereign, Bodawpaya, and his forest kingdom on the fringes of India. His description of the Burmese Kingdom echoes early modern Persian narratives that describe Southeast Asia as a strange, unknown, secret land on

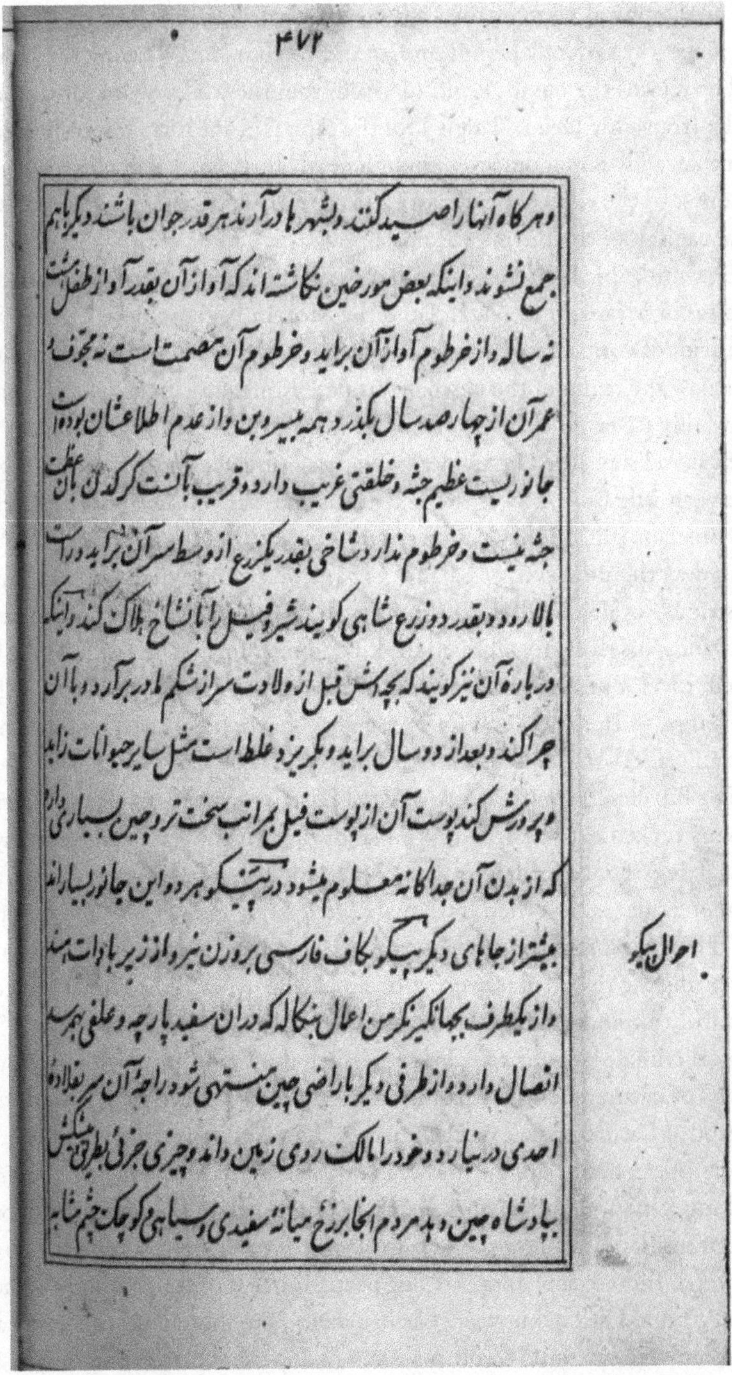

و هر گاه آنها را صيد كنند و شهرها در آرند هر قدر جوان باشند زكر باهم

جمع نشوند و اينكه بعض مورخين نگاشته اند كه آواز آن بقدر آواز طفل

نه ساله از خرطوم آواز آن برآيد و خرطوم آن عصمت است نه محذوف

عمر آن از چهار صد سال بگذرد و همه پير بين و از عدم اطلاع شان بوده

جانورى است عظيم جثه و خلقتى غريب دارد و قريب به آنست كه نى بآن

جثه نيست و خرطوم ندارد شاخى بقدر يك ذرع از وسط سر آن برآيد و در آن

بالا رود و بقدر دو زرع شاهى كه بيند شير و فيل را بآن شاخ هلاك كند و آنك

در باره آن نيز گويند كه بچه كش قبل از ولادت سر از شكم مادر برآرد و بآن

چرا كند و بعد از دو سال برآيد و بكر يزد غلط است مثل ساير حيوانات زايد

و پرورش كنند پوست آن از پوست فيل بمراتب سخت تر و چين بسيار دارد

كه از بدن آن جدا كانه معلوم ميشود در چنگ و هر دو اين جانور بسيار اند

**احوال پيكر**

بيشتر از جامه اى و ديگر پيكر كاف فارسى بروزن نيرو از زير بادات بمند

و از يك طرف به جهانگير نكرمن اعمال بنگاله كه در آن سعيد پارچه و علفى همرس

انفصال دارد و از طرفى و ديگر باراضى چين بنشستى شده راجه آن سر بعلاوه

احدى در نيارد و عمرو را مالك روى زبر داند و چيزى جزى بطريق پيشكش

پادشاه چين و يا مردم انجا برخ ميانه سعيدى و سياهى كو چك چشم شايد

FIGURE 7. Description of Pegu (Ahval-i Pegu) in *Tuhfat al-'alam* (Bombay, 1847).

the geographical edge of the Indo-Persian world. Like them, he refers to Burma as the *zirbad,* the unfamiliar and foreign "lands below the winds"; and he retains the name "Pegu" (derived from the Malay word for the lands of the Irrawaddy Delta, "Paigu") for the capital of the former southern Mon Hanthawaddy Kingdom, even though nearly forty years had passed since its conquest by the Konbaung dynasty and the rise of Ava and Amarapura as the royal capitals of the Burmese Empire.[26]

But unlike previous Persian accounts, which focused on the early modern empires of Mrauk U in Arakan and the Mon in Pegu, imperial spaces with centuries of contact with the Mughal world, 'Abd al-Latif's story brought into view the realm of the nascent Burmese Konbaung dynasty of the upper Irrawaddy River valley. In *Tuhfat al-'alam,* the Burmese Empire appears as a forest world stewarded by an ideal king, a *raja* and *padishah,* a lord and sovereign with rule (*hukm*) over the marvelous "rarities" (*nafa'is*) of the forest.[27] The Burmese ruler, Bodawpaya (1782–1819), is idealized as an ethical king and praised as the preserver of balance between city and wilderness. From his illustrious royal capital of Amarapura, the "Immortal City," on the upper Irrawaddy, his rule encompassed the kingdom's forests as he assumed the hallowed royal Burmese title of Hsinbyumyashin, "Lord of Many White Elephants."[28] This was a style of sovereignty that 'Abd al-Latif and the Indo-Persian readers of *Tuhfat al-'alam* could recognize.[29]

The Burmese Empire, wrote 'Abd al-Latif, was a valley of forested river systems tucked between the rugged lands of the Himalayas and the Bay of Bengal. It extended from Bengal to China, and it took three months to travel from one side to the other. Its climate (*ab u hava,* literally, "water and air") was the tropical monsoon (*mawsim baran*), and the people of the lowlands, inhabiting the river deltas, were cultivators who utilized the climate to grow plentiful rice and grain, and they caught fish in the seas and rivers.[30] The tropical climate created a verdant forest environment in which exotics and rarities of nature, such as elephants, rubies, and teak, were to be found.

'Abd al-Latif's passage on the Burmese Empire opens with a brief natural history of elephants, and he uses tales of these beasts as a vehicle to describe the kingdom's forest environment: these dense forests emerge as the habitat of unfamiliar animals, the tough-skinned pachyderms of the *jangal.* Although Indian elephants had long been exported to Iran through Central Asia, 'Abd al-Latif acknowledged that there were more wild elephants and rhinoceros "to be found in Burma, than in any other place," and only in the

Burmese Kingdom were there mahouts who were so skilled in taming and riding them.[31] Of these Burmese elephants, he writes,

> The elephant [*fil*] is a famous animal [*janivar-i ma'ruf*], found in the forests of Pegu. Wild elephants are hunted and tamed [*ram namayand*] and trained to carry loads and to be ridden. It is an exceedingly sensible animal, and elephant tamers and mahouts [*filbanan*] speak to the animals in a special language that they understand and obey.[32]

The Burmese had established methods for capturing them: "When herds of male and female elephants gathered in the forests for the birth of their newborn, hunters trapped the young and old, and brought them to the towns, and no matter how young they are they will never see their herd again." Recalling tales of "the mournful cries of young elephants separated from their families, sad and sonorous sounds, which bellow from their trunks," 'Abd al-Latif affirms that "it is an animal of great bulk and strange disposition" (*'azim jissah u khalqat-i gharib*).[33] This was followed by a description of another similar tough-skinned creature, the rhinoceros:

> And related to the elephant is the rhinoceros [*kargadan*], which is not as great in bulk and does not have a trunk. The animal has a horn emerging straight out of its head and it is said that it can be used to kill lions and elephants.... Its skin is harder than that of the elephant and has many folds and creases that are visible on its body.[34]

The rhino was a grotesque, wilder pachyderm of the king's forest reserved for the royal hunt. Elephants were eminently featured in Theravada Buddhist cosmography, folklore, and mythology. The animal was prized as a Buddhist symbol, with tuskers traditionally seen as representing cosmic and spiritual power. Particularly prized were white elephants, which Burmese kings throughout history strived to aquire and possess since their presence in the royal palace was thought to assure a long and auspicious reign. 'Abd al-Latif's observations of the power and prestige of elephants as charismatic megafauna reveal the mutual symbolism and meanings shared, although in different iterations, between Burmese and Mughal imperial cultures.[35] His descriptions of the elephant and its imperial connotations in Pegu convey the links between the Southeast Asian kingdom and the Mughal world through knowledge of the animal as a force of empire and of nature. They echo imperial chronicles such as the sixteenth-century *Akbarnama*

(Book of Akbar) of ʿAbuʾl Fazl in lauding the regal splendor of elephants, and in suggesting the good fortune to be had from taming such a powerful wild animal as an instrument of war, which added "materially to the pomp of a king and to the success of a conqueror; and is of the greatest use for the army."[36]

Likewise, ʿAbd al-Latif observed that dominion over the forest and its animals was an emblem of kingship among the Burmese. In theory, all elephants in the country, both wild and tame, belonged to the king; whoever captured one was required to give it up, for it stood as a royal symbol and held a sacred place in the Buddhist cycle.[37] Owing to their hallowed place in Buddhist cosmology, white elephants in particular came to be regarded as an auspicious sign of royal authority, with Burmese monarchs vying to own them. Thus, the description of elephants in *Tuhfat al-ʿalam* develops into an account of Bodawpaya, his modes of kingship, and court culture. The application to Bodawpaya of the Persian title padishah rendered the Burmese Empire recognizable within an Indo-Persian context. According to ʿAbd al-Latif, the Burmese padishah considered himself a conqueror of the world (*malik-i kul-i jahan*) and insisted that diplomatic letters be addressed as from the "slaves [*ghulam*] of Bodawpaya, lord of the white elephants [*sahib-i pil-i safid*], master of mines of rubies, diamonds, gold, and silver."[38] Symbolic possession of forests and mines, flora and fauna, signified the universal sovereignty of the Burmese king.

The Burmese court, ʿAbd al-Latif observed, was attended by intricate customs and strict protocol as signs of loyal reverence from its subjects:

> Among the strange customs of Burma is that every time the padishah appears in the court, the roads, the streets, and the markets, all those present must lie face down on the ground, with no one permitted to look at the king as he passes. The princes and headmen of the empire who enter into the audience hall of the *majlis* [court] of the king, also by necessity, must humbly bow down in this way. And if the king addresses one of his subjects, he is to raise his head, with both hands below his chin, and respond, after which he is to return his head to the ground. All the servants and attendants inside and outside the court lie upon the ground in this custom of obedience. Such loyalty to a king can be found nowhere else in the world.[39]

The symbolic power of the Burmese king was supreme, an aura projected vividly in elaborate court customs.[40] Such codes and rituals of honor and loyalty in the presence of the sovereign would have been familiar to a traveler from Qajar Iran and Mughal India. The placement of hands upon the chin and the not looking upon the king, known in Burmese as *shiko,* were akin to Indo-Persian customs of bending down to the ground during ritual prayer or in the presence of the king, known as *sajda.*[41]

Bodawpaya's stewardship of the rarities of the forests included its subterranean minerals and precious stones. According to 'Abd al-Latif, lustrous rubies (*yaqut*) were among the rarest and most valuable wilderness resources to be found in the Burmese Empire.[42] The rubies mined in the valley of Mogok, in the Shan mountains north of Amarapura, surpassed all others in the world, but it was the way of Burmese kings "to wrap the mines round with mystery and seclusion," and mining was heavily restricted.[43] The king commanded his subjects to leave rubies and diamonds unmined, as they were regarded as sacred signs in the landscape (*manzar-i lutf-i ilahi*). The precious stones were not to be touched but only worshipped, and if anyone came across a ruby on the ground, he was to take the gem and place it in a Buddhist temple (*butkhana*). In a reference perhaps to the Shwe Mawdaw Pagoda in Pegu or the Shwe Dagon Pagoda in Rangoon, 'Abd al-Latif writes, "There exists a temple in Burma, that is said to be from thirty thousand years ago."[44] People did not enter or go inside it; they worshipped from the outside. There were niches on the outer walls for worshippers to peer into the temple, which was said to be filled with brilliant jewels, "the number of which God only knows," left untouched. 'Abd al-Latif relates a story he heard from travelers returning from Burma: A peasant herding cows in his village had found a large and lustrous ruby on the ground. Not recognizing the precious stone, he took it home. When the Burmese king was informed of the discovery, he ordered the villager to be put to death and the ruby deposited in a Buddhist temple.[45] This ethic of the forest and its natural resources as preserved and protected by a universal sovereign is a recurring theme in 'Abd al-Latif's description of the Burmese Kingdom.

Bodawpaya's possession and stewardship of the natural rarities of the forest, such as rubies, enabled a connection between the kingdom and the networks of exchange linking Indo-Persian and Mughal tribute empires. This much is suggested by a letter from Tipu Sultan, ruler of the Carnatic and the Kingdom of Mysore, addressed to Bodawpaya as "the Rajah of Pegu," dated 17 Rabi' al-Avval in the Hijri year 1200, corresponding to January 22, 1786. Tipu Sultan's letter begins by referring to the existing chain of communication running between the two empires and inquiring into the welfare of the Burmese "rajah." Tipu Sultan announces that, "in token of friendship," he has sent to the Burmese king, in the "hands of two of his servants, Mahommed

Kasim and Mahommed Ibraheem, a present . . . of two horses and a *Mehtaby* dress" of silver. Having introduced his merchant envoys, Tipu Sultan makes an economic overture, seeking to trade in the coveted rubies of the Burmese Empire and expressing his desire to open "commercial intercourse between the two states of Mysore and Pegue, whereby an exchange of the commodities of each may be established, to the mutual convenience and advantage of both." He invites Bodawpaya to open trading relations between the countries through his agents and requests the purchase of "rubies of high value, fine colour, and of a superior kind," seeking "stones, weighing each from ten to thirty *fanams*."[46] Tipu Sultan's letter to the king, along with other Persian correspondence and documents preserved in various collections, reveals fragments of the lost history of Burma's interaction with Indo-Persian imperial, economic, and cultural networks.[47] These Indo-Persian exchanges were a continuation of the long-standing contacts between the courts of Southeast Asia and the Mughal world, with the Persian language as a key medium.

'Abd al-Latif observed that Bodawpaya's rights of ownership to the forest and its resources were not limited to exotics and luxuries, which held symbolic value for the sovereignty of the empire, but also included flora, which had become new global commodities highly sought after by early modern European commercial empires. In *Tuhfat al-'alam*, the Burmese Kingdom has bountiful reserves of teak trees (*dirakhtan-i saj*), and is the center of the global teak trade. "In most of the groves and forests of that region, the growth of teak trees, which they call *sakvan* in the Hindi language, is so thick that there is no room for birds to find passage," 'Abd al-Latif wrote.[48] Indeed, "forests of teak grew together to cover completely much of the surface of the land throughout the country."[49] During the dry season, Burmese foresters in the upland interior carved deep rings round the trunks of trees and left the trees to dry in the sun. When they had dried out enough to stay afloat, woodcutters felled the timber and mahouts guided tame elephants as they rolled the two-ton logs through the forest to streambeds in time for the monsoon season. When the rains came, the flooded streams rose up from the forest floor, carrying the teak adrift to the mouths of rivers like the Irrawaddy, where the wood was caught and lashed into rafts by gangs of men, who paddled them as they were borne for days down the rapids toward the sea many miles away.[50]

It was in part due to the quest to gain control of the teak trade centred in the Burmese upland interior that the kingdom came to feature in Anglo-French rivalries over trade and colonies in the Indian Ocean. Because of the growth in trade during the eighteenth century, teak came to be more extensively harvested, in particular for the construction of Asian and European merchant ships. Port cities near the Bay of Bengal teemed with merchants and mariners seeking the lightweight tropical hardwood for that purpose. In Rangoon, where the river rose by twenty feet during spring tides, Burmese carpenters used teak to build some of the sturdiest ships in the world, and by the late eighteenth century the harbor sheltered a motley fleet of ships belonging variously to Burmese princes and governors and European and Muslim merchants. In particular, the French and British East India Companies set a high value on Burmese teak for shipbuilding and sailed their vessels to Burmese ports in search of markets selling the water-resistant hardwood. Burmese teak supplied the wood for shipbuilding in the Bay of Bengal littoral.

'Abd al-Latif reported that British East India Company merchants loaded ships with precious goods and sailed them from the bustling harbor of Calcutta and other Indian Ocean ports to the Burmese Empire, where they traded their wares for planks of teak. For some time, the East India Company had dispatched embassies bearing gifts to the courts of the Burmese kings. The Konbaung dynasty accepted their gifts and reciprocated with fine Burmese crafts, but it refused to allow an agent of the company to be stationed on its coast. The Burmese padishah, 'Abd al-Latif wrote, appointed numerous assiduous customs officials who exacted severe tariffs on trade and placed restrictions on exports of teak. Burmese teak, like other resources of the kingdom's forests, belonged to the sovereign. Although they claimed possession of the forest and its multitude of rarities, this was an idealized reflection of the nature of the Burmese Empire. In practice, the king's forest was in the impenetrable and mountainous interior of the country, beyond the imperial cities, in the territories of autonomous subjects of the empire. The sumptuary laws, which governed and limited the commerce in teak and other forest rarities, were shaped were by the centrifugal nature of the kingdom. The kingdom was content to collect tribute and revenues on timber and to project its sacred power through the imperial architecture of carved teak palaces and monuments.[51]

Among the subjects of the empire, teak found use in the building of houses in cities and surrounding villages; the wood was preferred over the more common bamboo due to its propensity to withstand the dampness of the tropical monsoon climate. Still, most of the population lived in the countryside in houses of cane or bamboo, woven like latticework and covered with straw.[52] 'Abd al-Latif observed that because the neighborhoods consisted of houses and monasteries of teak, no fires or lights were permitted at night. As he described it, "Near sunset, a herald calls out 'al-nar, al-nar,' and when the sound reaches the people, everyone must immediately extinguish their fires even if their food is half cooked."[53] The governors' watchmen patrolled the streets and bazaars at night. Upon finding a fire lit inside any house, they immediately entered and looted (*gharat namayand*) the place, imposing a steep fine on the owner.[54]

In *Tuhfat al-'alam*, 'Abd al-Latif thus describes the Burmese Kingdom as a Mughal borderland, a sovereign forest world on the geographical and cultural margins of India and the Indian Ocean.

. . .

This view of the Burmese Empire as a forest realm ruled over and guarded by a universal sovereign was a narrative of Indian Ocean travel steeped in early modern Persianate knowledge of the edges of the Mughal world. 'Abd al-Latif Khan's passages about the kingdom's forest landscape reveal the persistence, and rearticulation, of Indo-Persian perceptions of Southeast Asia into the late Mughal and early colonial period.

Through description of the city and wilderness and the sovereignty of a sacred king over forest spaces and their rarities, exotics, and natural phenomena, 'Abd al-Latif rendered the Burmese Empire as the half-known fringe of the Mughal world—a place on the far side of the Indian Ocean. Tales of the nature of the Burmese Empire and its forests connected space and sovereignty, making the Southeast Asian kingdom recognizable within the Indo-Persian imaginary. From the temple-lined royal cities of the empire, the king's sovereignty reached out into the forests, bringing into his possession nature's rarities: elephants, the charismatic megafauna that were a sacred symbol of kingship; rubies, the precious gems from hidden mines in the mountains seen as divine signs on Earth, reserved for enshrinement in temples and sent as diplomatic gifts; and vast reserves of teak that brought the empire and its territories into contact with the European East India Companies and their commercial interests.

In this way, 'Abd al-Latif crafted a Mughal cultural geography that encompassed Buddhist Southeast Asia. In the Burmese Empire, he found the familiar in the strange, a world very different from his own but still recognizable, depicted as it was through Indo-Persian and Mughal conceptions of imperial space, nature, and sovereignty. The Burmese Empire was mapped through an Indo-Persian vocabulary as the physical and cultural edge of

Mughal India, retracing enduring interconnections between South and Southeast Asia. Early modern patterns of travel and encounter, and forms of travel writing, across the Indian Ocean persisted.

But *Tuhfat al-ʿalam* was also shaped by its times, marked by colonial India and Orientalist knowledge in its sketches of the sublime wildness of nature in the Burmese Empire. ʿAbd al-Latif's narrative reveals the ways in which preexisting currents of inter-Asian crossings and exchanges were redefined in the early colonial period through contact with the East India Company. His description of the Burmese Empire was informed by Orientalist knowledge and aesthetics in its views of vast and untamed landscapes. Notions of the exalted wildness of nature in "the exotic East," gleaned from the pages of the company's accounts of Southeast Asia, are embedded in *Tuhfat al-ʿalam*. The story itself is a sort of axiom illustrative of the wider balance between indigenous South Asian imperial formations and the East India Company. The repertoire of sovereignty among Indo-Persian empires—the Mughal dynasty and the surrounding princely states and raja kingdoms—betrayed the influence of colonialism and came to include the navigation of a looming colonial world. The Konbaung dynasty, as viewed through the lens of *Tuhfat al-ʿalam*, was also immersed in this rising colonial tide: an empire of city and wilderness below the winds of the Indian Ocean during times of change.

PART TWO

---

*Mughal Meridian*

# THREE

# *Immortal City*

## MICHAEL SYMES

AMARAPURA, THE "IMMORTAL CITY," was a royal capital built in 1783 on the banks of the Irrawaddy River to fulfill prophecies during the reign of the Burmese Konbaung dynasty. The new royal city, constructed on a leafy strip of land on the east side of the river, was prophesied by court astrologers as earthly redemption from the bloodshed caused by the ascension of the king to the Konbaung throne. The palace in the old imperial capital of Ava, just six miles downriver, was dismantled and rebuilt within the fortress of the new royal city, with four Buddhist pagodas protecting its corners.

In the spring of 1795, just before the occurrence of a lunar eclipse, an embassy representing the British East India Company arrived in the royal city. Its members had traveled up the Irrawaddy River delta, along its dense forest terrain during the rainy monsoon season, to reach the capital. Over six months had passed since the embassy had entered the Burmese Kingdom bearing a Persian letter of friendship from the British governor-general of India, Sir John Shore. But the kingdom's astrologers had forecast the coming lunar eclipse to be an "inauspicious moon," and the affairs of the court had been suspended until it passed.[1] The enigmatic king had disappeared in secrecy from the capital to be present at the building of a monumental pagoda on the Irrawaddy River. The embassy was still to discover the king's name; he was known to them only as Dharma Raja, denoting "the virtuous and beneficient king."[2]

In the black of night in the Immortal City, Baba Sheen, an Armenian merchant and royal interpreter in the service of the Burmese king, explained to the members of the mission that different cultures construct the sky in different ways. Baba Sheen presented a Burmese zodiac and astronomical almanac delineating "the sixty-eight Burma constellations," along with two circular diagrams of the lunar zodiac. Although he could not read the written part in the old Pali script, he was fluent in Burmese and sufficiently acquainted with the sketch of the constellations, called "Thadan", to describe the astral formations of the Buddhist imagined sky and its intricate representations of days of the week, cities and countries, and mythical creatures. Baba Sheen presented the chart of the Burmese constellations to the envoy of the East India Company mission, Michael Symes. The astronomical manuscript was placed among the collection of texts, reconnaissance, specimens, and artifacts gathered during the nine-month-long company mission and assembled as an archive of Orientalist knowledge on the Burmese Kingdom. A lithograph of the Burmese zodiac was printed in Calcutta in the journal *Asiatick Researches* in 1801.[3]

On its mission, the British embassy had ventured into the unknown and hidden realm of a shadowy king on the eastern fringes on India. Scarce verifiable knowledge existed in the English language of the kingdom's geography, history, language, literature, religon, or customs. Nothing like the diplomatic and scientific expeditition being led to the Burmese Kingdom in 1795 had been attempted before. Apart from scattered correspondences and surveys, the East India Company possessed only a fragmented knowledge and hazy conception of the kingdom. Most of what the company could learn about the empire came through Persian, its historical and geographical archive, and via Indo-Persian intermediaries versed in the language. Among these Indo-Persian secretaries, scribes, travelers, and translators could also be found agents of the East India Company who relied on Persian as the Mughal literary and administrative language needed to govern colonial India, as well as to conduct foreign relations and open trading agreements with neighboring states. This cast of colonial officers explored and surveyed the kingdoms of the Indian crossroads in the late eighteenth and early nineteenth centuries through their knowledge of the Persian language and immersion in its culture and its customs. These agents of the East India Company kept close contact with Indo-Persian societies, upon whose knowledge and guidance they depended for surveying the foreign lands and kingdoms of outer India. The envoy of the 1795 East India Company embassy to the Burmese Empire, Michael Symes, was among these company agent-explorers embedded, skilled, and immersed in the cultural terrain of Persian.

The Symes mission was conducted through Indo-Persian channels, and came to decipher and translate the foreign realm of the Burmese Empire by means of the Persian language as a medium of cross-cultural communication, connection, and reckoning. The record of the mission, Symes's *Account of an Embassy to the*

*Kingdom of Ava* (1800), although written in English and "inscribed" in honor of the East India Company, consists of a diplomatic exchange conducted through the lingua franca of Persian, based on Persian correspondence between the company and the Burmese government that is translated throughout the text and its appendix. *Embassy to the Kingdom of Ava* was also heavily based on information Symes gathered from Armenian and other members of the Indo-Persian societies residing in the Burmese Empire at the time of the mission. The very style of Symes's text—with its intricate descriptions, ornate narrative turns, and overarching framework of a journey to the realm of an idealized sovereign and kingdom—render it an Indo-Persian book of travels.

The historiography surrounding the Symes mission, although rich, suffers from a question of contexts. The existing literature leaves the embassy disconnected from the Indo-Persian world in which it was immersed. Introverted and narrowly contextualized, alternately as part of British imperial or Burmese nationalist historiography, important aspects of the mission have not been appreciated. Because the episode has been understood strictly within these confined terms, certain global connections and Indo-Persian correlations have not been examined, leading to a misappraisal of the culture and character of Symes and the nature of his embassy to the Konbaung dynasty. The story of Symes and his mission has remained shrouded in the "legend" of being beguiled by the Burmese Empire, a naivete that led to an idealized conception of the kingdom and ended in the embassy's failure. Such a disdainful view of the Symes mission is traceable in colonial narratives of East India Company encounters with the Burmese Empire, originating in Hiram Cox's *Journal of a Residence in the Burmhan Empire* and echoed in the works of subsequent colonial authors Henry Yule, J. G. Scott ("Scott of the Shan Hills"), and G. E. Harvey, among others.[4] It was not until the mid-twentieth century and publication of D. G. E. Hall's *Michael Symes: Journal of His Second Embassy to the Court of Ava in 1802* (1955) that the episode of the 1795 Symes mission received a deep reconsideration, and this work remains the most definitive and thorough analysis of both of Symes's embassies to the Burmese Empire. According to Hall, far from painting an idealized image of the Burmese Empire, Symes "tried to understand, and present, the Burmese point of view."[5] This chapter takes this angle further by examining the ways in which the Symes mission was dependent upon Indo-Persian linguistic and cultural codes, a certain common repertoire in which the Mughal and Burmese Empires were still immersed at the time. Persianate and Mughal cultural networks and currents defined the art of Symes's diplomatic exchanges with the Burmese court and shaped the style and substance of his travel narrative.[6]

## BORDERLANDS

The Burmese conquest of Arakan and the fall of the Mrauk U Kingdom in 1784 rendered the territories of the Konbaung dynasty and British Bengal adjacent, giving rise to border disputes.[7] Following the conquest of Mrauk U, thousands of former subjects from the fallen kingdom, driven by desperation and from ruined villages, took flight across the Naf River into the dense forests and tidal marshes of eastern Bengal and its littoral to seek refuge from Burmese rule. Taking shelter in the fringes of colonial Bengal, in the territory of the East India Company, the Magh borderers marauded and raided Burmese territory across the frontier. Magh borderers struggled for survival, and some "marauded" across the Burmese frontier in acts of resistance and an irredentist longing to restore the Kingdom of Mrauk U. The lands of their refuge were wild and forested, under the constant effect of the ocean's changing tide. During the monsoon season from March through October, the country was "impracticable" and "completely inundated during the rains."[8] Its forested and impenetrable hills abounded with tigers.[9] According to one observer, the Arakan-Bengal borderlands were "almost depopulated and in [a] perfect state of wilderness being covered over with impervious woods, or high grass, more fit for the shelter of wild beasts than the habitation of men."[10] Thousands of Arakanese migrants took refuge in the eastern borderlands of Bengal, making a living "chiefly by fishing, labouring in the woods, and partial employment amongst the Musulman *zamindars*." Some subsisted on shifting fire-field cultivation (often called "slash and burn") in marginal "wasteland" terrains. None of them possessed land or property; they were "woodmen of necessity."[11]

The Burmese government considered the migrants from Arakan across the Naf River in colonial Bengal to be fugitive subjects of their empire, and accordingly the Burmese crossed the frontier in expeditions to pursue Magh rebels and *sardars* (chieftains) who were taking refuge in East India Company territory.[12] In 1794, thousands of Burmese troops had crossed into company territory in pursuit of the Arakanese, or "Magh marauders," and were met by British troops before the refugees were turned over to the Burmese government. A Magh chieftain and cultivator named Apolung fled from Arakan across the borderlands into colonial Bengal. Apolung had witnessed the Burmese destruction of Mrauk U in 1784, recalling that two thousand Arakanese people were killed, while thousands more were led into slavery in the Irrawaddy River valley.[13] Nevertheless, Apolung had reluctantly taken an oath of allegiance to the Konbaung dynasty, and he had been assigned the "Broken Islands" off the coast of Arakan in exchange for an annual tribute of beeswax and elephants.[14] In 1793, the Burmese government demanded that Apolung harvest rice paddies for Rangoon, to be used as provisions for the army in Thailand. Apolung, who "inhabited in a woody country which did not admit of the cultivation of paddy," contributed a *maund* of elephants' teeth instead, but when this proved insufficient, he took vengeance by killing the king's messengers and becoming a fugitive.[15] Apolung turned to raiding and burning Burmese boats along the coast of Arakan, including the plunder of a royal barge belonging to the king on its way to Calcutta. When Burmese troops closed in on him, killing a number of his family and followers, he took flight into Chittagong with his retinue.[16] Labeled an incendiary, informant, and marauder, he was turned over by the East India Company to Burmese authorities and put to death in Amarapura.[17]

The uncertain plight of the Arakanese migrants is captured in a Persian letter to the British governor-general in Calcutta from "Tyta Kufy," a courtier from the fallen city of Mrauk U who fled into colonial Bengal to seek refuge from the Burmese Empire:

> *The Petition of* Tyta Kufy, *the confined Minister; inhabitant of Arracan (Rakhang), now of the district of Chittagong (Chatgam).*
>
> Since this humble slave, along with Pehlun Raja and Khutu, fled together from the kingdom of Arracan, and in order to save our lives, took refuge in the Company's territory of Chittagong; in consequence of which, a war ensued between the Company and the Raja of Pegue, during which, Colonel Erskine having seized us, delivered us over to the people of the aforesaid Raja, who having cruelly and shamefully treated Pehlun and Khutu, put them to death; but as your humble servant's life was predestined to be saved, he contrived to make his escape, and in order to preserve his existence, again took refuge under the shadow of the Company, and returned to Chittagong, and took up his residence in the village of Bhu; in consequence of which the superintendent of the said place, named Rahmut Allah, again seized your humble servant, and sent him to Mr. John Stonehouse, the judge of the aforementioned district, in consequence of which, the said gentlemen sent him, without any crime, to prison, where he is still confined and suffers much trouble. Your humble servant has neither mother, father, nor brothers, and

therefore hopes from the bounty and favor of the Governor General, may his prosperity endure, that he may be liberated from confinement, and a portion of land sufficient to enable him to procure food and raiment may be assigned him, and that the Governor considering him as one of his slaves, will order some provision to be made for him, in order that having sufficient to live on, he may be constantly employed in offering up prayers for the prosperity of the Company, and fulfil the duties of a slave. The Company are masters of the country; on this subject, whatever they command.[18]

The petition, which was translated by Charles Stewart in his *Original Persian Letters* (1825), conveys the uncertainties faced by the former subjects of Mrauk U and the changing landscapes of imperial power in Bengal and Arakan, spurred by the waning of the Mughal and Mrauk U Empires and the rise of the British company state and the Burmese Konbaung dynasty.

## PERSIAN LETTERS FROM THE BURMESE KINGDOM

The Irrawaddy River delta and its littoral had been an object of European ambitions and trade in the Indian Ocean since the early sixteenth century, when Portuguese traders vied for possessions up and down the Burmese coast; and from around 1627, the Dutch and British East India Companies had opened up branches there, the Dutch stationed at Syriam, Pegu, and Ava and the English at Syriam. With the Dutch based in the Indonesian Archipelago and the English in India, however, these company branches were closed in the 1670s. By the last decade of the seventeenth century, the French East India Company had launched its own pursuit of trading relations by establishing a factory in the port city of Syriam near Rangoon, at the nexus of the Bay of Bengal and the Irrawaddy River delta.[19] The British East India Company in Madras meanwhile opened a small settlement on the island of Negrais in the Bay of Bengal, off a cape at the mouth of the Irrawaddy Delta.

Between 1730 and 1740, agents of the British and French East India Companies became increasingly entangled in their imperial rivalry over access to the ports and markets of the Burmese Kingdom. Joseph Dupleix, the French governor of Pondicherry, dispatched his agent Sieur de Bruno to the capital city of Pegu in order to stimulate hostilities against the English, based on the island of Negrais, and to establish closer contacts with the Mon Kingdom, which was seeking allies to aid in its wars with the Burmese

Konbaung dynasty to the north. In their correspondence, Bruno and Dupleix ambitiously contemplated a French takeover of the port of Syriam and the Rangoon River, a branch of the Irrawaddy that would allow them control of the kingdom's foreign trade. Dupleix's Burmese adventure was short-lived, however, as authorities in Paris did not back his risky schemes. In 1755, after the founder of the Konbaung dynasty, Alaungpaya (r. 1752–60), advanced into Rangoon (then known as Dagon), Pondicherry rushed to send reinforcements to save Bruno and his Mon allies in Syriam and Pegu. But by that time Bruno's fate was already sealed. Taken captive by Alaungpaya, the agent was forced to write a false letter that decoyed two French ships upriver and into Burmese possession, before being executed and the French settlement at Syriam being razed.[20]

In 1757, the Mon Kingdom of Pegu fell to Alaungpaya and the nascent Konbaung dynasty, just as the British East India Company became established as the colonial power in neighboring Bengal. From then on, imperial interactions between the company state in Bengal and the bordering Burmese, Arakanese, and Mon Kingdoms intensified. In 1756, a royal letter of gold from Alaungpaya was sent to London, inviting the English to reestablish a base at Negrais and to open up trading relations between the two empires, but by the time the letter from the Burmese king arrived two years later, the Seven Years War was underway in Europe, and it received no reply.[21] Still, in 1757 the English dispatched an embassy to the court of Alaungpaya led by Ensign Robert Lester, managing to gain in return for annual shipments of cannon and gunpowder the right for the East India Company to maintain possession and build a fortress on the island of Negrais. Only two years later in 1759, however, fearing collaboration between the English and his waning foes the Mon, two thousand of Aulangpaya's troops destroyed the company settlement in Negrais, massacring most of its English and Indian inhabitants.[22] Through the end of his reign, Alaungpaya did not permit foreign factories to be built in any part of his empire.[23] By the time Captain Walter Alves traveled to Ava in 1760 to seek compensation for the incident at Negrais, Alaungpaya had passed away and his son Naungdawgyi was on the throne, eager to reopen trading relations with the East India Company but unwilling to rectify past harms. What is more, as long as the Marathas waged a war of insurgency against the company in western India, and as long as the southern Kingdom of Mysore in the Carnatic, under the rule of Haydar 'Ali and his son Tipu Sultan, challenged British imperial power in the subcontinent, there remained few resources for the company to spare on commercial expansion on the Burmese frontier, apart from halting attempts. The East India Company subsequently put its ventures there on hold for more than three decades.

The Burmese Kongbaung dynasty circa 1795 was among a constellation of interconnected "Mughal" empires, a "Mughal imperium" of dynasties, that reigned over vast spaces, ruled as tributary empires through a decentered and layered sovereignty and sharing certain modes of comportment and correspondence that drew upon Persian language and court culture. The establishment of the Burmese Konbaung dynasty in 1752, and its subsequent conquest of the neighboring littoral kingdoms of the Mon (or Hanthawaddy) of Pegu in 1757, Ayutthaya in Siam in 1767, and Mrauk U in Arakan in 1784, brought it closer to the Mughal and Indian Ocean worlds. Most important of all, the conquest of Arakan extended the boundaries of the Burmese kingdom to colonial Bengal under the rule of the East India Company. Through the conquest of Arakan, the Konbaung dynasty came to rule over a sizeable Indo-Persian population from India, Afghanistan, and Iran—known as "Moguls"—and was more closely tied to the world of South Asia and the Indian Ocean. The Konbaung Empire employed "moonshees," scholars and scribes of Persian, who wrote official correspondence to Mughal India and the East India Company and served the kingdom as translators and interpreters.[24]

The immersion of the Burmese frontier into the networks of the Mughal imperium may be traced in the Persian correspondence of the Konbaung dynasty during the 1780s and 1790s. These materials are scattered, fragments appearing in divers collections.[25] These Indo-Persian letters and exchanges were effects of the Burmese Empire's connections to the Mughal world and its embeddedness within a cultural continuum and court protocol spanning South and Southeast Asia.

By the 1780s, Bodawpaya and his illustrious royal capital of Amarapura on the upper Irrawaddy River had emerged as the center of the Burmese Empire. The fourth son of Alaungpaya and the prince of Badon, Bodawpaya (r. 1782–1819) saw himself as the coming of Gautama Buddha and ruler of a universal empire, taking on the long-standing royal Burmese title of Hsinbyumyashin, "Lord of Many White Elephants," and once seeking to build the largest pagoda in the world at the site of Mingun on the Irrawaddy River before abandoning the project.[26] Alongside this adherence to the tenets of Theravada Buddhism, Bodawpaya and the Kongbaung dynasty were conversant in the broader Indo-Persian cultural continuum of Mughal Asia. Through the exchange of Persian letters and the experience of the *darbar* (imperial court), the Konbaung dynasty established its place and presence within a layered Mughal imperial realm, a cross-cultural terrain of chieftains, princes, rajas, *nandaws*, and sultans and their network of overlapping kingdoms.

In order to represent his kingdom and project his sovereignty, Bodawpaya sent bold letters in Persian to the East India Company. The purpose of these letters was twofold. Persian letters asserted and inscribed the sovereignty and territorial boundaries of the Burmese kingdom, reaching from north to south along the Indian Ocean, with the king praised as "His Majesty of the grand city of Amarapura, Lord of Pegu, Arakan, Bassein, Mergui, Tavoy, Martaban, Siam."[27] Persian letters also forged openings to further trade and commercial exchanges between the Burmese Empire and the East India Company. Bodawpaya reigned over a tributary kingdom through the practice of a "layered sovereignty," since beyond the river deltas and the littoral, various independent peoples lived in the uplands, hills, and wilderness terrains of the country, beyond the pale of empire—the Shan, Karen, Kachin, Akha, Naga, Chin, and various other "tribal" confederations.[28] The power in the peripheries of Bodawpaya's empire was the sign of the strength of his kingdom, where he stood as the raja of rajas.

The Burmese king professed his sovereign power in a Persian letter he sent to the collector of Chittagong in 1787, forwarded by Sir William Jones to Governor-General John Shore. In the letter, the Burmese sovereign—identified by Jones simply as "Tatbu Arnu King of Ava"—detailed the territorial bounds of his kingdom, claiming to be lord of various "countries," "Rajahs," "people," and "subjects":

> I am lord of a whole people, and of 101 countries, and my titles are Rajah Chattrdary (sitting under a canopy) and Rajah Surey Bunkshee (descendant of the Sun). Sitting on the throne with a splendid canopy of gold, I hold in subjection to my authority many Rajahs; gold, silver, and jewels are the produce of my country, and in my hand is the instrument of war, that, as the lightning of Heaven, humbles and subdues my enemies; my troops require neither injunctions nor commands, and my elephants and horses are without number. In my service are ten pundits learned in the Shaster, and 104 priests, whose wisdom is not to be equaled; agreeably to whose learning and intelligence, I execute and distribute justice among my people, so that my mandates, like lightning,

suffer no resistance nor control. My subjects are endowed with virtue and the principles of justice, and refrain from all immoral practices, and I am as the Sun, blessed with the light of wisdom to discover the secret designs of men; whoever is worthy of being called a Rajah, is merciful and just towards his people; thieves, robbers, and disturbers of peace, have at length received the punishment due to their crimes; and now the word of my mouth is dreaded as the lightning from Heaven. I am as a great sea, among 2000 rivers, and many rivulets; and as the mountain Shumeroo, surrounded by 40,000 hills, and like unto these is my authority, extending itself over 101 Rajahs; further, 10,000 Rajahs pay daily attendance at my Durbar, and my country excels every country of the world; my palace as the heavens, studded with gold and precious stones, is revered more than any other palace in the universe. [29]

The political sway and authority of the Burmese king extended from the lowland delta to the upland mountain regions, encompassing different princely rulers and their vassals.

In the letter, the Burmese king continued by claiming an ancient descent from Raja Sery (perhaps Raja Chandra Suriya of the Dhanyawadi Kingdom), a line of sacred kingship and sovereignty reaching back for thousands of years to the legendary visit of Gaudama Buddha to the realm of Arakan:

Raja Sery Tamah Chucka governed with justice and ability and the people were happy under his administration. He was also favoured with the friendship of the religious men of the age, one of whom, by name Budder, resorting to his place of residence. . . . One Boiwdah Outhar, otherwise Sery Boot Taukwor, came down in the country of Arracan, and instructed the people and the beasts of the field in the principles of religion and rectitude, and agreeably to his word the country was governed for a period of 5000 years, so that peace and good-will subsisted amongst men. [30]

The Burmese emperor touted his own sovereignty as in line with this ancient lineage of just kings, while making reference to his recent conquest of the ancestral Buddhist land of Arakan:

I likewise pursue a line of conduct and religion similar to the above; but previous to my conquest, the people were as snakes wounding men, a prey to enmity and disorder. . . . As there is an oil, the produce of a certain spot of the earth, of exquisite flavour, so is my dignity and power above that of other Rajahs; and the high priest, having consulted with the others of that class, represented to me on 15 Aughur 1148, saying, do you enforce the laws and customs of Sery Boot Taukwor, which I accordingly did, and moreover erected six places of divine worship, and have conformed myself strictly to the laws and customs, governing my people with lenity and justice. [31]

Having announced the mandate of his sovereignty over the region of Arakan, bordering on British Bengal, the king made overtures toward an alliance in ties of trade and commerce with the East India Company:

> As the country of Arracan lies contiguous to Chittagong, if a Treaty of Commerce were established between me and the English, perfect amity and alliance would ensue from such engagements; therefore I have submitted it to you, that the merchants of your country should resort hither for the purpose of purchasing pearls, ivory, wax, and that in return my people should be permitted to resort to Chittagong for the purpose of trafficking in such commodities as the country may afford.[32]

The letter was sent with four pieces of ivory under the charge of thirty representatives who were to seek an answer to the proposal of alliance. William Jones, in forwarding his translation of the letter to Governor-General John Shore, surmised that "[Bodawpaya] may be a good neighbor, and we may be gainers by his gold and ivory." But Jones also raised a more ominous specter of an empire of diminishing power on the brink of decline: the Burmese king was "ambitious" and "would act the lion if he could, and end, as he is said to have begun, the Aurenzeb of the Indian peninsula."[33]

In January 1788, the Burmese king sent another Persian letter to the East India Company, this one under the title "Nandaw, Raja of Pegu," again announcing his reign over Arakan and the "peace and tranquility" that prevailed in the port city of Rangoon. The raja proposed establishment of "a trade relation" with the company and assured the protection and facility of its merchant ships entering the dominions of the Burmese Kingdom.[34] In a follow-up letter to the company, the *vazir* (minister) and *nayib* (regent) of the Burmese king summarized the market for trade in Rangoon, where "for some years past no ships have visited," spiking demand for Indian articles and goods. The vazir suggested that "some vessels may be sent to Pegu laden with the required articles so that they may be purchased in exchange for the produce of the country."[35] Other letters from Burmese court ministers arrived requesting shipments of cloth, horses, and a chariot for the king.[36]

Persian correspondence created a channel of communication to address misunderstandings and thus built a certain code of trust between the East India Company and the Burmese state. There existed ongoing traffic and trade between British Bengal and the Burmese littoral, but it was mired in confusion, uncertainties, and misconceptions, with lost ships and stranded merchants on both sides. Apart from its uncertainties regarding the power and motivations of the company, the Burmese court sought news of its missing sea captains and unreturned merchant ships. Company merchants, for their part, complained of the Rangoon and Pegu trade as unwelcoming, unpredictable, and semiclosed, noting "the Japanese customs" imposed on ships anchored in the harbor to surrender their rudder and guns onshore, as detailed in William Hunter's view of trade with the Burmese Empire in his *Concise Account of . . . the Kingdom of Pegu*.[37] The exchange of Persian letters became a medium of possible commensurability and resolution. When in 1789 the Burmese sea captains Nakhuda Rangyiah and Mitu Sayab had their ship *Lachmi Narnan* seized by Gabriel Vrignon, a French merchant of Calcutta, due to an unsettled debt, the company intervened, in "sincere friendship," by covering the dues that had been incurred in 1784 when the Pegu merchants 'Abdul Vahid and Shaikh Muhammad Dilavar had sailed the same ship, under the name *Moonky Danguian*, to Bengal. All this was detailed in a Persian letter from the company "to the King of Pegu."[38] Later, in the early 1790s, Persian letters maintained an open channel between the Burmese Empire and the company state in cases of dispute, such as when Burmese agents in Rangoon took possession of company ships, including the merchant George Tyler's ketch the *Phoenix*, and flew the Burmese flag on it. In retribution, Tyler seized the ship of the Burmese sea captain Bagy Nacodar, which was carrying four elephants from the king, and a different ship, the *Ali Madad*, belonging to Captain Muhammad Sharif.[39]

In 1793, the Marquess of Cornwallis ordered a private merchant, Captain George Sorrel, to carry a "half official" letter to the Burmese king. Traveling on a small country schooner, Sorrel reached the Burmese capital of Amarapura in March 1794, where he presented the official letter to his sponsor, the governor of Pegu, who delivered the correspondence to the royal court, where it was read in the presence of the king.[40] A letter from the emperor addressed to the governor-general was entrusted to Sorrel, but the royal response was lost in a shipwreck at the mouth of the Hugli River on the return journey to Calcutta.[41] Sorrel's visit to the Burmese court, however, was noted in a Persian letter from the governor of Pegu, who announced that "the ports of his country were open to all nations and the English merchants get preference" and who expressed the diplomatic desire "to continue and strengthen the bonds of friendship."[42] The scene was set for closer diplomatic and commercial contacts and relations. There was need of a cultural emissary, versed and learned in the still extant Indo-Persian Mughal diplomatic language and etiquette, to serve as intermediary between the East India

Company and the Burmese Empire. In 1795, newly appointed Governor-General John Shore designated Michael Symes as the envoy of an official embassy to the court of Ava, with instructions to establish diplomatic contacts and open up commercial relations with the Burmese Kingdom.

## "INDIA BEYOND THE GANGES"

On February 21, 1795, the East India Company cruiser the *Sea Horse* set sail from the Calcutta harbor across the Bay of Bengal to the royal city of Amarapura in the Burmese Kingdom.[43] Aboard the ship were the members of the first official English embassy to the Burmese court. The envoy of the mission, Michael Symes (1761–1809), was an Irish officer and diplomat in the Seventy-Sixth Regiment of His Majesty's Army, dispatched by Governor-General John Shore to lead the embassy. Symes had attended Trinity College in Dublin and at the age of nineteen became an East India Company cadet in Bengal in 1780, rising to the rank of captain in Madras in 1791. Symes was a skilled diplomat and talented Orientalist, who "spoke and wrote Persian and possessed a knowledge of the classics."[44] His linguistic skill in Persian was essential because that was the common language of diplomacy and courtly correspondence between the East India Company and the Burmese Konbaung dynasty. In his letters to the Burmese state during the course of the embassy, Symes "always wrote in Persian, and in English," while receiving responses in Burmese as well as Persian, penned by the "Mussulman moonshee" of the emperor.[45]

The embassy carried a letter, "written in English and in Persian," from Governor-General John Shore to the Burmese emperor. The letter was intended to promote confidence, "convey sentiments of friendship," and "facilitate commercial relations" between the East India Company and the Burmese Kingdom.[46] The governor-general instructed Symes that

> the primary objects of your mission are the conciliating of the King and his ministry by the removal of that jealousy and suspicion which they entertain of the British Government in India and convincing them that it is our wish to preserve the most friendly intercourse with them, which will naturally if not immediately tend to promote the Commercial Interests of both nations.

Upon opening diplomatic contacts and turning "the Disposition of the Court of Ava," Symes was "to attempt attaining any Specific Concessions in Commercial points."[47]

Accompanying the letter, the embassy imported an array of gifts of friendship to be presented to the Burmese king, gifts selected with a view to the opening up of commerce between the East India Company and the Burmese Empire. The Burmese Kingdom and the ports of its littoral were already permeated by networks of Indian Ocean trade. Trade routes linked the kingdom westward to India and the Bay of Bengal and eastward to the Malay Archipelago. Its port cities were established as valuable markets for the trade in luxury goods like ivory, precious gems and metals, and teak wood. But the kingdom had a tributary economy, and its commerce was bound by the prevalence of sumptuary laws. The East India Company dispatched Symes to explore an uncharted Buddhist kingdom and to gain trading concessions from its enigmatic court.[48] The mission's purpose was to build diplomatic contacts between the company and the Burmese court, to open up trade and commerce, and in the process to survey and size up the environs, geography, history, and culture of the Burmese Kingdom. Symes was delegated with the challenging task of establishing direct diplomatic and commercial contact with an outer Indian kingdom about which very little was known. He regarded the mission as a journey into a part of the Indian subcontinent that had "remained in inexplicable obscurity" into the late eighteenth century. "There are no countries on the habitable globe, where the arts of civilized life are understood, of which we have so limited a knowledge, as of those that lie between the British possessions in India, and the empire of China," of "India beyond the Ganges."[49] In this way, the embassy also entailed a project to survey, decipher, and map the Burmese Empire.

On this mission, Symes was accompanied by a talented crew. Scottish surgeon, surveyor, and botanist Francis Buchanan (1762–1829) joined the expedition, then just in the early stages of his research into the flora and fauna of India and its surrounding kingdoms. Having studied medicine at the University of Edinburgh, where he also learned about botany under John Hope, he became a medical officer in the East India Company. Dispatched as assistant surgeon in Bengal in 1794, the following year he traveled on the mission to the Burmese Kingdom in order to collect and assemble an herbarium of flora found in its forests, but his extensive reports also touched on the natural history, topography, culture, language, religion, history, and archaeology of the kingdom. Ensign Thomas Wood joined the mission as assistant and secretary, charged also with the task of surveying the Irrawaddy River and recording astronomical observations during the course of the journey.

The expedition comprised a diverse crew of Indo-Persian go-betweens, essential to the gathering, recording, and translation of knowledge from the Burmese Empire to the East India Company. They included a *havildar* (native sergeant), a *naick* (native corporal), and fourteen sepoys, along with Indian scholars and scribes—a "Hindoo Pundit" (scholar of Sanskrit), a "Mussulman Moonshee" (scholar and scribe of the Persian language), a Bengali plant collector, and the skilled botanical artist Singey Bey.[50] These Indo-Persian middlemen aboard the *Sea Horse* wrote and translated Persian correspondence between the company and the Burmese court, and they were essential to the expedition's scientific endeavors in surveying the Southeast Asian kingdom and rendering it legible and known. Their presence on the mission highlights the role of Indo-Persian communities as intermediaries who bridged the cross-cultural expanse of Mughal Asia and its fringes.

The *Sea Horse*'s first port of call was off the Burmese coast on the pristine Andaman Islands, the abode of the elusive and free "Sea Gypsies," where the crew lured two young native women aboard the ship with an offer of fish before they quietly disappeared "in the middle of the night . . . into the sea."[51] Reaching the mouth of the swampy Rangoon River on 20 March 20, 1795, the *Sea Horse* was met by a "watch boat" and thereafter proceeded again, guided by a pilot ship toward the port city. Sailing past "low and swampy" banks of the river, "skirted by high reeds and brushwood" on both sides, the *Sea Horse* anchored twelve miles below Rangoon to await the government fleet.[52] The following day, a fleet of twenty to thirty canoes appeared on the horizon, "long and narrow, with an elevated stern, ornamented with peacocks' feathers, and the tails of Thibet cows; each boat bore a different flag." Exchanging greetings with the royal officials in "the language of Hindostan," the *Sea Horse* again set sail toward the city, as the Burmese fleet "rowed with great velocity round her, performing a variety of evolutions, and exhibiting considerable skill in the management of their vessels."[53] As the *Sea Horse* entered the harbor and Rangoon came into view, Symes and his entourage discerned the golden spire of Shwe Dagon Pagoda, its rays gleaming through the city's sylvan landscape.

## "CUSTOMS OF THE COUNTRY"

Upon landing onshore, the members of the mission were taken to a bamboo house "on the verge of the river," constructed for their residence. The house was built entirely of bamboo and cane mats, covered with a lofty roof to give shelter from the rain and shade from the sun. Standing upon its balcony, Symes and his suite were ceremoniously greeted by music from a band of Burmese musicians, a *saing*, accompanied by a troupe of dancers and performers.[54] Despite the outward ceremony, however, the mission was treated with visible mistrust and suspicion by the Burmese government. The members of the mission were prohibited from entering the town and the market. A handful of Burmese guards trailed their every movement between the ship and their dwelling onshore, as Symes recounted, "following us, and vigilantly observing all of our actions." Symes complained, "Wherever we directed our steps, three or four Birman centinels followed us closely."[55] Although crowds of ordinary men and women gathered around them "from curiosity," the expedition members had little interaction with the people due to prevailing customs and taboos.[56] Symes noted in a letter back to Calcutta: "It is a matter of the Etiquette of this Country to hold as little publick correspondence as possible with a person delegated to a Superior power until the mission of the delegate has been announced and received the Sanction of the Supreme authority."[57] In addition to these restraints, all merchant ships in the harbor of Rangoon had received orders from the Rhoom, the government's public hall of justice, to not communicate or go aboard the *Sea Horse*.[58]

Having traveled to an unfamiliar foreign kingdom, with customs, peoples, and languages that he did not know or comprehend, Symes was left in isolation. His doubts about the prospects of the mission, inspired by the perceptible indifference and aloofness of the Burmese government, led to thoughts of calling off the embassy and returning to Calcutta discredited and in shame. The foreignness of the encounter with the Burmese Kingdom left Symes searching in vain for commonalities through the only possible shared medium of expression, the Persian language and its vernaculars, and those who understood them.

Symes's acclimation to the worlds of the Burmese Empire came through his contact with a representative of the government of Rangoon, who was also a member of the city's influential Indo-Persian society, Zedarutkio Johannes Moses "Baba Sheen." An Armenian of Iranian descent born in the Burmese Empire, Baba Sheen was assigned by the Burmese king as the chief interpreter and guide to the mission due to his knowledge of Persian and Hindustani. He makes his first appearance early in Symes's account as "a tall elderly man, of a graceful appearance followed by several attendants," whose "manners were easy and respectful" and who held the office of the "Ackawoon" of Rangoon. Although Baba Sheen was "a native of the Birman country, he was of Armenian extraction, and professed belief in our Saviour." His duty was to wait on the British mission and to serve as interpreter and guide. Symes's communications with Baba Sheen were at first facilitated through the latter's interpreter, "a Mussulman merchant, who spoke Persian." Baba Sheen soon revealed, however, that he himself understood Persian and "spoke the language of Hindostan," and he and Symes "soon understood each other so well, as no longer to stand in need of an interpreter."[59] Through Persian, Symes became "enabled to convey sentiments with more ease" and "to converse on the subjects of the deputation" with Baba Sheen.[60]

Baba Sheen assuaged Symes that the limits placed upon the embassy and its movements were not meant disrespectfully but were "the custom of their nation" and "in conformity to long established usage." Symes noted his intention of "acquiescing in every ceremonial that their custom prescribed" and admitted his "own want of knowledge of the customs" of the Burmese state.[61] In his letters to Calcutta, he wrote of his attempts to accommodate himself "in every part to the customs of the Country."[62] When more than a week had passed without official acknowledgment of the embassy from the royal court, and with the strict limitations placed on the expedition's freedom in Rangoon, Symes threatened to return to Calcutta and leave the mission incomplete. Symes objected to Baba Sheen that what was "conformable to custom" in the Burmese Kingdom was "incompatible" with the "customs" and "dignity" of the East India Company. "Their forms and ours differed so widely," Symes wrote, "and . . . were not likely to correspond."[63] While it would bring him dishonor in Bengal, Symes expressed his decision to withdraw to Calcutta. Knowing that this was not a hollow threat and that it would be sure to affect his own standing in the court of Amarapura, Baba Sheen sought to ameliorate the qualms of the British embassy. In a meeting with Baba Sheen and the *raywoon,* or governor of Rangoon, Symes prevailed on them to order the removal of the Burmese guards from the *Sea Horse* and grant permission for members of the embassy to freely enter the city and bazaar. The captains of the English ships in the port's harbor, accompanied by Baba Sheen, visited the embassy at its house on the river.[64]

The *maywoon,* or provincial governor of Pegu, had invited Symes and the members of the embassy to the "great pagoda" in his city to host them during the annual festival of the full moon, and it was decided that they would attend. Traveling with Baba Sheen as their guide, Symes and his cohort made the journey to the former capital of the fallen Mon Kingdom. Rowing along

FIGURE 8. Watercolor of Shwe Mawdaw Paya in Pegu, capital of the fallen Mon Kingdom in southern Burma, by an Indian artist, probably Singey Bey. Inscribed "Choemadoo the Great Temple of Pegu See Symes Ava pg. 186 Height 361." Said to be more than one thousand years old, the temple was built to enshrine two hairs of the Buddha, as well as his tooth relics. Add. Or. 568 (ca. 1800), British Library, London.

the winding, reed-fringed tributaries in between the Irrawaddy and Sittaung Rivers, the country seemed to open up to them for the first time, stirring their curiosity about the hidden kingdom they had entered. Upon reaching Pegu, Symes described the former Mon capital as an "ancient city" of "ruins" and "fragments," noticing in its crumbling walls the traces of its former "magnificence" and "fallen grandeur." The city had been razed during the Burmese invasion of 1757, only its temples left intact, above all the reverenced and monumental Shwe Mawdaw Pagoda. Since then, the reigning Burmese king had "issued orders to rebuild" Pegu and "invited the scattered families of former inhabitants to return and repeople their deserted city." Symes noted that "a new town has been built within the site of the ancient city," with paved streets and houses constructed of bamboo and straw mats.[65]

Early in the morning after their arrival in the city, the embassy made its way to Shwe Mawdaw Pagoda. On their way, the mission members stopped to view a passing procession of the maywoon's royal guard of "five or six hundred [armed] men," followed by the maywoon himself, "mounted on the neck of a very fine elephant," which he guided independently, "a parade of elephants" trailing behind him.[66] The elephant knelt on reaching the steps of the temple as the maywoon alighted and removed his shoes before entering the platform of the pagoda. "At the grand Pagoda," Symes reported in a letter to Bengal, there was "a seat prepared for us above."[67] Viewing the spectacular and extraordinary monument, the embassy began to perceive a glimpse of the cosmic Buddhist world at the core of the Burmese Empire and its sovereignty.

The sacred temple was the primary force and object that attracted the people of the city, a monumental trace of the lost kingdom of the Mons. It was called Shwe Mawdaw, "the Golden Supreme," a brick-and-mortar temple claimed to have been built to enshrine the relics of the Buddha, including two of his hairs. The temple was ascended by "flights of stone steps" to a parallelogram-shaped "double terrace, one raised above another." From the upper terrace, with over a hundred smaller spires around its base, the pyramid-like temple and its lofty pinnacle soared 361 feet above the city.[68] The structure was crowned by a *hti*, an intricate gilded finial that chimed in the wind. Symes described it in detail, noting that the Burmese king had gifted it as atonement and merit following the destruction of the city:

> The whole is crowned by a *Tee*, or umbrella, of open ironwork, from which rises a rod with a gilded pennant. The tee is to be seen on every sacred building that is of spiral form: the raising and consecration of this last indispensable appendage, is an act of high religious solemnity. The present king bestowed the tee that covers Shoemadoo. It was made at the capital: many of the principal nobility came down from Ummerapoora [Amarapura] to be present at the ceremony of its elevation. The circumference of the tee is fifty-six feet; it rests on an iron axis fixed in the building, and is farther secured by chains strongly riveted to the spire. Round the lower rim of the tee are appended a number of bells, which, agitated by the wind, make a continual jingling.[69]

Symes heard the sounds of the hti chime through the silent air of devotion around the temple. It was the first of his recurring encounters with the sacred Buddhist monuments and relics of the Burmese Empire. After a long silence during the attendance of the maywoon, beneath the afternoon shadow of the temple, Symes avowed the friendship of the British government of India and presented a copy of the governor-general's letter before the closure of the ceremony.[70]

For the next few days, with Baba Sheen as their master of ceremony and guide, members of the embassy were hosted at various festivals in celebration of the New Year, marking the annual cycle of the premonsoon stage of the rice harvest, at the height of the hot season, and they attended various musical concerts and dramatic performances (*pwe*). Symes and his retinue were treated to a grand spectacle of fireworks on an open plain, put on by troupes of pyrotechnicians from remote districts across the kingdom, as wagons drawn by water buffalo fired explosives into the sky from the hollowed tree trunks they carried.[71] In the open theater of the court of the maywoon, expedition members attended a dramatic performance of the ancient Indian epic of the *Ramayana*, which recounted the legendary struggles of the divine prince Ram across the forest in search of his lost consort Sita before becoming king. Symes recognized the drama and cast of characters as "the sacred text of the Ramayan . . . among the Hindoos," Indic mythology adapted to the Burmese Kingdom, although he noted, "it excelled any Indian drama."[72]

On the last day of the year, Symes, Wood, and Buchanan, guided by Baba Sheen, were invited to the residence of the maywoon for the annual water festival known as Thingyan. It was the custom during Thingyan, in order "to wash away the impurities of the past," for women "to throw water on" and "endeavor to wet every man that goes along the street." On entering the maywoon's, the members of the embassy had water scented with sandalwood poured over them out of a golden cup by the eldest daughter of their host, to mark the beginning the festivities. They were then "surrounded and deluged" by "ten to twenty women, young and middle aged, rushed into the hall from the inner apartments," leaving the men "tired and completely drenched." On their way back home, the members of the British embassy passed many women who seemed keen to douse them but let them pass on account of their being foreigners, "but they assailed Baba Sheen and his Birman attendants with little ceremony."[73]

When the travelers were not exploring the ancient city of Pegu, they spent their nights and days in between festivities in their bamboo-thatched lodge, where they became a spectacle to locals. Symes recounted that "men and women, prompted by harmless curiosity, surrounded the paling of the enclosure from morning till night," often entering the public hall and sitting respectfully on the wood floor as they observed the strange and unusual customs of the foreign visitors to the kingdom.[74]

## DAGON

The city had long been known by the name "Dagon," in reference to the chimeric temple perched on Singuttara Hill high above the town. According to legend, the pagoda enclosed the relics of four past Buddhas, including eight hairs of Siddartha Gautama. The city of the revered Buddhist temple of Shwe Dagon, "Golden Dagon," was renamed Yangon (later Anglicized as Rangoon, meaning "End of Strife") by the founder of the Konbaung dynasty, Alaungpaya, following the conquest of the lower Irrawaddy River delta from the Mon Kingdom in 1755. Returning to Rangoon following a nearly month-long sojourn in Pegu, Symes regarded the temple and its spire, crowned by a radiant and entirely gilded hti, as he climbed the temple steps under the sun.[75] He and the other members of the embassy spent their time, while awaiting the king's permission to proceed to the court of Amarapura, surveying the port city, its environs, and its trade.[76] Their main focus was to open up the traffic at the port and the commercial flows in and out of the city.

In May 1795, Symes wrote an extensive report to Calcutta on the trade of Rangoon and the Gulf of Martaban. Despite being cut off from "People of the means of procuring information" and perceiving an averseness to trust, Symes discerned some measure of "the flourishing state of Rangoon" and found "indisputable Proof of the Power of Trade." But the Rangoon trade was "in its Infancy" and "just rising from Obstacles" in its way. Although he still could not "specify the present state of this country" or know the name of its king, he lauded the harbors of Rangoon and its sprawling Indian Ocean gulf, commenting that "no country opens more Convenient Channels of Intercourse with the Nations of the East." The principal commodity to be procured was teak timber, which according to Symes "constitutes the present importance of the Pegu trade, and in which it must maintain its prominence. It is the staple that cannot be supplied from any other Quarter." But the teak grew in the high upland mountains of the kingdom, in the territory of autonomous ethnic populations, and was heavily taxed along its transport route down the rivers during the monsoon season. Other exports of the kingdom included such rarities as ivory, emeralds, rubies, sapphires, and jade. And Symes speculated that deposits of precious metals—gold, silver, and lead—were the "Commodities which in this Country lie concealed." It was common knowledge that although the mines of the dominion were supposedly rich, "the King does not suffer them to be worked except in certain Places near the Capital, and these very sparingly." The king collected a duty of 10 percent in kind on all commodities imported to the kingdom and 5 percent on all exports paid in cash.[77]

Symes attributed the fledgling state of commerce to the destruction caused by years of war between the Burmese, Arakanese, Mon, and Siamese Kingdoms and their effects on trade. Wars with rival kingdoms had depopulated and laid waste to the lands of the Burmese Empire from the Irrawaddy River delta to the littoral of the Gulf of Martaban. Despite the lure of teak, the uncertainty surrounding trade with the Konbaung dynasty and the "slow profits" to be had there, led many merchant ships to bypass it, "to go Eastward and seek larger Gains at a greater Risk and a more distant Market" in the Indies. The European and English merchants who arrived at the shores of Rangoon and resided in the city were "Persons who have taken Leave from the Laws of their Country and the Mariners who use it, for the most part, Men of no Capital, and confined Credit" who "carry their ships to Rangoon when they can afford to carry them nowhere else, in the Expectation of being able to procure a Cargo of Timber." Symes noted that trade and commerce were the priorities of "Armenians, Moors, and Parsees" in Rangoon, where there existed "no Substantial European House of Agency." Instead, the trade of Rangoon was conducted by interpreters and intermediaries—Armenians, Indians, Iranians, Parsees, and Portuguese who due to their knowledge of languages served as the "King's Linguists." Symes described their influential position in the trade of Rangoon: "As soon as a Ship arrives, an Interpreter is immediately assigned to it—he becomes the common provider to the Vessel, the Master's Agent in Mercantile Concerns, and the Government Spy, to give Notice of all the Transactions of that particular Ship."[78]

As the East India Company relied on "native" pundits and munshis to navigate their encounters across the Mughal world, so too did the Konbaung dynasty, as it veered closer to the Mughal world, turn to the network of Indo-Persian populations in its territories to conduct trade and diplomacy with European merchants and the outside world. The designation "Mogul" in Burma referred to Indian, Iranian, and Armenian merchants, overlapping with the appellation *kala* (foreigner).[79] Indo-Persian populations—Bengalis, Afghans, Persians, Parsis, Armenians, Arabs, Jews, and Portuguese known in Burma as "Moguls"—served as middlemen and interpreters in Anglo-Burmese contacts, interactions, and correspondence, which through the First Anglo-Burmese War (1824–26) occurred in the lingua franca of Persian and may be traced in Indo-Persian textual and visual representations produced through encounters between South and Southeast Asia. By the turn of the nineteenth century, these Indo-Persian communities were an increasingly recognizable part of the fabric of Burmese society in the port cities.

In Rangoon, Symes described the mix of people encountered, with particular emphasis on the social fabric and ethnic and religious diversity of the city:

> Here are to be met fugitives from all countries of the East, and of all complexions: the exchange, if I may so call the common place of their meeting, exhibits a motley assemblage of merchants, such as few towns of much greater magnitude can produce; Malabars, Moguls, Persians, Parsees, Armenians, Portuguese, French, and English, all mingle here, and are engaged in various branches of commerce. The members of this discordant multitude are not

only permitted to reside under the protection of government, but likewise enjoy the most liberal toleration in matters of religion; they celebrate their several rites and festivals, totally disregarded by the Birmans, who have no inclination to make proselytes. In the same street may be heard the solemn voice of the Muezzin, calling pious Islamites to early prayers, and the bell of the Portuguese chapel tinkling a summons to Christians. Processions meet and pass each other without giving or receiving cause of offence. The Birmans never trouble themselves about the religious opinions of any sect, or disturb their ritual ceremonies, provided they do not break the peace, or meddle with their own divinity Gaudma.[80]

Symes also noted the connections to trade and commerce held by these Indo-Persian communities in the Burmese Empire:

Obscure adventurers and outcasts from all countries of the east had flocked to Rangoon, where they were received with hospitality by a liberal nation: among these, the industrious few soon acquired wealth by means of their superior knowledge. The Parsees, the Armenians, and a small proportion of Mussulmen, engrossed the largest share of the trade of Rangoon; and individuals from their number were frequently selected by government to fill employments of trust that related to trade, and transactions with foreigners.[81]

Seeking to benefit from the commercial networks of these foreigners, the Burmese Empire "had of late years given toleration to all sects, and invited strangers of every nation to resort to their ports; and being themselves free from those prejudices of cast, which shackle their Indian neighbours, they permitted foreigners to intermarry, and settle among them."[82]

Many members of these Indo-Persian and Indian Ocean communities journeyed to the port cities of Burma as merchants, and some entered into influential posts within the Konbaung dynasty as supervisors of foreign traders and shipmasters, known by the Persian title Shahbandar, meaning "King of the Port and Harbor," or the Burmese title Akakwun, "Collector of Customs."[83] It should not come as a surprise that these Indo-Persian merchant groups were protective of their position when faced with East India Company expansion from colonial Bengal, even to the point of identifying with Tipu Sultan and allying with the French. Symes reported that in Rangoon certain "principal merchants"—two Muslims named Muhummed Shoffie and Moung Yaa and an Armenian merchant of foreign commodities, Jacob Aguizar—endeavored to tarnish the motivations behind the company and its missions to the Burmese king by recounting tales of the company's treachery against the greater imperial Kingdom of Mysore under Tipu Sultan and also seeking to build alliances with French "adventurers."[84] A Muslim from the coast of Coromandel by the name of Mounja presented Bodawpaya with a memorial in which he advised the king "to be jealous of the English and their Embassy; that they have their eyes fixed on his dominions, of which they only want a plausible pretext to make themselves masters."[85]

There was little doubt that the "Moguls" and their reports "made a strong impression on the minds of the King and his eldest son," rendering them suspicious of British motives and doubtful of their chances of overcoming the Kingdom of Mysore and bringing about the "destruction of Tippoo" even in the year following the fall of Seringapatam.[86] Based on such reports Bodawpaya sent spies to Seringapatam, seeking to build alliances with Tipu Sultan, as well as to the Mughal imperial court in Delhi and the Marathas in western India, as Muslims and Armenians at home warned Bodawpaya of the threat posed to his kingdom by the British company.[87] The records of *The Royal Administration of Burma* recount that the Konbaung had established contact with the rajas of Hindustan, who sent gifts of tribute to the Burmese sovereign and made an alliance "with the King of Burma in driving out the English, who, from their base in Bengal, were encroaching on Indian territories."[88] Bodawpaya and other representatives of the Konbaung dynasty keenly followed news of Tipu Sultan, his resistance against British expansion in the Deccan of India, and his alliances and diplomacy with the revolutionary republic of France, the isle of Mauritius, and other states. Word of the nawab of Mysore's exploits were not far from the shores of the Burmese Kingdom. In 1791, a Naqshbandi Sufi lascar from Bombay named Qazi Ghulam Qasim sailed the Indian Ocean between Bandar Aceh in Sumatra, Sri Lanka, and the Martaban Peninsula of the Burmese Empire while composing qasida in praise of Tipu Sultan in his Persian scrapbook, lauding him as the second coming of Alexander the Great, ruler of the East and the West.[89]

The Armenian merchants who settled in the Burmese Empire were of paramount importance to the kingdom's navigation of the outside world and the expanding web of the East India Company. The Burmese Armenian community were descendants of long-distance merchants from the city of Isfahan in Safavid Persia. From Isfahan, Armenian merchants conducted the foreign trade of the Safavid Empire and forged a wide-ranging global trade network spanning the Indian Ocean and the Mediterranean.[90] In the aftermath of the sudden fall of Isfahan and the Safavid Empire, as well as the dynastic instability that ensued in eighteenth-century Persia, many Armenian merchants migrated to other ports of trade in India and the Indian Ocean, including in

Southeast Asia. Since the latter seventeenth century, Armenian merchants and shippers in Madras had become influential in the trade with the Burmese and Mon Empires of the Irrawaddy River valley and the littoral across the Bay of Bengal. By the mid-eighteenth century, the Armenian community in the Burmese Empire had flourished to the point that they constructed a large brick church in the port of Syriam across the river from Rangoon.[91]

In the imperial capital of Amarapura, Symes met "an Armenian interpreter, named Muckatees, who spoke and wrote English fluently, [and] was ordered to make a copy in English" of the letter from the governor-general of India to the Burmese king.[92] Muckatees, whose name in Armenian was Mackertich, had mastered the difficult Burmese language and served the Burmese court as a translator and scholar. Symes added further details about the talented Armenian scholar's life and work:

> The Armenian interpreter of English, who had spent the greater part of his life in the Birman country, was a man eminently qualified for the task: he spoke, read, and wrote English, superior to any person I ever knew, who had not been in Great Britain. It is a singular fact, that the first version of the late Sir William Jones's Translation of the Institutes of Hindoo Law, should be made in the Birman language. When I arrived in Ummerapoora, the Armenian had just completed the work, by command of his Birman Majesty.[93]

The most prominent of the Armenian merchants in the service of the Burmese government was Baba Sheen, who played a critical role as intermediary, interpreter, and guide to the embassy from the East India Company. Writing of the character of Baba Sheen, whose name was a Burmese derivation of Baba John, in reference to his family name of Johannes, Symes praised his worldly disposition: "He was a man of general knowledge, and deemed by the Birmans an accomplished scholar; he was better acquainted with the history, politics, and geography of Europe, than any Asiatic I ever conversed with; his learning was universal, being slightly versed in almost every science."[94] This view was repeated by Francis Buchanan, who referred to "Joannes Moses, *Akunwun* of *Haynthawade*" as "the most intelligent man with whom we conversed" and reproduced the Burmese Armenian's "delineation of the sixty-eight Burma constellations, with a short explanation in the *Burma* language" in his essay "On the Religion and Literature of the Burmas," published in the journal *Asiatick Researches* in 1801.[95] The collector of an extensive library of Burmese palm-leaf manuscripts and books in Persian and European languages, Baba Sheen (publishing under the name

Johannes Moses) also compiled the *Pawtugi Yazawin,* a Burmese chronicle of the Portuguese centering on the exploits of Felipe de Brito y Nicote in Syriam during the early seventeenth century, coediting the text with Father Ignazio de Brito of Rangoon.[96]

Due to his skills as a merchant and knowledge of the outside world, Baba Sheen had been appointed Akakwun of Rangoon. In this post he pursued commercial trade and was active in the import and export of goods in and out of Rangoon, as well as trade up and down the Irrawaddy River to the cities of the delta and the interior. Baba Sheen received no salary for serving as customs officer; it was expected that he would profit from his position of authority in the commerce of the port city. As Akakwun, he was in a precarious position subject to the whims of the emperor; "he was obliged annually to make the King considerable presents, and had more than once been stripped by his Majesty of all he possessed."[97] Between 1795 and 1812 in his capacity as Akakwun, Baba Sheen received and served as interpreter and guide to the various British East India Company missions sent to the Burmese Empire. There was a certain irony in Baba Sheen's transactions with the company, whose expanding sphere in the Bay of Bengal and the Burmese littoral threatened to displace the thriving Armenian, Parsi, and Muslim merchant communities then resident in the port cities of the Burmese Empire. It was this situation, and the general suspicion that surrounded British motives in the Burmese Kingdom, that affected the equivocal nature, subtle resistance, and mysterious attitude of Baba Sheen toward the East India Company and its representatives.

Though he belonged to the Armenian community, Baba Sheen was born and acculturated in the Burmese Empire. He was an Armenian Christian, but he was tolerant in his beliefs and accepting of different religious practices, even participating in Buddhist processions for admitting young monks into the priesthood, a sign of the open religious environment that prevailed in Konbaung Burma.[98] The last references to Baba Sheen appear in the letters of the missionary Ann Judson nearly two decades later in 1815 and cast him as an old harbinger of Indo-Persian culture in the Konbaung dynasty. He seemed less fond of the presence of the Baptist missionaries than even the East India Company's agents. Judson describes him as the "old Armenian," noting his frequent visits to the Baptist Mission, where he argued with the missionaries over what he saw as their dangerously rigid evangelical Christianity and insistence that a man had to be born again in order to be saved. "How can a man be born again?" inquired Baba Sheen, while dismissing the zealous missionaries over their poor grasp of the Burmese language: "Ay, you cannot speak the language fluently. I find it difficult to understand you. When you can talk better, come and see me, and I shall get wisdom."[99]

## IMPERIAL ECLIPSE

Astrologers of the Burmese Kingdom had for some time forecast that a lunar eclipse would occur in August 1795. They foretold that this would be an "inauspicious moon" and advised that "affairs of state" be delayed until the eclipse had passed.[100] Such customs of auspicious and inauspicious astral conjunctions weighed heavily upon the decisions of the Burmese court and the ceremony of introduction with the embassy from the East India Company until long after the eclipse had subsided. Amid pervasive doubts and suspicions regarding the intent of the British mission, and the guardedness of the Burmese court and its various protocols, Symes suspended Thomas Wood's astronomical research so as to not raise alarm.[101] With the impending eclipse of the moon, the mission humbly awaited the king's permission for the auspicious day to proceed to the royal capital, the Immortal City of Amarapura. The secrecy that surrounded the Burmese emperor left the mission uncertain even as to the king's true name; even after the conclusion of the embassy, the company was not able to "procure the real name of the reigning monarch ... whose real name, as his reign still continues, it may not be lawful to mention." They called him Dharma Raja, denoting "the virtuous and beneficient king."[102]

In late May, the rains of monsoon season had arrived and heavy rainfall had set in when the court granted the British embassy permission to proceed to the royal capital. Symes and the mission departed Rangoon on "the favorable auspice of a lucky day," on May 30, in traditional boats especially fitted to defend against the rain, while Baba Sheen, the Armenian interpreter and guide for the mission, accompanied them on the journey in his own vessel.[103] The journey upstream from Rangoon to Ava lasted thirty-five to forty days and entailed laborious rowing to counter the rapid tide of the Irrawaddy. With the freshness of the rains and "the Enclosures of the Hills," the embassy's passage upriver was rough and Symes's baggage boat sunk along the way.[104]

On July 9, following thirty-nine days of travel, the mission reached the ancient city of Pagan, the crumbling spires of its ruined stupas appearing along the banks of the river. Built on a plain along a bend in the Irrawaddy River, near its confluence with its main tributary, the Chindwin River, the city had been the site of the first Burmese Empire from the ninth to thirteenth centuries, when it was invaded by the Mongols. Symes described the ruins of the lost city and its fading traces of its former imperial grandeur: "We approached the once magnificent city of Pagahm. We could see little more from the river than … its numerous mouldering temples, and the vestiges of an old brick fort, the ramparts of which are still to be traced." But amid the ruins and debris, he clearly recognized what the city had formerly been: "Pagahm is said to have been the residence of forty-five successive monarchs, and was abandoned 500 years ago in consequence of a divine admonition: whatever may be its true history, it certainly was once a place of no ordinary splendour."[105] Pondering the time when ancient Pagham was an imperial metropolis before its decline and fall, Symes perceived the city's vanished glory, in particular its Theravada Buddhist monuments. Walking through the ruins on the lost city's "narrow, winding" streets, he passed "a range of temples" and "religious edifices," including the gilded Shwe Zigon Pagoda. Many of the oldest enshrined below their arched domes massive images of Gaudama, often depicted "sitting cross-legged on a pedestal, adorned with representations of the leaf of the sacred lotus."[106]

Symes reported to Calcutta that in Pagan, the embassy was received with the "Mark of high Distinction" by imperial officials, including the Portuguese Shahbandar, or "Master of the Port," Joseph Xavier da Cruz, also known as Jhansey, and representatives from the king, as well as "a Multitude of Musicians." The king also sent "a Royal Barge and two War Boats" for "the safe conveyance" of Symes and his suite to the capital. After two days in Pagan, the embassy continued its upstream journey, reaching what was once the capital city of Ava within a week, on July 17. It was another lost city. Ava had emerged after the fall of Pagan as an erstwhile capital of Burmese kingdoms based on the upper Irrawaddy until the Konbaung dynasty abandoned it due to astrological prophecies in 1783. At "the Place where Ava formerly stood; not many Years ago the Capital of the Empire and Residence of the King—It is now quite deserted with nothing to be seen except … the Ruins of the Fort Wall with Several Pagodahs." When the reigning king moved the capital nine miles upriver to Amarapura upon ascending to the throne, the city of Ava fell into decay, with its "name … almost forgotten." Indeed, the mission had voyaged to nowhere, to a city that did not exist any longer as it once had, with a dead name that was not, in Symes's words, "Comprehensive of the whole Empire unless in Compliance with the Practise of Strangers."[107]

The new imperial capital, the Immortal City of Amarapura, lay in a swampy environment. Symes observed that "the swollen state of the river, gave to the waters the semblance of a vast lake, interspersed with islands. . . . The foundations of Ummerapoora seemed to be immersed." The river channeled into the lake of Taungthaman, above which rose "the spires, the turrets, and the lofty Piasath" of the new royal city.[108] This was the new imperial metropolis. But the king was not there. Rather, he was at a place on a bank of the Irrawaddy River known as Mingun, overseeing construction of the Pahtodawgyi, a massive pagoda to house a tooth of the Buddha.[109] A sign of imperial prowess, the Mingun Pagoda was built by slaves captured following the Konbaung dynasty's conquest of Arakan and the Kingdom of Mrauk U, which followed on the heels of the earlier conquests of the Mon Kingdom of Pegu in 1757 and the Ayutthaya Kingdom of Thailand in 1767. Despite his expansionist and daring imperial outlook, the king was reclusive and enigmatic during the time of the British mission. As explained by Symes's contemporary and acquaintance in Rangoon, the Italian monk Vincentius Sangermano, the Burmese sovereign believed himself to be a sacred king on the path to becoming a Buddha. According to Sangermano's account, which was heavily tinged by Orientalist tropes of "Eastern" despotism and tyranny, the Burmese sovereign called "Badonsachen," saw himself in the image of Gautama and "abandoned the royal palace . . . retired into solidtude" and "withdrew himself from the palace" to overlook the building of the Mingun Pagoda.[110] After passing the fallen and faded former capitals of the kingdom, the members of the embassy had reached the imperial city of Amarapura to find that the king was not there.

The coming lunar eclipse heightened the mystery surrounding the king's absence. Symes explained in a letter to Bengal, "The time of our arrival happened at an unfavorable Juncture for expediting Business" because "an Eclipse of the Moon was to take place," and due to this "Phenomenon" astrologers and sages postponed the affairs of the court until the new moon, which would not arrive until the last day of August in the Burmese month of Tawthalin. The embassy would have to await "an auspicious day" in order to be received by the king and deliver the Persian letter from the governor-general.[111] Symes speculated that the eclipse supplied an excuse for the court to delay a formal reception of the embassy. In the meantime, Wood was permitted to once again resume his astronomical observations. At night, he would walk into the open plains along the banks of the Irrawaddy River "in order to have a distinct view of the heavenly bodies," causing local peasants and villagers to believe "him to be a necromancer, and his telescope and time-keeper instruments of magic." They crowded around him in curiosity, believing that he "held communication with the Natts," supernatural nature spirits worshipped by the Burmese.[112] The king, who was deeply interested in knowledge of the stars and "adept in the science," sent "a gracious message" to the mission seeking to know the company astronomer Wood's calculation of the exact time and shading of the expected eclipse of the moon.[113]

While waiting to be granted permission to meet the king, the members of the embassy occupied themselves by exploring the environs and monuments of Amarapura. Wood continued his astronomical research, while also drafting a map of the Irrawaddy River from Rangoon to Amarapura and a plan of the fortress of the royal capital. Buchanan and the Indian artist Singey Bey focused on detailing the natural history, particularly the botany, of the Irrawaddy River delta, and Buchanan also delved into the study of the Burmese language and Buddhist religious practices. Symes explored the Buddhist built environment and material culture in the vicinity of the royal city: its stone temples, carved teak monasteries (*kyaung*), and sacred relics such as the Mahamuni image of Gautama. Although not yet granted an audience with the king, he surveyed the royal fortress and the intricate imperial halls and chambers within. Having seen the debris of past imperial cities by the wayside, Symes may have suspected that this royal city of an unseen king would also one day fade from glory.

## THE LION THRONE

In August 1795, after the lunar eclipse, the British embassy was granted a formal reception at the imperial court, the durbar, in the royal capital. When the time came, Thomas Wood, Francis Buchanan, and the artist Singey Bey rode to the Burmese court on fine horses of the "Pegue breed," while Symes, befitting his rank as representative of the governor-general of India, was conveyed upon an elephant.[114] As the representatives of the mission marched to the fortress city and the royal palace within, they became a part of and spectators to a ceremonious procession. Inside the gates of the city, "a troop of tumblers" and "dancing girls" performed to the music of a Burmese orchestra. Dismounting and removing their shoes, the members of the embassy and their attendants then entered the audience hall to await the princes of the royal family, who arrived on the backs of elephants shaded by "gilded parasols," followed by their various entourages, including musqueteers, "halberdiers," carrying gilded spears with golden tassels, and officers "dressed in velvet robes," trailed by a parade of elephants. The crown prince arrived last to the sound of "a great drum," attended by his "numerous body guard of infantry" and party of mounted "Cassay troopers," as well as the ministers and nobility, whose "robes and caps . . . varied according to their respective ranks."[115] Symes described the entrance of the heir apparent to the court, which he imagined as reminiscent of the order and grandeur of the Mughal court in Delhi at its height:

> The Prince, borne on men's shoulders, in a very rich palanquin . . . [was] screened from the sun by a large gilded fan, supported by a nobleman, and on each side of his palanquin walked six Cassay astrologers, of the Brahmanical sect, dressed in white gowns and white caps, studded with stars of gold; close behind [were] his water-flaggon, and a gold beetle-box, of a size which appeared to be no considerable load for a man. Several elephants and lead horses with rich housings came after . . . and a body of spearmen, with companies of musketeers, one clothed in blue, another in green, and a third in red, concluded the procession. . . . All things seemed to have been carefully predisposed and properly arranged.[116]

Symes continued: "If it [the court] was less splendid than imperial Delhi, in the days of Mogul magnificence, it was far more decorous than any court of Hindostan at the present day."[117]

With the crown prince present, a Burmese translation of the embassy's letter from the governor-general of India was brought in on a silver tray and read aloud by a *sandohgan*, or royal reader. The reader then recounted the array of gifts of friendship presented by the mission for King Bodawpaya, gifts selected with a view to the opening up of commerce between the East India Company and the Burmese Kingdom. The presents included

> two pieces of gold muslin, two pieces of silver muslin, four pieces of white flowered muslin, four pieces of silk, ten pieces of printed silk, six pieces of plain satin, two pieces of flowered satin, two pieces of velvet, six pots of rose water, one crystal stand, six crystal water cups, two pairs of candle shades, two crystal bowls, two large mirrors, three guns, two pistols, six pairs of gold slippers and twenty five pieces of broad cloth, one electric machine, and one copy of the Bhagwat Gita.[118]

A royal officer then inquired in the Persian language about the embassy's itinerary and length of stay in Burma, and whether England was "at peace or war" or "in a state of disturbance," to which Symes responded that though Great Britain was in conflict with France and "the continent of Europe was the seat of war," England remained in "perfect tranquility." After being served a feast of "laepack, or pickled tea leaf, and beetle" and "not less than a hundred different small dishes," which members of the embassy found "very palatable," they were informed by the sandohgan that there was "no occasion ... to remain any longer," and following the departure of the princes and their retinues from the court, the members of the embassy returned to their camp in a nearby grove.[119] Symes and members of the British embassy were struck by the magnificence of the Burmese imperial court and left "highly gratified by the splendid scene" of the ceremonious durbar, "in every respect suited to the dignity of an imperial court."[120]

Symes. however, was immensely disappointed and utterly snubbed by the absence of the Burmese king, a complicated situation that left him unable to successfully carry out his mission. Word reached Symes that the royal court had deemed the embassy as representing "a provincial and subordinate power ... not an equal and sovereign state," and had resolved that an audience with the king would not be granted.[121] A French ship from Mauritius had arrived in Rangoon flying the Burmese flag and Symes suspected it had transmitted false news of the impending defeat of the British Empire in Europe and India. It was rumored that a French fleet was on the way from France across the Indian sea to join in an alliance with Tipu Sultan, ruler of the southern Indian Kingdom of Mysore, against the British. Symes feared that such misinformation from the French was supported by "Armenian and Mussulman merchants" protective of their trading status and privileges in the Burmese Empire.[122] With the origins of the mission and its intent in doubt, and rumors regarding the imminent ruin of the British Empire, the embassy was shunned and dishonored by the Burmese king.

In this difficult predicament, Symes again turned to his knowledge of Persian to get the embassy through diplomatic and commercial negotiations. Throughout the course of the mission, as repeatedly recorded in his account and letters, Symes relied heavily on Persian to communicate and conduct official affairs, as well to decipher and understand the physical and cultural world of the Burmese Kingdom. Persian had been his indispensable tool, his medium of exchange and interaction, since the mission's arrival in Rangoon, and it had remained so in the embassy's subsequent journeys across the empire. Persian was the common language of diplomatic and commercial intercourse between the Burmese Kingdom and India. Through the repertoire and codes of Persian, the mission was able to traverse the Burmese Empire and conduct its negotiations with the royal court. To begin with, Symes carried a Persian letter from the governor-general to the Burmese sovereign that was the "ticket" to his mission. Then through his munshi, Symes drafted Persian letters to the Burmese court as his official diplomatic means of contact, while relying on those who knew and understood Persian to articulate the purpose of his mission. "I always wrote in Persian," he recalled in his travel account, knowing that Persian was readily known as a language of discourse in the Burmese Kingdom, particularly among the Muslim, Parsi, and Armenian merchants settled there. Knowing that the Burmese court had interpreters of the language, he relied on those representatives of the kingdom who "understood his meaning in Persian."[123] Even his etiquette was shaped by Persian court protocol; in official ceremonies he greeted and gestured "after the manner of the Mahomedan Salaam."[124] Persian correspondence was particularly essential when it came to articulating views on critical matters such as the Arakan border and those who crossed it, the opening of commercial relations between the East India Company and the Burmese Empire, and Anglo-French imperial rivalries. It was also a language of scientific research and translation, as Symes collected Persian versions of Arakanese *sastras*, or books of law, in order to access and translate the Burmese codes of the "Derma Sath."[125]

Thus, when the fate of the mission and its objectives seemed uncertain, Symes turned to his knowledge of Persian and its codes of diplomacy and persuasion. In his interactions with the Burmese court, he used Persian to express, alternately, humility and boldness. He drafted a lengthy "memorial" in Persian and English, expressing in a tone of reverence to the Burmese sovereign his object of being deputed to deliver "the explicit Declaration of Friendship from Sir John Shore, Governor-General of India," and outlining the essential points of the mission, which were to ease rising tensions over the Bengal-Arakan boundary and to open official political and commercial relations.[126] When informed that the embassy would not be granted an audience with the king, Symes addressed a more blunt Persian letter, sharper in tone and substance, to the chief *Wongee*, or First Counselor, and the grand council of the kingdom, calling for their "serious consideration." With the mission's time of departure approaching, Symes abandoned all pretense and assumed a more forceful posture and frank tone, so "that nothing may hereafter be attributed to misapprehension." In his Persian letter to the council, Symes challenged the notion that he was the representative of a subordinate commercial settlement seeking the favor of the Burmese crown, as were the French, but rather was the agent of a powerful Indian empire:

Of the power and resources of the British in India, you cannot be so misinformed to suppose, that they are under the necessity of soliciting the friendship of any nation on earth, out of a prudential regard to their own security, or from an inability to maintain a cause of justice and their national honour, in opposition to all the force that could combine against them. It is not from a petty island [a reference to the French in Mauritius], which may send out two or three piratical privateers, that a government, whose dominions extend from Ceylon to the mountains of Tibet, from Bengal to the Western Sea, can have anything to dread: apprehension, therefore, had no share in the present mission; and, I desire to have it clearly understood, that I come not to seek a favour, but to cement friendship; not to supplicate, but to propose.[127]

Symes concluded his letter by noting that should his embassy return to India dishonored, without having been granted an audience with the Burmese king, there could be no expectation that another such overture would be made should disputes arise in the future.

In late September 1795, seven months after the British embassy's arrival in the Burmese Kingdom, Bodawpaya at last agreed to a reception in his presence at the imperial court in Amarapura. On the morning of September 30, the embassy suite accompanied by Baba Sheen entered the royal fortress and proceeded first to the Rhoom, the public hall, and then on to the Lotoo, the royal audience hall. Removing their shoes, they entered the Lotoo, where the grand council of the kingdom was assembled, taking a seat at the foot of the carved and gilded Lion Throne, the focal center of the royal court. A visible symbol of Burmese imperial power, the Lion Throne was reserved for important occasions and the reception of representatives from foreign sovereigns. It projected and demonstrated the absolute authority of the Burmese sovereign before he had even been seen. Singey Bey painted the dreamlike scene in the royal audience hall, which appeared in Symes's *Embassy* as a lithograph titled "View of the Imperial Court at Ummerapoora, and the Ceremony of Introduction."

With the crown prince and several *chobwas* (tributary princes) assembled, the audience awaited the appearance of the king. After a quarter of an hour, the carved folding doors that screened the throne were opened to reveal King Bodawpaya, clad in a winged suit of golden armor weighing nearly fifty pounds and a jewel-studded conical cap, scaling the flight of steps to the Lion Throne.[128] The members of the mission witnessed that "on the first appearance of his Majesty, all the courtiers bent their bodies, and held their hands joined in an attitude of supplication," and were themselves made to take part in the custom of shiko—to prostrate themselves before the king. When the names of the individual members of the mission were read, each of them took

FIGURE 9. The royal audience hall in Amarapura during British East India Company embassy's ceremony of introduction with King Bodawpaya. Drawn by Singey Bey, an Indian artist in the East India Company. Michael Symes, *An Account of an Embassy to the Kingdom of Ava, Sent by the Governor-General of India in the Year 1795* (London, 1800).

"a few grains of rice" in his hands and, joining them together, bowed to the king as low as he could. The manner of assembly was orchestrated to display the unmatched majesty and superiority of the Burmese throne, without equal on Earth. When the ceremony was completed, the king departed the throne through the folding doors without taking "verbal notice" of the embassy.[129]

After Bodawpaya had departed the throne and the court had disbanded, an attendant presented Symes with a royal letter in Persian to the governor-general of India, enveloped in a lacquered "case of wood and covered with a scarlet cloth."[130] The correspondence was in response to the governor-general's letter, delivered by Symes, seeking to establish regular diplomatic relations and commercial interchange between the two contiguous empires across the Bay of Bengal, an exchange that would allow the East India Company open access to the timber trade out of Burma. The letter in response, which displayed the Burmese court's own usage of Persian diplomatic parlance, opened with a passage lauding the unmatched natural resources and commodities of the empire and how such rare nature belonged to the Burmese sovereign:

The Lord of Earth and Air, the Monarch of Extensive Countries, the Sovereign
of kingdoms ... of wide extended regions, Lord of great cities ... where merchants trade and the inhabitants are protected; Proprietor of all kinds of precious
stones, of the mines of Rubies, Agate, Lasni, Sapphires, Opal; also the mines of
Gold, Silver, Amber, Lead, Tin, Iron, and Petroleum; whence everything desir-
able that the earth yields can be extracted, as the Trees, Leaves, and Fruit of
excellence are produced in Paradise; Possessor of Elephants, Horses, Carriages,
Fire Arms, Bows, Spears, Shields, and all manner warlike weapons; Sovereign of
valiant Generals and victorious Armies, invulnerable as the rock *Mahakonda.*
*Mahanuggera, Ummerapoora,* the great and flourishing Golden City, illumined
and illuminating, as the Habitation of Angels, lasting as the firmament, and
embellished with Gold, Silver, Pearls, Agate, and the nine original Stones; the
Golden Throne, the seat of splendor, whence the royal mandate issues and pro-
tects mankind; the King ... master of the white, red, and mottled Elephants;
may his praise be repeated, far as the influence of the sun and moon.[131]

In his letter, the Burmese king presented himself the absolute ruler of a sovereign realm, an empire of great cities and subkingdoms, a land of nature's
rarest bounty.

The king's letter continued by recounting the arrival of the Symes mission
in Rangoon, dispatched as an embassy to "the Golden Feet" by "the illustrious Governor General, the Representative of the King of England, the
Governor of the Company at Calcutta in Bengal." The letter recorded that
"in the Birman year one thousand one hundred and fifty-seven, or year of the
Higera one thousand two hundred and ten, and the sixteenth of the Birman
month of Toozalien [Tawthalin], or fourteenth of the Mussulman month,
Suffir [Safar]," Symes and the members of the embassy, bearing letters and
gifts, were "attended to the Presence." Symes had conveyed the diplomatic
position of the East India Company, the letter continued, and had written a
"memorial" delineating the political and commercial purpose of his mission,
by which "his Majesty was exceedingly pleased."[132] In carrying out his mission, Symes had strived to promote a mutual agreement concerning the
Arakan-Bengal frontier and the Magh borderers who crossed it to take refuge
in company territory in Chittagong, and he sought to open up trade and
commerce between English merchants and the Burmese Kingdom.

The letter from Bodawpaya was accompanied by an addendum in the
form of a Persian *farman,* or decree, assenting to a commercial opening of
trade with the East India Company:

I direct, that all merchants of the English nation, who resort to Birman
ports, shall pay customs, duties, charges, warehouse hire, searchers, agreeably

to former established usage. English merchants are to be permitted to go to whatever part of the Birman dominions they think proper, either to buy or sell, and they are on no account to be stopped, molested, or oppressed, and they shall have liberty to go to whatever town, village, or city they choose, for the purpose of buying, selling, or bartering; and whatsoever articles of the produce of this country they may be desirous of purchasing, they shall be allowed to do so, either in person, or by their agents[;] ... and should the English Company think proper to depute a person to reside at Rangoon, to superintend mercantile affairs, maintain a friendly intercourse, and forward letters to the Presence, it is ordered, that such person shall have a right of residence; and should any English merchant be desirous of sending a representation, the officers of the Government, in any port, district, and town, shall forward such representation; or if a merchant should be inclined to present in person, a petition at the Golden Feet, he shall be allowed to come to the Golden Presence for that purpose[;] ... and as, in the stormy season, English ships are often dismasted driven into Birman ports by stress of weather, ships in this unfortunate predicament shall be supplied with all necessary wood at the current rates of the country.[133]

The letter ended with an auspicious royal promise: "It will therefore be right that the illustrious Governor General do acquaint the King of England, of the friendship that is, on this occasion, established, and which it is hoped will be permanent."[134] Bodawpaya's letter more than hints of changes and shifts in the Burmese Empire's conception of its place within wider networks of the world economy, as well as the opening of the immense reserves of teak in Burmese forests. To commemorate the embassy and the agreed-upon mutual understanding, the members of the mission were generously honored with gifts showcasing the rarities of the kingdom—ruby and sapphire rings, amber beads, raw precious stones and gems, ivory, lacquerware, and cloth.[135] The embassy had seemingly accomplished its mission of opening up the Burmese Kingdom to commercial and diplomatic relations with the East India Company.

The members of the embassy spent their last days in the Immortal City of Amarapura pursuing their research on and surveys of the kingdom, as well as in attendance with members of the court. Taking satisfaction in the course of his three months in the capital, Symes reposed on a gilded teak "war boat" with the "Maywoon of Pegue," riding on the prow of the craft as the East India Company artist Singey Bey sketched the scene from the shore.[136] In late October, with the king's letter in its possession, the embassy departed the royal capital and headed back down the Irrawaddy River to the Bay of Bengal for the return voyage to India.

FIGURE 10. A Burmese teak war boat rowed down the Irrawaddy River. Michael Symes is seated in the prow with the provincial governor, or *maywoon,* of Pegu. While honored by his position in the front of the vessel, Symes is visibly not reposed beneath the shade of the royal parasol, reserved for the *maywoon.* Drawn by Singey Bey, an Indian artist in the East India Company. Michael Symes, *An Account of an Embassy to the Kingdom of Ava, Sent by the Governor-General of India in the Year 1795* (London, 1800).

On November 27, 1795, the *Sea Horse* set sail from Rangoon for Calcutta, more than nine months after the embassy had first arrived in the Burmese port city. When the ship reached Calcutta on December 22, news of the mission's success spread fast, and early in the new year the *Calcutta Gazette* published a notification concerning trade with the Burmese Empire.[137] The Symes mission had opened up trade between the East India Company and the Burmese Empire, and the sovereign had authorized English merchants to conduct trade in the kingdom. But the king's openness to trade and commerce with the company soon faded. The following year, in 1796, when Captain Hiram Cox was sent as the English Resident at Rangoon, relations between the company and the Burmese Kingdom fell apart and were broken off, with Cox leaving his post in frustration in 1798. In 1802, Symes returned to Ava on a second embassy to reestablish commercial relationships and to settle persistent and increasingly dire misunderstandings between the Burmese Empire and the East India Company over the porous Arakan-Bengal frontier and the fugitives who crossed it.

It was during these years that Symes's narrative of the mission, *An Account of an Embassy to the Kingdom of Ava*, was printed London in 1800 and became the most detailed English description of the country known at the time. The work, produced by Symes and the small but talented scientific wing of the mission, addressed the history, geography, culture, and economics of the Burmese Empire; surveyed the Irrawaddy River, providing the first reliable chart of it; and classified the kingdon's flora, fauna, and natural environment. As this chapter has detailed, *An Account of an Embassy to the Kingdom of Ava* was heavily based upon knowledge gained from Indo-Persian intermediaries and immersed in the ways of Persianate knowledge and genres. Complete with an appendix of translated Persian letters, the work was in part an Indo-Persian travel book, a sort of safarnama written in English, that extolled the wonders of unknown Indian Ocean realm seen in the course of a long journey. As such, Symes's travelogue paralleled other eye-opening and scientifically detailed colonial travel accounts of early nineteenth-century Asian empires, such as Mountstuart Elphinstone's *Kingdom of Caubul* and John Malcolm's *Persia,* establishing Symes as the foremost authority on the Burmese Kingdom. And like those works, *An Account of an Embassy to the Kingdom of Ava* was a narrative that signaled imperial entanglements to come, most immediately the First Anglo-Burmese War of 1824–26, and the ensuing annexation of Arakan and Tenasserim by the East India Company.

# FOUR

# *Forest Worlds*

## SINGEY BEY

THE MONSOON RAINS HAD SET IN and the Irrawaddy River had begun to swell when Singey Bey, an East India Company artist on a botanical expedition from Calcutta to the Burmese Kingdom, boarded a thatched-roof boat in Rangoon for the journey upriver into the country's upland interior in May 1795. It was pouring rain, and the wind and current pushed back against the boat, forcing the oarsmen to use long bamboo poles to propel the vessel through the winding river and past shifting sandbanks. At times the current swept the boat back onto the sands and the Burmese rowers had to struggle to set it on course again. Slowly the boat made its way upriver into the mountainous interior and its dense forests, where it was the season of the passage of teak down the river from the uplands to the sawmills and harbors of port cities on the Bay of Bengal, from where the timber was exported across the Indian Ocean.

During the dry season, Burmese foresters carved deep rings around the trunks of the trees and left them to dry in the sun. When the trees had dried enough to stay afloat, woodcutters felled them and mahouts guided tamed elephants in rolling the two-ton logs through the forest to streambeds in time for the monsoon season. When the rains came, the flooded streams rose up from the forest floor, carrying the teak adrift to the river mouths, where the wood was caught and made into rafts by gangs of men who guided them as they were borne by the torrential currents down the rapids for days toward the sea many miles away. Traveling upstream, Singey Bey and his companions saw the rafts of massive teak drifting past them down the river as they explored the lush reaches of the Irrawaddy and its upper delta on their way to the "Immortal City," Amarapura, the royal capital of the Burmese Konbaung dynasty. The monsoon forests of the Irrawaddy displayed their verdant diversity of plant life, the banks of the river teeming with green, an array of flora and flowering species. Drifting up the river, Singey Bey entered the forest worlds of imperial Burma.

Singey Bey's botanical and landscape drawings were sketched during the 1795 East India Company Embassy to the Burmese court and appeared as lithographs in the printed account of the mission, presenting views of the encounter with the forest environments of Southeast Asia. In the Burmese Empire, Singey Bey came into contact with a forest kingdom beyond the Indian Ocean monsoons brimming with wildness and plant and animal life. On the mission, Singey Bey strived to "draw figures and trace every line ... with a laborious exactness" that accurately represented the environs and peoples encountered along the embassy's journey through imperial Burma, most notably botanical drawings, which conveyed the abundant flora and fauna, and the biodiversity, of its forests in the late eighteenth century.[1] But looking through the dense sylvan terrain, he saw something more: a forest landscape marked by the signs, relics, images, and material culture of Theravada Buddhism and its cycles of the birth, destruction, and rebirth of the natural world.

The science of botany has most often been portrayed in scholarly literature as a European preoccupation, and a range of works in the field of the history of science treat it purely as such, for although at times these works allude to the influence of indigenous knowledge, such mentions rarely go beyond the surface.[2] In the field of colonial South Asian history, however, the place of local and indigenous knowledge in the emergence of the botanical sciences in India has been more substantively examined in works by Richard Grove, David Arnold, and, most significantly, Kapil Raj.[3] In some regards, this is due to the nature of the archive on South Asia itself, which leaves little doubt about the ways in which knowledge was shared and mutually constituted. From early modern works such as Garcia da Orta's *Coloquios dos simples e drogas he cousas medicinais da India,* printed in Goa in 1563, based on Indian knowledge of plants and flora, and Hendrik Van Reede's *Hortus indicus malabaricus,* a compilation the local botanical knowledge of lower-caste Indian toddy tappers and tree climbers, printed in Amsterdam between 1678 and 1693, to eighteenth-century East India Company botanies based on the work of native collectors, scribes, and artists, the archival trail has revealed complex and tangled interconnections. The role of such exchanges in the production of knowledge about Indian flora has been conveyed in the existing scholarship on colonial botany in South Asia. This chapter builds upon these existing studies of indigenous knowledge and colonial botany in India through the microhistory and life story of a Bengali botanist and artist, as well as the visual traces of Mughal encounters with Southeast Asia and the forest landscapes of the Burmese Kingdom.

## BURMESE TEAK AND THE EAST INDIA COMPANY

In the course of their maritime trade in the Indian Ocean during the eighteenth century, the East India Company set a high value on teak from the forests of the Burmese Empire for shipbuilding and, in competition with French merchants, sailed their vessels to the Southeast Asian kingdom's littoral in search of the Asian tropical hardwood. Teak was felled from mountain forests and floated down rivers during the monsoon torrents to the port cities of the empire, supplying the wood for shipbuilding in Calcutta, Madras, and the Coromandel Coast. The quest for teak led to a rapid increase in trade between India and the Burmese Konbaung dynasty across the Bay of Bengal during the late eighteenth century. It was largely in the quest to form "commercial connections" conducive to the teak trade that in 1795 the East India Company sent an embassy to the Burmese court at Ava.[4]

The dense monsoon forests of the Burmese upland interior held three-quarters of the world's reserves of teak (*Tectona grandis*), known in Burmese as *kyun*. When the monsoon rains set in, teak timber from Burma's upland interior was floated downstream for days downriver to port cities near the Bay of Bengal, which teemed with merchants and mariners seeking the lightweight tropical hardwood for the building of ships. In the port city of Rangoon, where the river swelled by twenty feet during the spring tides, Burmese carpenters used teak to construct some of the sturdiest ships in the world.

But sumptuary laws placed strict regulations on access to the natural resources of the Konbaung dynasty, including its teak forests. Teak wood, like other resources of the Burmese forests, belonged to the kings who claimed to be lords of the kingdom's mines of precious stones and forests of trees.[5] Access to teak was also limited due to more practical reasons related to the tributary nature of the empire and the fact that much of the country's forest remained out of reach and in the territories of independent, and at times insurrectionary, hill "tribes," such as the Shan, and the crown was only able to collect tribute on timber and other forest resources.[6] The imperial use of teak was restricted to the sacred Buddhist regalia of carved golden teak palaces, pavilions, and monasteries in imperial cities, as well as the ornate royal barges like mythological creatures, and war boats that plied the Irrawaddy River. Among the subjects of the empire, teak found use in the building of houses in cities and surrounding villages. Those who could procure teak preferred the wood to the more common bamboo because it was well adapted to the dampness of the tropical monsoon climate. Still, most of the population lived in the countryside in houses of cane or bamboo, woven like latticework and covered with straw.[7] By far, the most prevalent use of teak by ordinary people was in the building of boats and canoes for rowing Burma's rivers. A variety of vessels, modeled on the *loung-goh*-type boat, plied the rivers and coastal waters of the kingdom. These were canoes hollowed out of the trunks of teak trees, with the center chipped out and plank sides added to the solid keel.[8]

Foreign merchants and firms faced considerable challenges and obstacles in acquiring access to precious teak reserves, given that the Burmese crown placed strict limitations and surveillance on all trade. Foreign trading vessels and merchant ships could not enter the river leading to the port of Rangoon without a Burmese pilot coming on board. Upon reaching the Rangoon harbor, the ship's rudder, cannon, and muskets had to be taken ashore, while an officer from the merchant ship had to report to the customs office and present a list of cargo. The crown charged a duty of 12 percent for all imports into the kingdom, and there were also prohibitions against carrying specie out, as merchant ships that sold their cargo to take in another in teak—prepared either as planks or masts—were charged a duty on the export of timber.[9]

By the eighteenth century, however, the teak trade became globalized, as the hardwood came to be more extensively harvested for commerce, in particular for the construction of Asian and European merchant ships. In 1689, the French East India Company, seeking to penetrate the teak trade and access the best natural material for the building of wooden ships, opened a small factory in the port city of Syriam opposite Rangoon on the Bay of Bengal; subsequently, French shipbuilding techniques were adopted along the Irrawaddy Delta, as Talaing and Burmese carpenters replicated the French model of ships then common in the river and sold them to "sultans and Indian merchants."[10] Between 1730 and 1740, agents of the British and French East India Companies became increasingly active in their imperial rivalry and increased efforts to build teak ships at Syriam to serve trade out of Madras and Pondicherry. Under the adventurous schemes of Joseph Dupleix, governor of Pondicherry, French attempts to corner the Burmese teak trade peaked. Writing of Burmese teak, "Les bois y sont pour rien, les ouvriers causent toute la dépense" (The wood is free to take, the workers cause the only expense), Dupleix regarded the extension of French influence in the Burmese littoral of the Bay of Bengal to be a highly profitable measure to offset the British Indian Empire. It was during this period that the merchants La Noë and Puel built the famed teak ships the *Fulvy* and the *Fleury*.[11]

By the 1790s, the Rangoon harbor had evolved into a full-fledged global teak market, and it sheltered a motley fleet of ships belonging variously to Burmese princes and governors and European and Muslim merchants and mariners.[12] According to Vincentius Sangermano, an Italian missionary resident in Ava and Rangoon from 1783 to 1806, it was for cargoes of teak wood, "more than anything else, that vessels of every nation come to Pegu from all parts of India. . . . In Pegu and Ava there are such immense forests of it, that it can be sold to as many ships as arrive at a moderate price."[13] Planks of the wood were so buoyant in weight and so durable that, reportedly, teak ships filled by water during ocean storms still did not sink. The teak trade supplied an essential commodity for the British East India Company, and in the 1790s "some of the finest merchant ships ever seen in the river Thames, arrived from Calcutta, where they were built of teak timber" exported from Konbaung Burma. The *Cuvera,* the *Gabriel,* the *Superb,* and other vessels of Burma teak stood out from all other vessels as they delivered valuable cargoes from the Indian Ocean to London. The East India Company commerce in teak was extensive enough that it required 200,000 pounds sterling of Indian goods annually in exchange for Burmese teak, either as masts for ships or as cut planks of different sizes. The teak trade with the Burmese Kingdom was essential to the British company's prospects in maritime trade, since it was impossible to build "a durable vessel of burden . . . in the river of Bengal, except by the aid of teak plank, which is procurable from Pegue [Burma] alone."[14] The loss of the timber trade with the kingdom would effectively spell the end of the prosperity of the company's Bengal mariners and merchants. By the late eighteenth century, British East India Company shipbuilders had become established in Rangoon in order to benefit from the teak trade.

A tributary economy and its networks of exchange in natural resources were on the verge, within decades, of being eclipsed by the formation of a colonial economy based on the commodification, commercial extraction, and export of raw material—teak timber—from the forests of the Burmese Empire to the world.[15] The lure of earnings from the teak trade led Burmese villagers to migrate to port cities like Rangoon to find work sawing timber at the dockyards. As one villager from Shwebo named "Quester after Silver" recalled in an epistle written to his family back home,

> Therefore, pulling up my loin cloth with its flowery pattern of light yellow, and loosening it a little, I climb a high sawing platform, and from sunrise to sunset, with sweat from my brow falling on my big toes, I push and pull the saw, up and down, cutting the logs into thin planks. In no time and with no mistake, every hundred planks put twenty Kyats in my pocket.[16]

During the nineteenth century, as the British East India Company vied for access to the forests of the Burmese Kingdom and their output, three Anglo-Burmese wars were fought. After the First Anglo-Burmese War of 1824–26, the East India Company annexed Arakan and Tenasserim; following the Second Anglo-Burmese War of 1852, lower Burma, including Rangoon, fell; and the conclusive Third Anglo-Burmese War of 1885 resulted in the end of the Konbaung dynasty and the conquest of Mandalay, the Irrawaddy, and Upper Burma, opening the way to Burma's upland teak forests as a colonial economy cohered around the teak trade.

## INFINITE FOREST

Little is known of Singey Bey, the East India Company–trained Bengali artist from Calcutta who sketched the forest environment of the Burmese kingdom, apart from the paintings he left behind, lithographed in Symes's *Account of an Embassy to the Kingdom of Ava*. Because nothing but his drawings remain, very little can be determined about his personal life. Even his name, "Singey Bey," does not take us very far. The forename "Singey," derived from "Singh" and meaning "Lion" in Sanskrit, possibly reveals a Rajput or Sikh provenance, while "Bey," from the Turkic word *bayg*, meaning "lord" or "prince," suggests his immersion and standing within the Indo-Persian cultures of the Mughal Empire. There exist no concrete facts, however, as to how he arrived in colonial Bengal and came to be a company artist in Calcutta.

Much of what we can trace about the life of Singey Bey comes from the network of naturalist "native artists" trained and employed by the East India Company to draw the flora of India around the time of the establishment of the Asiatic Society of Bengal in 1785 and the Calcutta Botanic Garden in 1787.[17] Singey Bey was among a class of native artists trained by the East India Company during the 1790s in the delineation of botanical specimens across

India and Asia. These artists produced realistic drawings of plants that identified and made visible the flora of India using the Linnean system of classification. With establishment of the Calcutta Botanic Garden in 1787, developed as a laboratory for the scientific study and exchange of global plants, thousands of botanical species were collected from Central, South, and Southeast Asia, and local Indian artists were commissioned to meticulously paint the different plant varieties. The scientific skill and the knowledge of plants possessed by Indian artists employed by the East India Company and the Calcutta Botanic Garden contributed to the creation of the field of colonial botany.[18]

The Indian artists painted the plants of Asia in their natural and living state, and their drawings accompanied the dead specimens and botanical descriptions that were sent back to London. William Roxburgh (1751–1815), a Scottish surgeon and botanist trained at the University of Edinburgh under the tutelage of John Hope, was among the first East India Company naturalists to investigate the world of Indian flora, with a particular focus on "commercial crops and plants . . . plants he knew to be economically viable to the British" and "plants that Indians valued as sources of food, drink, writing material, structural materials, and household items."[19] In 1789, Roxburgh employed two unnamed Indian artists to draw hundreds of plants, and upon his appointment to the Calcutta Botanic Garden in 1793 he recruited a crew of Indian artists to create more botanical illustrations of the world of Indian flora. Singey Bey was among the first generation of these Indo-Persian naturalist and botanical artists in late eighteenth-century Bengal, and he was likely one of the artists recruited by Roxburgh whose names have survived; others include Vishnu Prasad, Gorachand, 'Ali Mardan, Rungiah, Haludar, Mahangu Lal, Guru Dayal, and Lakshman Singh, because they signed their works.[20] Before the time of Michael Symes's embassy to Ava, Roxburgh introduced Singey Bey to Francis Buchanan, who had also studied medicine and botany at Edinburgh under Hope and who would later succeed Roxburgh as superintendent of the Calcutta Botanic Garden.

It was arranged for Singey Bey to travel with Buchanan on the East India Company expedition to the Burmese Empire and the Andaman Islands in 1795, in order to make drawings of plants and vegetation. Singey Bey's botanical drawings were to accompany Buchanan's detailed observations and extensive reports, which were sent to the British Museum in London along with numerous plant samples.[21] Singey Bey was part of this milieu of naturalist artists working in colonial Bengal, and his travels into the Burmese Empire in 1795 became the basis of his major botanical and artistic work. During the mission, Singey Bey's "labours were principally directed by Dr. Buchanan in the delineation of plants," and several of his botanical drawings, as well as those of the Burmese kingdom's landscapes, architecture, and costumes, appeared as lithographic plates in Symes's *Account of an Embassy to Ava.*[22] Symes praised Singey Bey's sketches for being "as faithful as a pencil could delineate" and for the artist's ability to "draw figures and trace every line of a picture, with laborious exactness."[23]

Working alongside Buchanan, Singey Bey executed many "drawings of plants" that were essential to the mission's venture to collect and classify the rare botanical specimens and flora of the Burmese Kingdom and its vast monsoon forests. These botanical paintings were part of the Linnean project to classify and order the kingdom of plants according to the taxonomy of phylum, genus, and species. Buchanan and his Bengali plant collector compiled "a copious and valuable collection" of specimens, while Singey Bey drafted "delineations of each plant, executed on the spot."[24] In all, fifty-three large colored drawings of Burmese flora by Singey Bey were sent, along with a manuscript written by Buchanan describing more than five hundred plants, to the Department of Botany in the British Museum, and sketches of eight of the rarest species encountered were selected for reproduction in Symes's travelogue.[25] In the humid forests of the Andaman Islands, Singey Bey drew the stalks, leaves, and petals of *Thalia canniformis,* called *Thayng payng* in Burmese. Along the sylvan banks of the Irrawaddy, he traced *Bauhinia diphylla,* known locally as *Pa-lam.* In the former Mon capital of Pegu, he sketched *Agyneja coccinea,* known to the Burmese as *Ta-hmayng-tsoop kyee.* In the forests around Rangoon, he drew *Gardenia coronaria,* known as *Yaeng-gap; Sonneratia apetala,* called *Kam-ba-la; Epidendrum moschatum,* known as *Thee-kua nee;* and *Heritiera fomes,* locally named *Kanatso.*[26]

But there was more to the botany of the Southeast Asian empire than taxonomical concerns. Singey Bey and Buchanan also encountered the Buddhist cultural context of the Burmese Kingdom's forest terrain, coming upon signs of the sacred presence of Buddhism and its culture in the forests and physical environment. The two men entered a landscape seen as sacred, endless, and infinite in Buddhist cosmography. Upon finding a specimen of the water lotus *Pontederia dilatata* in the forests of Rangoon, a plant known as *Ka-duak kyee* to the Burmese, Singey Bey faithfully diagramed the flowering stem, floral segments, pistil, stamen, corolla, petals, leaves, and seeds, true to the emphasis on the scientific identification of plant specimens.[27] And

FIGURE 11. *Agyneja coccinea*, known to the Burmese as *Ta-hmayng-tsoop kyee*. Drawn by Singey Bey, an Indian artist in the East India Company. Michael Symes, *An Account of an Embassy to the Kingdom of Ava, Sent by the Governor-General of India in the Year 1795* (London, 1800).

still, this description, drawn with precision by Singey Bey and written in Latin by Buchanan, did not capture all that the lotus was. Along their journey, the members of the mission had seen the plant before, engraved into temple walls showing Gautama Buddha "sitting cross-legged on a pedestal, adorned with the leaf of the sacred lotus carved upon the base."[28] The forest world of the Burmese Empire was more than the taxonomy and sum of its parts.

Singey Bey's botanical drawings merged with depictions of Buddhist iconography, relics, and material culture, and the botanical research of Buchanan became tied to a broader exploration and study of Buddhist religion, literature, and languages in Burma, which resulted in long pieces printed in publications of the Asiatic Society.[29] The expedition's botanical and scientific research drew upon and recorded vernacular Burmese knowledge of the natural world, which was discernible in the works the mission produced.[30]

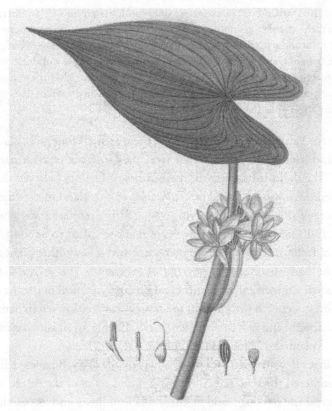

FIGURE 12. The water lotus, *Pontederia dilatata,* called *Ka-duak kyee* in Burmese. Drawn by Singey Bey, an Indian artist in the East India Company. Michael Symes, *An Account of an Embassy to the Kingdom of Ava, Sent by the Governor-General of India in the Year 1795* (London, 1800).

The forest was the pantheon of nirvana. Buchanan outlined the wilderness context of Buddhism, and its setting in the forest, in his article "On the Religion and Literature of the Burmas," published in *Asiatick Researches* in 1801. Within the Pali imaginary, the forest was part of infinitely recurring and cyclical worlds. According to Buchanan, "The Universe is called by the Burmas, *Logha,* which signifies successive destruction and reproduction . . . after it has been destroyed either by fire, water, or wind, [it] is again of itself restored to its ancient form."[31]

In the Buddhist cycle of destruction and creation, there was neither a beginning nor an end to the passing of worlds. These worlds were destroyed by the elements in an endless pattern like a wheel:

The Burma writings do not conceive one world, but an infinite number, one constantly succeeding another; so that when one is destroyed, another of the same form and structure arises, according to a certain general law, which they call *dammada,* and which may be interpreted fate. . . . These worlds never had a beginning, and never will have an end: that is to say, that the successive destructions and reproductions of the world, resemble a great wheel, in which we can point out neither beginning nor end.[32]

Within the Pali conception of the world, there existed "four great islands" on Earth and each possessed a sacred tree, the "insignia of each particular island." The Buddhist subjects of the Burmese Kingdom believed that they inhabited the southern island of "*Zabudiba,* or the island of the tree *Zabu; diba,* in the Pali language, signifying island."[33] The tree *zabu* was a flower of fiction, and since there was no species of plant so called to be found in the forests of India and Burma, Buchanan identified it as another plant around which he had observed the offering of reverence. The prince Gautama Buddha had attained enlightenment and nirvana (*niehban*) under the canopy of the forest, beneath the shade of the *Indica ficus* tree known in Sanskrit as the Mahabodhi and in Pali as *Gnaung-bayn.* Buchanan classified it as both a species of plant and "a relic of the God."[34]

As Singey Bey surveyed the botany and plant life of the Burmese Kingdom, he encountered the material culture and sacred relics of the forest, signs of the ethereal and passing world of Theravada Buddhism and its cosmic cycles of life, death, and rebirth. In the course of walks through the forested banks of the lower Irrawaddy, he came across stone impressions bearing the footprint of Gautama Buddha. It was believed by Theravada Buddhists that Buddha had appeared and set foot upon the Burmese forest. The stones depicted the creation of the world and were engraved with emblematic signs and hieroglyphics of the flora and fauna of the forest and ocean. These stones were objects of great veneration; as Buchanan noted, "In the Burma language these stones are called *Kye do bura,* or the respectable royal foot."[35] Singey Bey saw and illustrated an extraordinary Buddha footprint of stone, etched with conch shells for the toes, the lotus in the various stages of flowering as the heel, and elephants, serpents, and other forms of the Buddha's past incarnations across the arch. In his travel account, Symes described the relic in rich detail to accompany Singey Bey's illustrated plate:

In the course of our walks, not the least curious object that presented itself was a flat stone, of a coarse gray granite, laid horizontally on a pedestal of

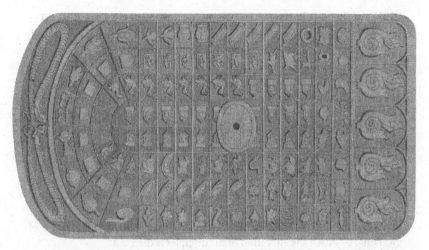

FIGURE 13. Stone imprint of the foot of Gautama Buddha, with conch shells and flora and fauna, depicting the creation. Drawn by Singey Bey, an Indian artist in the East India Company. Michael Symes, *An Account of an Embassy to the Kingdom of Ava, Sent by the Governor-General of India in the Year 1795* (London, 1800).

masonry, six feet in length, and three feet wide, protected from the weather by a wooden shed. This stone was said to bear the genuine print of the foot of Gaudma [Gautama]. . . . On the plane of the foot upwards of one hundred emblematical figures are engraven in separate compartments: two convoluted serpents are pressed beneath the heel, and five conch shells, with the involutions to the right form the toes: it was explained to me as a type of the creation, and was held in profound reverence. There is said to be similar impression on a rock on Adam's Peak, in the island of Ceylon; and it is traditionally believed, by the Birmans, the Siamese, and the Cingaleze, that Gaudma or Boodh, placed one foot on the continent, and the other on the island of Ceylon. The neighboring Rhahaans had no objections to my painter's taking a copy of it, a task he performed with great exactness.[36]

Singey Bey and the members of the mission traveled through a forest landscape marked by the sacred signs and iconography of Buddha, ancient relics imprinted with symbols of the flora and fauna of an eternal wilderness.

In other excursions, the mission came across stunning cosmic temples of stone purported to house the relics of Gautama Buddha. These monumental spired structures that seemed to grow from the forest floor were sites of profound veneration among Buddhist subjects of the Burmese Empire. Buchanan explained,

Godama [Guatama] commanded his images and relics to be worshipped. The largest and most celebrated temples are generally in the form of a pyramid, and are supposed to contain some of those relics; such as a tooth, a bone, a hair, or a garment. To these temples, as containing the sacred relic, the prayers of the devout are addressed, and their offerings presented. The pyramids are often of a great size, constructed of solid brick-work plastered over, and generally placed on a prodigious elevated terrace. The base of the pyramid is frequently surrounded by a double row of small ones; and the summits of whole are always crowned with umbrellas, made of a combination of iron bars into a kind of fillagree-work, and adorned with bells. Many of these pyramids are from three to five hundred feet high. In the larger temples the umbrella, with at least the upper part of the pyramid, and often the whole, is entirely gilded over: and then the title of *Shué*, or golden, is bestowed on the edifice. Other temples of nearly a similar structure, but hollowed within, contain images of Godama, to which the adoration of his disciples is directed.[37]

Singey Bey passed by one such sacred temple in Pegu—Shwe Mawdaw Paya, or Golden Supreme Temple—painting the pagoda on the spot during the day of the full moon festival.[38]

Even in botanical representations of teak, which the East India Company coveted dearly, there was more than met the Linnaean eye—these too harkened to reverence for Buddha. Singey Bey spent considerable time on drawing and making delineations not merely of the teak plant but also of its material culture in the Buddhist iconography and relics of the Burmese Kingdom.[39] Teak was known to botanists as *Tectona grandis,* a deciduous tree native to the forest interior of Burma, where it was called kyun.[40] According to Buchanan's Latin entry, teak "often grows along the banks of the Irawaddi at Prome, Sagaing, Ava, and the mountain basin of Taong Dong."[41] On his tour of the lower delta of the Irrawaddy, the river running through the heart of the country, Buchanan described the supply of teak from the upland interior during the monsoon season: "Down this [river] are floated during the rains the best Teak timbers that are brought to the Rangoon market. In the dry season the timbers are cut down and shaped in the hills near the sources of the river."[42] Along the way, Buchanan's plant collector, "a peasant boy from Bengal," sent every day into the fields "to gather herbs," found a rare variety of teak known among the Burmese as *tala-hat.*[43] A sketch of this rare species of teak, classified as *Tectona hamiltoniana* (in homage Buchanan's Scottish family name), possibly drawn by Singey Bey as part of the Ava mission's botanical venture, is reproduced in the third volume of Nathaniel Wallich's illustrated natural history of exotic botany,

*Plantae asiaticae rariores.* The painting depicts the flowering plant of *Tectona hamiltoniana* in full, complete with leaves and stem and with close-up illustrations of the flower, the opened corolla, the fruit, and the nut (open and closed) drawn along the bottom of the painting.[44]

In tracing the botany of teak in the Burmese Empire, Singey Bey also faithfully detailed the uses of the hardwood in the kingdom's Buddhist material culture and architecture. The mission passed magnificent teak monasteries, built entirely of wood, ornately carved with mythological figures, emblems, and patterns and richly gilded in gold. Buchanan noted that the grandest Buddhist monasteries, called kyaung, were located near cities.[45] In the former capital of Ava on the upper Irrawaddy River, the mission arrived at the elaborately carved teak royal monastery known as Kyaungdawgyi, housing a large Buddha image. To members of the embassy, a few miles from the Burmese court, it appeared as a stunning sight of the material culture of teak rooted in the Buddhist traditions and forest environment of the empire:

> We observed at some distance on the plain, another religious edifice of distinguished splendor, it was dignified by the title of Kioumdogee [Kyaungdawgyi], or royal convent. . . . We were conducted into a spacious court, surrounded by a high brick wall, in the centre of which stood the kioum, an edifice not less extraordinary from the stile of its architecture, than magnificent from its ornaments, and from the gold that was profusely bestowed on every part. It was composed entirely of wood, and the roofs, rising one above another in five distinct stories, diminished in size as they advanced in height, each roof being surrounded by a cornice, curiously carved and richly gilded. On ascending the stairs, we were not less pleased than surprised, at the splendid appearance which the inside displayed; a gilded balustrade, fantastically carved into various shapes and figures, encompassed the outside of the platform. Within this, there was a wide gallery that comprehended the entire circuit of the building, in which many devotees were stretched on the floor. An inner railing opened into a noble hall, supported by colonnades of lofty pillars. . . . A marble image of Gaudma, gilded and sitting on a golden throne, was placed in the centre.[46]

The resources of the forest were made into emblems of Buddhism and projections of imperial sovereignty. Singey Bey illustrated the wooden ships of teak in the royal Burmese fleet as they plied the Irrawaddy River and its tributaries. These included the *Shwepandawgyi*, the 150-foot "Golden Royal Craft" of gilded teak with the head of Karawaik, the bird mount of Vishnu, carved into its bow, the vessel used to convey the king in state on the water.[47]

FIGURE 14. *Shwepandawgyi,* the royal barge of King Bodawpaya, made of gilded teak. Drawn by Singey Bey, an Indian artist in the East India Company. Michael Symes, *An Account of an Embassy to the Kingdom of Ava, Sent by the Governor-General of India in the Year 1795* (London, 1800).

## THE KING'S FOREST

Word of Singey Bey's artistic exploits spread across the Burmese Empire. He produced botanical drawings of the kingdom's forest culture with such "great exactness" that the Burmese who saw them along way "instantly recognized" the plants "which they use very generally in medicine."[48] During the course of Singey Bey's journey, the Bengali artist gained a reputation "by his botanical drawings" of Burma's plant kingdom. The Burmese monarch Bodawpaya, who was kept closely informed of the embassy and its members, began to hear rumors of the talented Bengali artist traveling the country with the East India Company. The artist's skills in rendering "botanical drawings" came "to the knowledge of his Birman Majesty, or, in the Birman phrase, having reached the Golden Ears."[49] Seeking a specimen of Singey Bey's art, the Burmese king sent a glass painting to the embassy depicting the methods of mahouts in the act of catching wild elephants in the forest, drawn by a Siamese painter in his court, indicating that it was to be copied onto paper by Singey Bey as a royal gift.

FIGURE 15. Mahouts capture wild elephants in a Burmese forest. Drawn by Singey Bey, an Indian artist in the East India Company. Michael Symes, *An Account of an Embassy to the Kingdom of Ava, Sent by the Governor-General of India in the Year 1795* (London, 1800).

The vast forests that covered the Burmese Empire were the habitat of a multitude of wild elephants. Elephants, with and without tusks, were prized throughout the kingdom. When tamed, they were put to use clearing forest, armed and mounted with artillery during war, and most often, ridden upon by princes and royals in ceremonies of court. The reigning monarch Bodawpaya was fond of elephants and reportedly possessed thousands of the animals, including breeds of rare white elephants, which were held to be sacred and highly auspicious due to the belief that Gautama Buddha had been incarnated as the sacred animal in one of his past lives.[50] For this reason, Bodawpaya claimed the title of Hsinbyumyashin, "Lord of Many White Elephants."[51] On the banks of the Irrawaddy in the Elephant Village, the Burmese king kept five thousand to six thousand female elephants for the task of taming the younger and newly captured ones.[52] He now sought an image of elephants being captured and tamed drawn by the talented Indian artist visiting his empire.

Singey Bey's intricate rendition of the painting appears as an engraved lithographic plate titled "Method of Catching Wild Elephants in Ava" in

Symes's *Account of an Embassy to the Kingdom of Ava*. In the painting, hunters riding flat on the backs of tame elephants enter unnoticed amid a wild herd in what appears to be a teak forest, trapping younger wild elephants by running a noose along their paths and roping them in, snaring their feet.[53] As Maurice Collis explained, drawing upon the *Glass Palace Chronicle* tale of King Usana and his head trapper, the old man U Naga, this was the most daring method of trapping elephants, far more daring and dangerous than simply enticing the powerful animals into a fenced enclosure:

> There were two ways of catching elephants. The most ordinary was to surround the herd with a ring of beaters and drive it into the mouth of a wide V, through the base of which a narrow passage led into a palisaded enclosure. There the animals were gradually tied up, starved at first and then fed and handled until they became docile. This method was the safest, as it was the most profitable, for by it fifty elephants might be taken at once, but it lacked the excitement of the other way, which was to penetrate the herd perched on the neck of a tame female elephant and cautiously creeping in choose the best animals and lasso them round the legs. Courage and skill were essential for this; it was far from safe, but it was splendid sport.[54]

In the forefront of the painting, Singey Bey depicts a row of mahouts riding in pairs and casting ropes in the tracks of the wild elephants, while in the center and background the captured animals with their feet entangled struggle to break free of the reins, the other end of which are tied to the bodies of the tame elephants ridden by the mahouts. As the wild elephants are overpowered, the others in the herd desert them and take refuge in the trees. The hunters, mounted on their tame elephants, are seen dragging the fallen wild elephants and warding off the blows of their heavy trunks with hooked sticks. All around the depicted scene are woods, what appears to be an old and mossy forest. After such a hunt, the captured animals were then borne away, bound to two tame elephants and led to the villages and towns, where after a few weeks they would be made docile. Through this sporting method of catching wild elephants, the Irrawaddy Delta came to find a steady supply of elephant labor to be used in such tasks as the transport of teak timber. Singey Bey drew every line of the painting of the scene of elephants being captured "with a laborious exactness," and the end result was much to Bodawpaya's satisfaction.

The Burmese king was so eager to procure more pieces of the artist's meticulous work that he requested his employment at the court to draw the celebrated image of the Mahamuni, plundered from the fallen Kingdom of Mrauk U in Arakan after its fall in 1784 and moved to the new capital city Amarapura on the Irrawaddy River. According to legend, the twelve-foot-high Mahamuni image was cast in bronze in the presence of Gautama Buddha during his fabled visit to the Salagiri Hill in Arakan. The image, once located twenty-five miles north of Mrauk U near the site of the ancient capital of Dhanyawaddy, became the most sacred devotional relic for Theravada Buddhists who made pilgrimage to the Mrauk U Kingdom of Arakan.[55] The Mahamuni was to protect Arakan until the end of the cosmic cycle and Bodawpaya, a deeply committed though enigmatic Buddhist king with aspirations as a future Buddha and a penchant for control over the *sangha* (monastic community), feared its powers.[56] Before sending troops for the conquest of Arakan, the Burmese king dispatched two spies, disguised as monks traveling to worship at the shrine, to report back and cast a magical spell on the image, purportedly neutralizing its power. In 1784, thirty thousand troops under the crown prince of the Konbaung dynasty, joined by the retinues of his brothers—the princes of Prome, Taungoo, and Pagan—marched on Arakan over rugged mountain passes and through the tidal rivers and creeks adjacent to the Bay of Bengal, capturing Mrauk U with little resistance. The Mahamuni image was the most treasured of their plunder, and it was carried away in three pieces on rafts to the coastal city of Thandwe, over mountain passes to Padaung, and then floated down the Irrawaddy River toward Amarapura, where Bodawpaya and the court appeared in person to meet the statue on its arrival.[57] The Mahamuni was enshrined at the Arakan Pagoda in Amarapura, where captive families were reportedly kept as slaves to the image.[58]

It was this Buddhist relic looted from the depths of the tidal mangrove forests of Mrauk U as "a part of the spoils of Arracan" that Singey Bey was asked to draw.[59] He and the members of the embassy found the magnificent metallic idol, sitting in the Bhumiparsha *mudra,* or the earth-touching position, "on a pedestal within an arched recess," with "the walls gilded, and adorned with bits of different coloured mirrors."[60] Symes reported that "peculiar sanctity is ascribed to the image, and devotees resort from every part of the empire to adore the Arracan Gaudma ... this brazen representative of the divinity."[61] Singey Bey was "employed on it a week and when it was finished, his Majesty condescended to express his approbation of the performance." A lithograph of Singey Bey's painting of the Mahamuni appeared

FIGURE 16. The Mahamuni image of Gautama Buddha. Drawn by Singey Bey, an Indian artist in the East India Company. Michael Symes, *An Account of an Embassy to the Kingdom of Ava, Sent by the Governor-General of India in the Year 1795* (London, 1800).

in Symes's travelogue as "Image of the Birman Gaudma in a Temple at Ummerapoora."[62]

During the occasion of the embassy's reception at the imperial court in Amarapura, Singey Bey was honored with an invitation to attend the royal durbar among the representatives of the English mission, riding to the Burmese court on a Pegu horse.[63] Singey Bey sketched the spectacle of the imperial court and the representatives of the British mission's audience with the Burmese king.

* * *

In late November 1795, the *Sea Horse* set sail from Rangoon across the Bay of Bengal for Calcutta. From there, the trail of Singey Bey disappears and the details of his life fade into obscurity. On December 22, he disembarked the ship at the Calcutta harbor. Three years later, in 1798, he again joined Francis Buchanan for another botanical expedition in Chittagong on the eastern Bengal borderlands. But he disappears from the record after that. It remains unclear if Singey Bey was the unidentified Bengali artist who journeyed with Buchanan into the Himalayas and the mountain kingdom of Nepal in 1800–1803 and produced a portfolio of more than one hundred botanical watercolor paintings of plant species collected from the Kathmandu Valley. All that remains certain about Singey Bey are the traces of his art and lithographic paintings of the forest worlds of the Burmese Empire, engraved in a suite of plates depicting the kingdom's forest landscape, immortalized in Symes's *Embassy to the Kingdom of Ava.*

FIVE

# In the Wilderness of Pali

### SHAH 'AZIZALLAH BUKHARI QALANDAR

ALONG A 360-MILE LITTORAL of the eastern Bay of Bengal, in a land of ancient Indic kingdoms, lay the ruins of the Buddhist empire of Arakan and its capital city of Mrauk U (1430–1784). Mrauk U was a monumental city and center of an Indian Ocean trading empire extending from the Irrawaddy to the Ganges. It was renowned as the realm of the golden Mahamuni image, for according to legend, Gautama Buddha had flown with his retinue from India to the Kingdom of Dhanyawaddy (580 BCE–326 CE) in Arakan and converted King Chandrasuriya, whose subjects cast an image of the Buddha in bronze and with pomp and ceremony placed it on a hill. With the passage of time and the reign of the Wesali Kingdom (327–818), the Mahamuni image came to be venerated as a sacred relic and site of pilgrimage, as well as a symbol of Arakanese sovereignty. The imperial reverence for the Mahamuni became invoked in 1430, when King Min Saw Mon Narameikhla, also known by the Indo-Persian Muslim name Sulayman Shah, captured Arakan with the aid of Afghan warriors after two decades in exile in the Muslim sultanate of Bengal in Gaur. Founding the capital city of Mrauk U to mark the establishment of a new sultanate, King Narameikhla/Sulayman Shah became guardian of the Mahamuni image, the renowned and sacred Buddhist relic of Arakan. Until its fall in 1784, Mrauk U was the royal capital of a syncretic Buddhist kingdom on the frontiers of Islam.[1]

At the crossroads between South and Southeast Asia, Mrauk U was an empire of paradoxes. As an imperial formation, it was a blend—at once an agrarian city-state and a maritime trading sultanate.[2] The imperial city of Mrauk U, located in the tidal valley of Dhanyawaddy, in the alluvial delta of the Kaladan and Lemro Rivers, was the upstream port and ceremonial city of the agrarian hinterland, its fields used for the cultivation of rice paddies.[3]

132

Although its setting at the foot of the steep and densely forested Arakan Yoma Mountain Range acted as a barrier to the Irrawaddy River delta of the interior, Mrauk U faced the ocean and the Bay of Bengal, as the empire's littoral and port city of Chittagong became immersed in the mesh of the Indian Ocean world and its trading networks.[4] The empire's main export was rice, derived from cultivation of its fertile alluvial plains, supplemented by the trade in elephants, ivory, and precious stones from the forest interior. In exchange, a multitude of goods from the Indian Ocean reached the shores of Arakan. Opium, salt, tobacco, textiles, and most notoriously slaves, arrived from India; cowries came from the Maldives Islands to be used as currency; and pepper and spices were shipped from Bandar Aceh and the Malay Archipelago.[5] Merchants from South and Southeast Asia, the Middle East, and Europe settled in the royal capital of Mrauk U. Portuguese friar Sebastien Manrique described the city's cosmopolitan character in his seventeenth-century *Travels*:

> The Court was full of men from various foreign countries.... They came in numerous vessels loaded with every sort of rich merchandise and hailed, not merely from neighbouring countries, such as Bengala, Pegu, and Martaban, but also from the empire of Siam, known as Sornau, and the kingdoms of Champa and Camboja. Ships had also come from various part of India, as from the kingdoms of Musalipatam, Negapatsam, and the Maldive islands, attracted to this duty-free market. Nor had ships failed to come from the rich islands of Sumatra, such as Greater and Lesser Java, Achem, Macassar, and Bima.[6]

During the sixteenth century, the bazaars of Mrauk U bustled as a lively emporium, attracting merchants from across the Indian Ocean to Arakan.

The immersion of Mrauk U within Indian Ocean networks of trade and Indo-Persian cultural currents also created complexities of identity and difference in the empire. A Theravada Buddhist kingdom steeped in the Indo-Persian court culture of neighboring Bengal and Mughal India, Mrauk U cultivated a heterogeneous social fabric that brought together Buddhist and Muslim populations and a syncretic mixture of Pali and Persian languages and cultural worlds.[7] The landscape and built environment of Mrauk U—from the early construction of the domed Lemyethna Temple to the Santikan Mosque under King Narameikhla/Sulayman Shah—marked this mixture of Pali and Indo-Persian cultures onto the space of the new imperial city. In parallel to its religious syncretism, the kingdom's imperial customs and diplomacy were considerably oriented toward the Indo-Persian and Islamicate

Mughal world, following the style of a sultanate. The Buddhist kings of Mrauk U adopted Persian names, minting their titles as "shahs" onto bilingual coins bearing the *kalima,* the profession of the Islamic creed, and they conducted diplomacy in Persian.[8] The Mrauk U court became host to renowned Indo-Persian poets from Bengal, such as Alaol (fl. 1651–71), an Indian captive who became a poet and translator in the court of Mrauk U and praised the openness of the kingdom in a verse of his *Padmavati:* "From diverse lands, diverse peoples having heard of the wealth of Roshang come under its King's shadow."[9]

By the eighteenth century, the Mrauk U Empire had fallen into decline due to its loss of naval power in the Bay of Bengal and chronic dynastic instability.[10] Rival Buddhist kingdoms in Southeast Asia, including the Burmese and Mon dynasties of the upper and lower Irrawaddy River delta, vied for the remains of the once illustrious empire and mounted expeditions to Arakan with the purpose of carrying off the Mahamuni image for their capitals. In 1784, the Burmese Konbaung dynasty conquered Mrauk U, as its armies plundered the city and carried off in triumph the Mahamuni image, the longstanding symbol of Arakanese sovereignty. The sacred bronze image was cut into three pieces and brought back, along with 20,000 captives, to the new Burmese capital of Amarapura, the "Immortal City," in the Irrawaddy Delta.[11] In the aftermath of the fall of Mrauk U, many former subjects of the empire fled from Burmese rule into the forested hills and tidal borderlands of Arakan and colonial Bengal. Taking refuge in the territory of the British East India Company, Magh borderers "marauded" the Burmese frontier, aspiring to restore the kingdom of Mrauk U. The fall of Mrauk U and the ensuing anarchy on the Arakan-Bengal border prompted the East India Company and its scientific branch, the Asiatic Society, to seek knowledge and gather reconnaissance on the once powerful but now fading kingdom of Arakan. Because Persian persisted as the language of correspondence and exchange between Mughal India and Arakan, it was left to the company's Persian munshis to survey the Magh borderland.

During the 1780s and 1790s, one group of Indo-Persian munshis in the service of the East India Company set out to decipher the syncretic Theravada Buddhist beliefs and rituals of Mrauk U through translation of Pali literature into Persian. Shah 'Azizallah Bukhari Qalandar was among this cast of munshis, employed by East India Company Orientalist John Murray MacGregor to recover Mrauk U's Theravada Buddhist laws and customs.[12] Scarce information remains on Shah 'Azizallah. But what is known is that through contacts with Arakanese monks and migrants, who read to him from Pali texts, he translated into Persian an archive of Buddhist literature from the Pali language, ranging from legendary and mythical histories of the Buddha and his teachings, including Theravada texts on the origins and end of the universe and the previous lives of the Buddha (known as the *jataka*), to ethnographic descriptions of the Magh peoples, their history, customs, and laws, and botanies on the known trees and plants of the Bengal borderlands. The Pali-into-Persian manuscripts written by Shah ʿAzizallah detail the Indo-Persian encounter with the "Pali imaginary" of the Mrauk U Empire in Arakan.[13]

Through the translation of Buddhist cosmographical texts from Arakan, Shah ʿAzizallah entered the Pali Buddhist imaginary of Mrauk U, recasting Gautama Buddha within a Persianate and Sufi view as a mystic prince seeking truth in the wilderness. Just as mystical Persian Sufi literature saw the wilderness as a space of Sufi wandering in search of truth, in Pali cosmographic literature the forest environment is the place where enlightenment and nirvana are sought; the forest is part of the ethereal and passing world of Theravada Buddhism and its cosmic cycles of life, death, and rebirth.[14] In Shah ʿAzizallah's reading, the *jataka*s become mystical Sufi parables, reminiscent of the Persian literary form of the *hikayat,* the tales of an ascetic Sufi prince who left earthly possessions behind to seek nirvana. According to these legends, Gautama Buddha was a king who gave up earthly ambitions and took on ascetic life, seeking solitude and meditation under the canopy of forest trees. Shah ʿAzizallah's translations from Pali into Persian reveal how Muslims understood and made sense of Buddhist religion and ritual in the Kingdom of Mrauk U. Even more, Shah ʿAzizallah's translations convey an Islamic view of Buddhist rituals and customs and of literary genres in the Pali cultural world of Arakan.

These traces of the presence and participation of Muslims in the history of Mrauk U and its ties to the Indo-Persian Mughal world are now almost forgotten amid the contentious interconfessional politics and violence in Rakhine State in Myanmar, which has marginalized and oppressed the region's Muslim populations. Although Muslim presence in Arakan stretches back centuries, Muslims are now regarded as foreigners (kala) and a vestige of the colonial era, with signs of their presence in the region becoming destroyed and effaced. It has been difficult to reconcile the hardened identity boundaries of the present with the syncretic nature of the past and to appreciate Arakan as a place of contact and exchange between Buddhism and

Islam. The writings of Shah 'Azizallah are traces of an almost irretrievable past, rare views of the lost world of the Mrauk U Kingdom, where the landscapes of Buddhism and Islam merged.

The frequent references in literature to Mrauk U as a "lost" or "forgotten" empire seem romantic on the surface but actually convey something real regarding the historical memory of the kingdom. As the Muslim ruins and remains of the empire decay in the forest, lost to natural disasters, destroyed by human violence, and ravaged by the passing of time, its Persian written histories have been overlooked. At the nexus of South and Southeast Asian "area" studies, the history of Arakan (and Myanmar) falls in between the lines of area studies and its rigidly imposed geographical frontiers.[15] Arakanese history continued along colonial and Orientalist frameworks, with the early publications of Arthur Phayre and Maurice Collis remaining the standard works of reference on Mrauk U until the late twentieth century.[16] Since the 1990s, a wave of new scholarship by Sanjay Subrahmanyam, Michael Charney, Jacques Leider, and Stephan van Galen, among others, has revived and solidified the study of Arakanese history from various historiographical perspectives: through the exploration of Mrauk U as connected to the early modern Indian Ocean trading world, by chronicling the political and economic history of the Mrauk U Empire, and via the examination of the kingdom's cultural, artistic, and architectural history.[17] The recent publication of Thibaut d'Hubert's *In the Shade of the Golden Palace: Ālāol and Middle Bengali Poetics in Arakan* (2018), a study of literary encounters and exchanges between Bengal and Arakan, represents the fruition of these nuanced recent works on the history of early modern Mrauk U.[18]

This chapter takes up the history where the existing literature has left off, during the late eighteenth century and the early colonial period in years of the twilight of Mrauk U. While recent studies have focused almost exclusively on the early modern period, particularly the sixteenth and seventeenth centuries when Mrauk U was at its height, the last decades of the eighteenth century, the fall of the empire, and its aftermaths remain in the shadows. Narratives of Arakan's history during the last decades of the eighteenth century still veer toward schematic outlines of decline, conquest, colonization, and ultimately incorporation into the modern Burmese state. After 1784, Arakan's complex past is hastily assimilated into narratives of Burmese colonial and national history, with its center of gravity in the Irrawaddy River delta.

The following discussion steps into this eighteenth-century lacuna in Arakanese history through an exploration of Indo-Persian exchanges with the Kingdom of Mrauk U. Following preliminary views of Indo-Persian commercial and imperial interactions with Mrauk U—including analysis of Persian letters from the court of the king of Mrauk U and the early colonial archive on the Arakan-Bengal borderlands—the chapter delves into Indo-Persian, Islamic perceptions of Buddhism in eighteenth-century Arakan through the Pali-into-Persian translations of Shah 'Azizallah Bukhari Qalandar. The Persian translations of Theravada Buddhist texts by Shah 'Azizallah are lost pages from the Buddhist-Muslim encounter in the borderlands of Arakan and Bengal and rare traces from the enigmatic, fallen Kingdom of Mrauk U. The translations produced by Shah 'Azizallah, as well as other munshis in the service of John Murray MacGregor, convey a syncretic religious landscape where, despite the existence of notions of difference, Buddhism and Islam cover overlapping cultural terrains and become intertwined. The Pali-into-Persian translations of Shah 'Azizallah reveal the mutual and shared worlds of ritual and belief that existed between Theravada Buddhists and Sufi Muslims in early modern Arakan.

## MERCHANTS TO THE GOLDEN CITY

In 1728, the royal court of the Kingdom of Mrauk U in Arakan sent Persian letters to an Armenian merchant in Chennaipattan across the Bay of Bengal. The letters, one of which is a decree, or *farman*, inscribed with the Pali seal of Chandrawizaya Raja ("the Moon of Victory," r. 1710–31) and addressed to the merchant Khwaja Georgin, have lain in obscurity in the British Library in the collection of the physician and naturalist Hans Sloane. In *Catalogue of the Persian Manuscripts in the British Museum*, Charles Rieu dismissively deems the letters, classified as Sloane Mss. 3259 and 3260, as "barbarous Persian" and dates them in the Arabic month of Sha'ban in the Hijri lunar year 1090 (1679).[19] But although the month written in the letters is indeed the Arabic Sha'ban, the year 1090 is not Hijri but rather Maghi, or Magh, as is clearly inscribed in the manuscripts, corresponding to the year 1728. Without doubt, the farman is the Persian translation of the earliest dated Burmese palm-leaf manuscript in the British Library, a single long palm leaf that is a permit issued by King Chandrawizaya in response to a "foreign trader" seeking permission to trade in Arakan. The Burmese palm leaf is marked by the same two faint royal seals in Pali that also appear on the Persian farman and is addressed, according to the British Library card

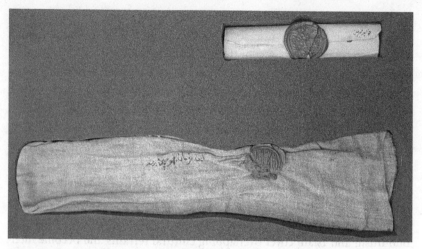

FIGURE 17. Persian *farman* from King Chandrawizaya of the Buddhist Kingdom of Mrauk U in Arakan to Khwaja George in Chennaipattan, 14 Sha'ban 1090 Magh (1728). Rolled with a wax seal and above the cloth it was sent in, addressed: *in farman bih Khwaja Georgin birisad* (this decree is to reach Khwaja George). Ms. 3259, Sloane Manuscripts Collection, British Library, London.

catalog, to one "Khoja Joro Jin."[20] The connection between these Burmese and Persian documents has previously gone unnoticed, as have the implications of the existence of a Persian farman from the court of a Buddhist sovereign in Southeast Asia.

The history of Indo-Persian contact with Southeast Asia remains obscure, but for centuries a global system of interimperial trade linked the Indo-Persian Mughal world to the Southeast Asian mainland and archipelago. By the fifteenth century, Islam had become established through trade and pilgrimage in the Indonesian Archipelago, while on the Southeast Asian mainland Buddhist empires blending Islamic and Indo-Persian influences rose to power. Although the kingdoms of mainland Southeast Asia did not convert to Islam as in the archipelago, the growth and spread of Theravada Buddhism stimulated trade and interaction with Islamic, Indo-Persian societies.

In the early modern period, trade, diplomacy, and the prevalence of Persian as a literary and cultural language of the court closely linked empires in South Asia and the Southeast Asian mainland. In the Kingdom of Ayutthaya (1351–1767) in Thailand, during the reign of King Narai (1656–88), a thriving community of Persian merchants from Safavid Iran attained influence and prestige in the Thai court.[21] Farther north, along the eastern littoral

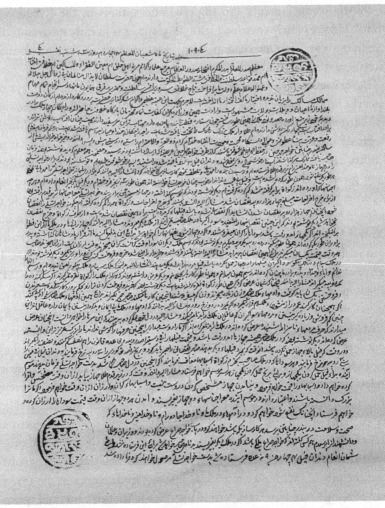

FIGURE 18. Text of Persian *farman* from King Chandrawizaya of the Buddhist Kingdom of Mrauk U in Arakan to Khwaja George in Chennaipattan, 14 Sha'ban 1090 Magh (1728). Ms. 3259, Sloane Manuscripts Collection, British Library, London.

of the Bay of Bengal, the Theravada Buddhist Kingdom of Mrauk U (1430–1784) in Arakan shared imperial, cultural, and commercial ties to the Indo-Persian and Mughal worlds.[22] Although Buddhist, the Mrauk U Empire was steeped in the culture and trappings of Islamic kingship; its kings adopted Persian names; minted their titles as sultans and padishahs onto multilingual Pali-Persian coins bearing the kalima, the profession of the Islamic creed; and recognized the kingdom's sovereigns as rajas and shahs.[23] The "Persianization" of courtly comportments and imperial conceptions in the Kingdom of Mrauk U were closely entwined with developments in early modern Indian Ocean trade and commerce, in particular as they pertained to relations and exchanges with Mughal India.[24]

The existence of the farman from the court of King Chandrawizaya suggests the immersion of the court of Mrauk U within Indo-Persian networks and currents of trade and correspondence, as well as Persianate and Mughal forms of imperial fashioning, into the eighteenth century. The farman denotes a royal decree, command, edict, or order—a public legislative document given in the name of the sovereign. The farman was a form of legal document and genre of courtly correspondence that prevailed among the chanceries of Persianized Turko-Mongol Islamic empires in the Middle East, Central Asia, and South Asia.[25] But Persian farmans were not known to have been written in the courts of the Buddhist sovereigns of Southeast Asia. The decree of King Chandrawizaya reveals, if only through a glimmer, how a Pali kingdom in mainland Southeast Asia adopted elements and aspects of a Persianate and Mughal imperial repertoire.

In Mughal travel and encounter literature, as noted in earlier chapters, the Southeast Asian mainland and its littoral were conceived as the far edge of the Indian Ocean, a zone of wondrous forest kingdoms and their rarities under the stewardship of an idealized sovereign. The courts of the sovereigns of Arakan, being fluent in the Persianate commercial, diplomatic, and literary currents of Mughal India and the Bay of Bengal, also represented and projected their empire as a forest kingdom of matchless marvels and rarities of nature ruled by a sacred and universal sovereign. This theme of a wondrous forest empire of manifold exotics and luxuries finds echoes in the 1728 farman of King Chandrawizaya permitting trade with merchants and agents in India across the Bay of Bengal.

King Chandrawizaya's decree reads,

In the year Maghi 1090 on Tuesday the 14th day of the month of Sha'ban al-Mu'azzam. Maghi narration [naql-i Magi]. From the Exalted Seat of the Moon of Honor, the Glory of the Great Sources of Knowledge and the Generous People of Creation, the Source of Certainty for the Poor and Indigent, the Source of Descent from the Caliphate, the Destined Source of Sovereignty and Kingship [Saltanat], the Proof of Government [al-zavabit al-hukumat]. By the grace of the Banner of Knowledge, may His glory be exalted, our state has kindled without decline since the reign of His Majesty the Eternal Sultan Min al-Man [Raja Min Saw Mon]. After the passing of the almighty, over time the crown of sovereignty [*taj-i khilafat*] and honor has become set upon my head. The important routes and provinces of the country are in order and under my authority. Therefore, for the sake of this great and generous royal threshold I give thanks to the presence of God [*Hazrat-i Parvardigar*]. The pillars of the kingdom have been hung high, reaching fame and reputation, visible from province to province [*vilayat bih vilayat*]. The ministers, nobles, and subjects of the kingdom remain loyal and devoted. Having brought the rajas of other kingdoms, with all their pomp, under the sway of the blade in building an empire of 190 kingdoms, the rays of the North Star [*Sitara-yi Qutb*] and the moonlight glow unto me, and my light burns so bright, it is like a brother to the sun. In the great golden Kingdom of Rakhang I have found a throne. The Raja of Rajas [*Raja-yi Rajagan*] Chandrawijaya Raja, the Moon of Victory, is my title. By the order of this decree [*hukm-i farman*], I give the sublime shelter of honor and the first order of kindness and friendship [*mifarmayam raf'at va 'izzat panah va 'atufat va 'avali-yi dastgah-i muhabbat va mavvadat*], and have awakened my subjects to bestow great honor, confidence, and goodwill upon Khwaja Georgin of the port of Chennaipattan. He is under celestial protection [*hifz-i ilahi*] and it is my hope that he has good fortune. It was a source of happiness and pleasure to receive a letter from Khwaja Georgin requesting a farman from the Lord [*farman-i sahib yafta*] and seeking three counts of ivory [*dandan-i fil*]. He had written that his brother Khwaja Tasalli had been sent as a captain of a ship in obedience to the Step of the Golden Foot [*Qadam-i Tala*] with kindness and grace. By the will of God, your brother Khwaja Tasalli has engaged fully in trade and has been shown mercy and given every benefit. Three flawless elephants with tusks [*fil-i bi 'ayb-i dandan dar-i khub*] have been sent in chains, as requested by Khwaja Georgin, along with another additional chained elephant with tusks I have sent as a gift. And I have purchased all the goods that were imported after charging the *zakat* tax. You had written that during the last monsoon, your brother Khwaja Tasalli had come to this kingdom on the ship of Mr. Chapman and incurred a loss of four thousand rupees but I can assure you that any such loss was not due to charges [*kharj-i ikhrajat*] or taxes [*zakat*] collected but due to elephants dying on the way. You mention that merchants [*sawdagarha*] who hear of these losses avoid our kingdom and sail elsewhere instead, giving us a bad name, to which I inform you that the merchant mariners [*jahazraniha*] of this kingdom are dismayed of this talk, as the more merchant ships arrive here, the less goods will cost and the more they will profit. We follow the customs of our previous kings [padishah], our fathers and brothers, and doing as they have done in the past, we will charge a one-tenth tax in silver rupees, as you have also requested. You mention the trading customs of the kingdoms Siam and Pegu, and that if merchants load a healthy elephant on their ships from there and it dies on the journey another elephant will be sent, but I have not seen these places and am not familiar with their ways. I only know the customs of my own kingdom and the traditions of my ancestors, father and brothers, which I follow. Your letter references rumors told by foreign merchants that the subjects of this kingdom are ignorant and dishonest, but if this were true and my subjects lacked such manners, my reign would be short lived and the kingdom in disorder. Certain unwise foreign merchants have spread rumors that in our kingdom there exist faithless and wicked people, and the words of unreliable merchants have given our kingdom a bad name. If you are a friend to us, you will not heed these words and hold us dear. You have also written that many ships come and go in the direction of our land, and that if as lord of the kingdom I wish to permit one ship to arrive to purchase elephants and another ship to purchase rice during the start of every monsoon season [har sar-i mawsum], that I present a farman to Khwaja Tasalli. You should know that once under the protection of the Step of the Golden Foot, I will recognize and acknowledge any of your ships that reach this kingdom, and I will bid upon the goods they import. If you hold us in esteem and trust [i'tibar], during the next monsoon season dispatch two ships laden with goods, and I will send the ships back to you with merchandise ensuring that you will find profit. And in my kingdom, I have sea captains [nakhuda] who can deliver blessings [sihhat va salamat] to Chennaipattan and conduct trade and transactions. In the story of Khwaja Sara', it was said by all the ministers and scholars that if Khwaja Sara' was in one land and a gift was sent to another land, it would give the Sahib a bad name, and due to this, nothing was sent. But your gift of 9 ivories weighing 4 mans has been sent to you along with this farman by the hand of Khwaja Tasalli.[26]

In its form and materiality, the farman of King Chandrawizaya represents a Persian-Islamic genre of correspondence produced within an Indic-Buddhist setting and context. This is most visibly indicated by the multilingual nature of the letter, as the Persian script of the text is marked in Pali script by two royal seals at the beginning and the end. The royal seal reads in Arakanese, raja dhippati rhwe nan sa khan, "Supreme Lord, Master of the Golden Palace."[27] Although there are no other extant seals to compare to this seal, which is also stamped onto red wax on the cloth that the letter was sent in, this seal resembles the multilingual Pali and Persian coins of Mrauk U. In its form and structure, the Pali seal of Chandrawizaya conforms even more closely to the Persian seals of the Mughals, most notably in its circular shape and its pattern of lines and latitudes. Its Pali script is presented in the form of Persian seals of the Mughal Empire, appearing on paper as opposed to the palm leaf, or parabeik, upon which the Pali script is traditionally found. The unusual material culture of the letter is matched by corollaries in the structure of the farman, which bears the signs of traditional Southeast Asian documentary formulas. The decree of Chandrawizaya follows an accepted schematic structure of the Persian farman genre: the invocation of God and the introduction of the title of the sovereign and his reign; the disposition of the royal mandate; and the call to recipients and subjects to recognize and execute the command. Farmans were imperial directives issued on various political, administrative, and economic subjects. The decree of Chandrawizaya most closely resembles the form and content of the Mughal trade or commercial farman, granting concessions and allowing royal protection to foreign merchants and companies to conduct trade in the empire.[28] In its structure the Arakanese farman, however, was also clearly adapted to local vernacular forms and idiosyncrasies. One revealing sign of this variation in structure occurs with the great emphasis placed on the date, given at the beginning of the document, customary among Southeast Asian courts focused on auspicious times and dates.[29]

King Chandrawizaya's farman was addressed to the Armenian merchant Khwaja Georgin, or Khwaja George, of Chennaipattan, and delivered by the hand of his brother Khwaja Tasalli, a sea captain known for journeying across the Bay of Bengal to Pegu and Arakan along the littoral of the Southeast Asian mainland. From other extant sources of the period, fragments of the identities of the merchant brothers may be pieced together. *Records of Fort St. George* (a publication of the Madras government) in 1728 mentions a court case between the Madras merchants George Christianezar and Philip Muzavin, with one "Coja Tessaly" undertaking to represent George Christianezar in the case.[30] Khwaja George again appears in the record as "Coja George Christianeza" in a case involving another Armenian merchant in Madras, "Coja Joan," in 1736.[31] Traces of Khwaja Tasalli, Khwaja George's brother and representative to King Chandrawizaya of Mrauk U, appear in Madras government records that note that during the spring monsoon season of 1707, an Armenian sea captain by the name of "Coja Tassaree" returned from a voyage to Pegu to the Coromandel Coast.[32] Again, in the summer of 1732, it is recorded that a captain named "Tassalee" had "sailed for Arracan."[33] Khwaja George and Khwaja Tasalli were thus prominent merchants in the port of Chennaipattan when it was governed by East India Company as the Madras Presidency of Fort St. George. The merchant brothers seem to have been key intermediaries and middlemen in the trade with the Southeast Asian mainland across the Bay of Bengal, as indicated by their efforts to negotiate and open up trade with the Kingdom of Mrauk U in Arakan.

The farman suggests the immersion of Armenian merchant networks originating from Safavid-era Isfahan within the currents and conventions of the Persianate world, its commerce, its letters, and its courtly etiquette, which Armenians from New Julfa carried to the eastern shores of the Indian Ocean. Armenian high merchants (*khwaja*) and sea captains (*nakhuda*) sought trading concessions contained in Persian farmans from Indian Ocean sovereigns. As Sebouh Aslanian has detailed in his book on global Armenian trade networks, within a decade of the founding of the Armenian quarter of New Julfa in Isfahan during the seventeenth century, Armenian merchants became settled in Burmese ports, where in subsequent years they gained a monopoly on the ruby trade and came to play "an important role both as merchants and diplomatic go-betweens to various Burmese kings" through the eighteenth and nineteenth centuries.[34] From rubies to elephants, Armenian merchants found access to the trade of the forest treasures of Southeast Asian kingdoms.

The farman from King Chandrawizaya conveys the integration of the Kingdom of Mrauk U within the networks of the Indo-Persian world. The raja's decree reveals the role of Persian as a medium of communication for the conduct of trade and to express mutual and shared courtly ethics of sacred kingship and sovereignty.[35] At the heart of such transactions was the trade in elephants, a mutual symbol of kingship in the Mughal Empire and the Buddhist kingdoms of the Southeast Asian mainland. Elephants were the royal mount, part of the spectacle and repertoire of the projection of kingship and sovereignty in the court and out on the hunt. Taming elephants conferred the sovereign's possession over the sacred forest and its rarities. Most significantly, for centuries war elephants were a decisive force in battles in South and Southeast Asia. Their exchange as imperial megafauna between courts was a mutually understood transaction.[36] In this way, the trade in elephants between Arakan and Chennaipattan was a ritual and tributary exchange between imperial formations, with Armenian merchants serving as intermediaries between the Mughal Empire (along with the East India Company and South Asian princely states) and the Kingdom of Mrauk U, all of which were immersed within an Indic repertoire of imperial regalia. The trade in elephants and ivory was in part spurred by this symbolic exchange between sovereigns, a sign of kingship, power, and the harnessing and domestication of the forest realm. The trade in elephants and ivoriy between South and Southeast Asia was thus embedded within Indo-Persian customs of imperial fashioning and the projection of royal power.[37] The exchange of elephants was part of an economy of interimperial exchange.

Beyond imperial regalia and power, elephants were also prized for their tusks, the source of ivory (*dandan-i fil*). The market for ivory evolved from ivory's use as a material object, from carved royal thrones and panels to jewelry and ornament. Ivory was an object of luxury and its consumers were royals, kings, and princes, who displayed it on their thrones, palanquins, cabinets, and courtly objects d'art. Ivory also found application among religious establishments, particularly in Buddhist art and iconography. Owing to this widepread usage, there was a Bengali saying that "even a dead elephant is worth a million rupees," as merchants made great profit from the ivory trade.[38] The heavy demand and limited supply of ivory prompted merchants to search for new markets, and the forest kingdoms of the Southeast Asian mainland were reported to be the habitat of multitudes of wild elephants. Khwaja George and Khwaja Tasalli were merchants in the lucrative trade of elephants and ivory. Through a grasp of Persianate and Mughal customs and cultures of transactions, the Armenian merchants became intermediaries in the trade between Indic courts and sovereigns in South and Southeast Asia. King Chandrawizaya's correspondence with Khwaja George and Khwaja Tasalli illustrates details of the ivory trade and its intricate protocols. Above all, it hints at the heightened imperial reach over the forest habitat of elephants by the eighteenth century, due to the great wealth that could be made from the trade of just a few precious pieces of ivory.

King Chandrawizaya's farman was the golden ticket, the legal document that permitted Armenian merchants from India to enter Arakan and trade with the Kingdom of Mrauk U. This royal decree was the permit, a license of access to the commerce of an empire on the margins yet nevertheless entwined within the networks of the Indo-Persian world. It was the literary instrument, the writ of passage that permitted transactions with empires fluent in Persian courtly and commercial parlance. Its social and cultural context was the Persianized Indic court of Mrauk U, the realm of an idealized universal sovereign with a sacred reign; as such, the farman of King Chandrawizaya gave "divine protection" to Khwaja George and Khwaja Tasalli to conduct trade in the kingdom. The legal right of "divine protection" (*hifz-i ilahi*) given by the king's writ opened the gates of the "bazaar" of Mrauk U to trade and transactions. The farman served as a written sign of the king's "trust" (*i'tibar*) and guaranteed that Khwaja George and his brother Khwaja Tasalli were recognized by "the grace and kindness of the

Golden Foot" (*Qadam-i Tala*).[39] A second, shorter letter, written in a different hand and lacking the Pali scripted seals, was addressed to Khwaja George and sent from an unnamed merchant of Arakan following up, reiterating, and substantiating King Chandrawizaya's decree of opening to trade.[40]

The commercial relations between King Chandrawizaya and the Armenian merchants of Chennaipattana, however, were to be short lived. In 1731, three years after these exchanges and the promise of the opening of trading relations, the king was assassinated; the throne of Arakan would subsequently pass between fourteen different monarchs until the eventual fall of the kingdom in 1784. The prospect of trade with Arakan became haphazard as reports appearing in the British East India Company archives detailed the insecurities and turbulence caused by Arakanese raiding and piracy in the Bay of Bengal. The Burmese Konbaung dynasty's violent conquest of Mrauk U in 1784 only accentuated the climate of chaos as Arakanese refugees from the fallen kingdom crossed the frontier into the Bengal borderlands, bringing the Burmese Empire and the East India Company to the verge of war. It would not be until 1795 that the East India Company would send its first official embassy to the Arakanese and Burmese littoral to seek the opening of commercial relations, with particular emphasis upon the lucrative teak trade. But the mission, led by Orientalist officer Michael Symes, accompanied by his Indo-Persian munshis and go-betweens, still followed long-standing precedents and patterns of Persianate correspondence. In seeking sanction of the court of King Bodawpaya of the Konbaung dynasty for company merchants conducting trade along the Burmese coast, the mission relied on the medium of Persian correspondence, procuring a Persian farman from the Burmese king to open up the teak trade, a farman that only exists (for now) in its English translation in Symes's travelogue, *An Account of an Embassy to the Kingdom of Ava*.[41]

### LAND OF THE BANDIT KING

For much of the remainder of the eighteenth century, reports of the violence and turbulence in Mrauk U and their effects on India and the Bay of Bengal would find echoes in the British East India Company archive on the Southeast Asian kingdom. The empire's openness to foreign commerce and heterogeneous culture coexisted with and was in ways predicated upon the violent practice of slave raiding and trading in the Bay of Bengal.[42] Partnering with Arakanese mariners and Portuguese mercenaries, and their swift fleet that rowed through the rivers and along the coasts of the Bay of Bengal region, the Kingdom of Mrauk U sponsored raids and the taking of captives from India to be sold into slavery in Southeast Asia. Raiding and the slave trade advanced Arakan's frontier in Bengal vis-à-vis the rival Mughal Empire and bolstered its agrarian and commercial economy. The royal fleets of Arakan raided the Bengal littoral for captives to be put to work cultivating rice paddies in the Kaladan River delta, to enter the ranks of the imperial army as soldiers, to serve as ministers and men of letters in the royal court, or to be trafficked through Dutch East India to till the plantations of Java.[43] In Bengal, the Arakanese came to be known as the "Magh," a term of contempt and fear commonly associated with the violence of their slave raids and the anarchy of the Bengal-Arakan frontier.[44]

The British East India Company came to know and establish direct contact with Mrauk U only in the waning days of the kingdom during the eighteenth century. This was a century of royal instability and political upheaval in Arakan, culminating in the Burmese conquest of Mrauk U in 1784. Much of the East India Company's knowledge of Mrauk U and its history, as well as its tangled past interactions with Mughal India, was recovered through Persian imperial chronicles that mapped the Kingdom of Arakan as a savage realm on the geographical and cultural margins of India, a foreign land on the eastern shores of the Bay of Bengal.[45] In the tumultuous waning years of Mrauk U and after its fall in 1784, the company sought reconnaissance on the turbulent Arakan-Bengal borderland through the recovery of Persian chronicles detailing the relations between the Mughal and Arakanese empires.

Charles Stewart (1764–1837), a military officer and Orientalist with the East India Company in Bengal, knew this Mughal genre and its outlook on the Arakan frontier well. Stewart had entered the company's Bengal Army in 1781, later serving as professor of Persian at Fort William College in Calcutta from 1800 to 1806, at which time he returned to England and assumed a professorship of Arabic, Persian, and Hindustani at the East India College in Hertfordshire. His prolific scholarly works include an 1809 descriptive catalog of the library of Tipu Sultan, the nawab of Mysore; a translation of Mirza Abu Talib Khan's book of travels in 1810; an 1821 translation of the fables of *Anvar-i Suhayli;* and a collection of original Persian letters published in 1824. Through the translation of the Persian chronicles of the Mughal Empire,

Stewart retraced the violent past of the Arakan borderland and littoral in his *History of Bengal* (1813).

*The History of Bengal* was based on the archive of Persian Mughal imperial chronicles. According to Stewart, "The greater part of this work is composed of translations made by myself from Persian Historians."[46] These included "the Persian Manuscripts from the East-India Company's Library" and "the antient documents" among "the Records of the India House," evanescent records kept "in a damp situation, the ink daily fading, and the paper mouldering into dust ... documents fast vanishing from sight."[47] At the outset, Stewart includes a "List of Persian Books Used in the Compilation of This Work," referring to such early modern Mughal imperial chronicles as *Tarikh-i Firishta, Akbarnama, Jahangirnama, Shah Jahannama, Alamgirnama,* and *Muntakhab al-lubab.*[48] Indeed, Stewart "had no reason to complain of a paucity of materials; but rather of such an abundance," which posed "some difficulty in compressing the narrative within one volume." These Persian histories were not figments of arcane "Oriental learning" but rather comprised, in Stewart's estimation, "the best information that could be obtained" on the history of Bengal.[49]

When it came to the history of the coast and islands of Arrakan and the Magh Kingdom of Mrauk U, Stewart described them within the context of Mughal imperial history and the making of the offshore borderlands of Bengal. Through the annals of Persian histories, Stewart's *History* looks back on the seventeenth-century Bay of Bengal as a "middle ground" of interimperial encounters and exchanges between the Mughal Empire and the Kingdom of Mrauk U. The subjects of the Magh Empire of Arakan are represented as a people of rude customs who practiced "the grossest idolatry" and who were dismissed disdainfully as offensive and "very reprehensible" by Emperor Jahangir when they appeared in the Mughal court.[50] Most disconcerting of all for the Mughals were the slave raids of the Magh Empire along the littoral and islands of the Bay of Bengal. Collaborating with Portuguese mariners and adventurers in piracy, the "native princes" of Arakan, with their swift wooden boats that freely entered river mouths and creeks from the sea, commanded the Bay of Bengal coast and the adjacent islands at the mouth of the Ganges River, such as Sandwip. From the perspective of the Mughals and their imperial chroniclers, the "incursions of the Mugh" pirates left the Bengal littoral of the Indian Ocean precariously unsettled.[51] Into the 1630s, the Magh pirates and their Portuguese associates continued their depredations and piracy. They "had become so insolent, that they committed many acts of violence upon the subjects of the empire, and presumed to exact duties from all the boats and vessels which passed." Moreover, they "were in the habit of kidnapping or purchasing poor children, and sending them as slaves to other parts of India ... and [they] committed innumerable aggressions on the inhabitants of the districts on the eastern branch of the Ganges."[52]

In portraying a treacherous Arakanese frontier, Mughal chronicles recounted the tragic flight of the Mughal prince Shah Shuja' to Mrauk U in 1660 in the aftermath of his struggle against his brothers to succeed their father Shah Jahan on the Mughal throne. Pursued by the army of his victorious brother Aurangzeb, he fled with his family and retinue of famed Afghan archers, known as the "Kaman," to the court of Arakan. As legend has it, the Mughal prince, who was promised ships to sail from Arakan to Mecca, Safavid Iran, and the Ottoman Empire, refused to give his daughter in marriage to Chandrasudhamma Raja (r. 1652–84) of Mrauk U, eventually resulting in the prince's murder, the imprisonment of his family, and the absorption of his Kaman archers into the palace guards of Mrauk U. In response to these events and the chaos caused by Arakanese slave raiding on the Bengal littoral, the Mughal emperor Aurangzeb appointed Shaista Khan, the Amir al-Umrah—son of the celebrated *wazir* Asif Jah, and nephew of Empress Nur Jahan—as governor of the province of Bengal. By 1666, the Mughal fleets had driven the Magh pirates from the Ganges River and its tributaries, and they "took by storm" the fortresses at the mouth of the river and the islands off the coast of the Bay of Bengal, also capturing the key port city of Chittagong.[53]

Mughal histories of the Bengal borderlands and the Kingdom of Mrauk U informed and shaped the East India Company's perceptions of Arakan as a turbulent frontier zone. Arakanese raids persisted into the eighteenth century, with reports appearing in the East India Company archives. The *Calcutta Review* reported that during a single month—February 1717— Arakanese pirates "carried off from the most Southern parts of Bengal 1800 men, women, and children." The report added that "in ten days they arrived in Arracan and were conducted before the sovereign, who chose the handicraftsmen and about one-fourth of the number, as his slaves." The rest were returned "with ropes around their necks" to the slave traders who took them to the market to be sold for "20 to 70 rupees each."[54] The colonial government took measures to fend off the raids from the Magh. Arakanese mariners and slave raiders, and their Portuguese associates, continued to cause such great alarm on the Bengal coast that in 1770, "a chain was run across the [Hugli] river at Mukwah Fort, where the Superintendent of the Botanical

Garden resides to protect the port of Calcutta against pirates."[55] The piracy and depredations of the Arakanese off the coast of Bengal in 1778 caused alarm among colonial officials.

The archive of the East India Company highlights the climate of chaos that followed the fall of Mrauk U in 1784 and how these disorders spilled over into the Arakan-Bengal borderlands. In the ruins of the Mrauk U Empire of Arakan, the company's Persian munshis and scholars surveyed a world fallen apart. Their letters detailed disorder, upheaval, flux, and turbulence on a perilous and violent colonial frontier rife with "marauders" from a fallen empire; numerous files described the roving banditry and frontier exploits of "Magh marauders" with names like "Apolung" and "Kingberring."[56] This is a well-known genre of the British colonial archive in South Asia and the Indian Ocean world, one focused upon and haunted by the security, legibility, and panic of violence on the uncertain fringes of empire.[57]

The turbulence of Arakan could even be felt at its very geological core. In the spring of 1762, a destructive earthquake shook the Bay of Bengal region. The quake, violently felt in Bengal, Burma, and Pegu, was centered in Arakan.[58] A Persian eyewitness described the earthquake in a report to Harry Verelst, Esquire, an East India Company agent in Chittagong who forwarded the letter, along with a translation, to the English governor of Fort William in Bengal, Henry Vansittart, and the company representative, Warren Hastings, in Calcutta. The English translation of the report described the violence and devastating effects of the earthquake:

> An Account of the Earthquakes that have been felt in the Province of Islamabad, with the Damages attending them, from the 2d to the 19th of April 1762: Translated from the Persian, and communicated to Henry Vansittart, Esq. President and Governor of Fort William in Bengal, by Mr. Verelst, Chief of the Hon. East India Company's Affairs at Islamabad.

> The weather being very close and warm for some days preceding, on the 22d of the month of Chytt 1168 Bengal aera, answering to the 2d of April 1762, on Friday about 5 o'clock in the afternoon, we were alarmed by an earthquake; which beginning with a gentle motion, increased to so violent a degree, for about two minutes, that the trees, hills, and houses shook so severely, that it was with difficulty many could keep their feet, and were thrown on the ground.... On the plains, by the rivers, and near the sea, it was chiefly felt with great severity.... The ground opened up in several places in the town, throwing up water of a very sulphurous smell ... in some parts so deep that they could not fathom its bottom; the water immediately overflowing the whole town.[59]

Dwellings were destroyed and a great number of people "were lost," while surviving inhabitants "ran into the woods and were not heard of."[60] The writer concluded that the "disorders that have come to pass in these regions, and which continue to happen, insomuch from the time of Adam until now, in this place, no one has heard of the like." What he saw was beyond comprehension and words: "If I should describe them with a thousand instances and relations, and make mention of so many particulars, still there would not be part in ten that I could bring within the compass of writing."[61] This report of geological turbulence was part of a colonial archive that deemed Arakan a foreign land and a kingdom of unfamiliar customs, as well a violent frontier zone of piracy, slave raiding, and banditry.

Still, there was a different, and more literary and esoteric, Indo-Persian element in the colonial archive on the Mrauk U Empire of Arakan, one that sought out Orientalist knowledge of the empire, its Pali literature, and Buddhist culture. The interests of these Indo-Persian writers, in line with the East India Company Orientalists who employed them, were antiquarian, philological, and legal and concerned with the recovery of knowledge in Pali and its translation into Persian.

## PALI INTO PERSIAN

The colonial Persian archive on the Mrauk U Kingdom of Arakan was produced amid the early period of the British East India Company's Orientalist pursuits during the late eighteenth century, when the recovery of Sanskritic knowledge was sought through its translation into Persian. It was a project of colonial knowledge gathering provoked by the East India Company's practical need to access and codify indigenous law through the Persian language following its territorial conquest of Bengal. An early venture in this genre of Indo-Persian legal compilation was a Sanskrit compendium of legal codes from the Dharmasastras collected by eleven pundits, translated into Persian by the munshi Zayn al-Din 'Ali Rasa'i and then into English in 1776 by Nathaniel Halhed as *A Code of Gentoo Laws*.[62]

The endeavor to collect and codify Indian law and religion became more pronounced with the establishment of the Asiatic Society in Calcutta in 1784. The society, along with its journal, which first appeared under the title *Asiatick Researches* in 1788, formed a venue "for inquiring into the history and antiquities, the arts, sciences, and literature of Asia."[63] The society's founder, renowned Orientalist and jurist Sir William Jones, had learned Arabic and Persian, the courtly language of Mughal India, while at Oxford during the 1760s, and he began study of Sanskrit shortly after arriving in Calcutta. These Asian languages, Jones and others believed, unlocked codes of Indic and Islamic law that could then be fixed by the East India Company. The Sanskrit Dharmasastra texts were seen to contain the varied world of Hindu law, while Arabic and Persian texts conveyed the tenets of the Islamic legal canon.[64] Jones translated *Al Sirajiyya; or, The Mohammedan Law of Inheritance* from Arabic in 1792, following it the next year with the culmination of his work on Indian codes of indigenous law, his translation of the Manava Dharmasastra, *The Institutes of Hindu Law: or, The Ordinances of Menu.*[65]

While this colonial project to codify indigenous law in the end instigated the creation of fixed boundaries between Hinduism and Islam, Sanskrit and Persian, at the time in late eighteenth-century Bengal it also held a quite different promise. For Jones and other members of the Asiatic Society, the effort to recover knowledge from Sanskrit and Persian also held certain theoretical possibilities of deciphering the common origins of languages, cultures, and religions. In the course of studying Asian languages, Jones discerned structural affinities between Sanskrit, Persian, Greek, and Latin.[66] In the essay "On the Hindus," the third-anniversary discourse to the Asiatic Society in 1786, Jones elaborated on these theories of linguistic, cultural, and religious syncretism and interconnection, writing of the people of India, "Of these cursory observations on the *Hindus,* which it would require volumes to illustrate, this is the result: that they had an immemorial affinity with the old *Persians, Ethiopians,* and *Egyptians,* the *Phoenicians, Greeks,* and *Tuscans,* the *Scythians* or *Goths,* and *Celts,* the *Chinese, Japanese,* and *Peruvians.*"[67] Influenced by notions of Biblical chronology and genealogy, Jones searched for stories of a great flood across religions, such as the Hindu legend of Vishnu's warning the world of a fathomless deluge, as proof of the flood of Genesis and the descent of all the world's inhabitants from Noah before they and their languages were scattered.[68]

This age of Orientalism and translation in Bengal forms the context of the creation of John Murray MacGregor's Pali-into-Persian archive on the Theravada Buddhist culture of Arakan. The empire of Arakan and the cultural and religious heterogeneity of its capital city of Mrauk U, alternately known in Persian as Rakhang or Roshanga, presented a rich laboratory for examining the shared linguistic structures, legal codes, and belief systems between Asian cultures. In the ethnically and religiously varied environment of Mrauk U—a Theravada Buddhist empire and Pali cultural world steeped in Indo-Persian Islamic culture—British Orientalists and their Indo-Persian munshis treaded into a borderland of cultural difference that mirrored then-current theories of the commonalities between the civilizations and their shared belief systems.

John Murray MacGregor (1745–1822) was a Scottish officer in the East India Company and was appointed auditor-general of Bengal from the 1770s through the 1790s. In Bengal, Murray learned Persian, avidly collected Asian-language manuscripts, and became a prominent member of the Asiatic Society in Calcutta.[69] His collection of manuscripts included a vast archive of texts from Arakan, known as the "Magh manuscripts," consisting of Buddhist literary, religious, legal, and natural history tracts written in the Pali script of the Burmese language on Indian paper, with Persian titles on their wooden cover boards, held in the British Library.[70] The Persian translations of these manuscripts are kept at the Staatsbibliothek in Berlin and were produced by Murray's indigenous collaborators, munshis whose task it was to gather the Buddhist literature of the Mrauk U Kingdom from mystic monks known as *rawali* and to translate narratives from Pali into Persian.[71]

The colophon of a number of these Persian-Pali manuscripts bears the name of a munshi—"Sayyid Shah 'Azizallah Bukhari Qalandar." Signs of his name also appear on folio pages in the Arabic literary form of *huwa al-'aziz,* at once invoking a Sufi word for God (*huwa*) and leaving a trace of the scribe's own identity, "the dear one" (*'aziz*). He wrote with a wide-brushed *qalam* (pen) in the *shikasta-amiz nastaliq* script on tanned Indian paper. From the name of the munshi, Shah 'Azizallah Bukhari Qalandar, it can be surmised that he was an antinomian Sufi wanderer and mendicant (one skilled with the pen), an Iranian *qalandar* from or descended from the Central Asian oasis city of Bukhara and most possibly a disciple of the Naqshbandi Sufi *tariqa*. In 1783, he accompanied "John Murray Sahib" on a journey down the Ganges River from Calcutta to Agra, and to the Taj Mahal, keeping a written account of his travels.[72] Three years later, in 1786, during a period when he was unemployed (*dar ayyam-i bikari*), he traveled through northern India on the instigation of Murray and wrote a brief narrative of the journey.[73]

During the 1780s and 1790s when Shah 'Azizallah was active as a munshi, he composed original reports and copied existing works of literature for Murray's collection. These included compiling statistical reports about the *zamindar* (landowners) of Bengal, writing histories of the Maratha Wars, recording chronologies of the kings and rajas of India, as well as copying letters, farmans, and histories of Mughal sovereigns and recovering texts about the natural history and cultures of Bengal and surrounding lands.[74] The most unusual and substantive materials in Shah 'Azizallah's body of work were a set of translations and narratives on the Pali Buddhist literature of the kingdom of Arakan and its capital city of Mrauk U, or Roshanga. There are traces in the manuscript suggesting that Shah 'Azizallah and other munshis employed by Murray recovered the Pali literature of Arakan through collaboration with a certain Arakanese Buddhist monk named Kyaw Jain. In the colophon of a Persian translation of a Pali cosmography, it is noted that the manuscript was written "from the reading of Kyaw Jain [az khwandan-i Kyaw Jain], an Arakanese monk [rawali; thakur] settled in the Niyapara Pargana of Islamabad [Chittagong]."[75] The ending of another manuscript on medicine attributes its source as "being spoken in the language of Kyaw Jain, rawali thakur" (bi zabani Kyaw Jain in rawali va thakur).[76]

Through contacts with rawali Buddhist monks from Arakan, Shah 'Azizallah, along with other munshis employed by Murray, translated into Persian an archive of Buddhist literature in the Pali language, ranging from legendary histories of Gautama Buddha and his teachings, including jatakas on the past incarnations of Buddha; Theravada cosmographies on the origin and end of the universe; books of law, medicine, and botany; original compositions on the ethnography of the Magh people and their Buddhist beliefs, rituals, and practices; and Persian glossaries of the Pali language of Arakan. Shah 'Azizallah's familial origins in Bukhara and Central Asia suggest a possible exposure and familiarity with Buddhism, the traces of which had existed in Central Asia since late antiquity. The Persian translations of Pali Buddhist texts produced by Shah 'Azizallah during the 1780s to 1790s convey a syncretic climate of Islamic-Buddhist cultural contact and exchange. Through Persian translations of tales of the Buddha's ascetic wanderings in the wilderness and his past lives, he rendered Buddhism and Islam as corresponding in belief systems and ritual practices in the Bengal-Arakan borderlands.

## THE CITY OF LIGHT

During the late eighteenth century, Persian speakers in Bengal and Arakan knew the royal city of Mrauk U by the name Rakhang or Roshang, in reference to the "city of light," and its inhabitants were known variously as Rakain, Roshan, or Rooinga. The subjects of the kingdom included Buddhists, called Rakain Leet, and Muslims and Hindus, called Rakain Kula.[77] For Shah 'Azizallah Bukhari Qalandar, Rakhang was a city (*shahr*) and a kingdom (*mulk*).[78] From the royal city of Rakhang, which gave its name to the region of Arakan, the realm extended to the lands of Bengal, Assam, and Hanthawaddy, encompassing "101 kingdoms" (*yak sad u yak mulk*).[79] The peoples (*mardum*) of Rakhang were separated into an array of different ethnicities and identifications of belonging—Burma, Sakra, Buddhu, Achin, Makh, Akkya, Jamiya, Chakma, and many more.[80] The subjects of the empire spoke an old language (*az qadim ast*) distinct from Sanskrit.[81] Kingship was the basis of sovereignty in the empire and its rulers were titled raja.[82] These are the basic geographical contours and political details that Shah 'Azizallah provides on the empire of Rakhang in his Persian ethnographic tract "Sual-i ayin va ravaj-i qawm-i Makh va javab-i an" (Questions and answers on the prevalent customs and religions of the Magh peoples).[83]

It was the Buddhist rituals, customs, and practices of Rakhang that Shah 'Azizallah explored in detail. Buddhism defined the physical and cultural landscape of Rakhang. For centuries, its rajas had built an urban ceremonial space through construction of images, monuments, gates, fortresses, wells, and resting houses in tribute to Gautama Buddha and his relics.[84] Shah 'Azizallah deemed that the people of Rakhang worshipped idols (*sanam*) and practiced idolatry (*but parastish*).[85] These idols were all relics and images of Gautama Buddha, called in the Pali language Buddha Thakur, or "Lord Buddha," and Shah 'Azizallah noted that the Magh did not build and worship idols to other deities as did the Hindus.[86]

According to legend, as related in a Persian translation of a Pali Buddhist cosmography titled "Kitab-i Buddha Thakur" (Book of the Lord Buddha), Gautama Buddha made a journey to the kingdom of "Roshanga," at which time the sacred Mahamuni idol was made in his presence to serve as a relic to protect the kingdom until the end of the cosmic cycle. The "raja" and "padishah" of Roshanga, upon hearing the recitation of Buddha's teachings— referred to in the translation as "Qur'an"—became omniscient, and knowing that Buddha would depart from his kingdom, they sought to have an image (*shabiya*) of the Buddha made. Buddha replied, in a curiously monotheist and Muslim fashion, that although in the past idols were worshipped by the people, over time they lost the true path of belief (*iman*), and thus the Buddha idols were made hidden and concealed (*khafiya*) by angels (*firishtigan*), since the worship of idols (*but parasti*) was not part of the path to nirvana (*nivala*).[87] Buddha conceded, however, that if an idol for worship was sought, then he would allow one to be made. Overjoyed, the raja ordered that precious metals and stones be gathered from his treasury, including rubies (*la'l*), the brilliant gem (*shab chiragh*), emeralds (*zumurrud*), diamonds (*almas*), carnelian (*'aqiq*), coral (*marjan*), and gold (*tala*), and brought to adorn the Buddha image in its casting.[88] The idol, completed in the year 147, was called Mahamuni, "meaning the idol of Buddha Thakur."[89] Persian descriptions of the popular reverence for the Mahamuni and images of Buddha in Rakhang bore traces of the undeniable tension between Buddhism and Islam surrounding perceptions of idol worship. However, Shah 'Azizallah and other Muslims who encountered Buddhism in Rakhang did not adhere to any stringent Islamic iconoclasm and rather came to nuance their understanding of Buddhism as not being idolatrous in its essence (as revealed in Gautama's reluctance to allow the casting of the Mahamuni in the passage above), meaning, practices, and rituals.

Further, the way of Buddhism was not limited to Buddhists alone and there existed a syncretic communication of the Buddhist Pali imaginary across different religions. Shah 'Azizallah sketched views of Muslims in the society of Rakhang, noting the relative ease with which the empire's Muslim subjects crossed over into the Buddhist plane of ritual and belief. Muslims in Rakhang could enter the spiritual fields of Buddhism "by bringing their faith and hearing the mantras" (*az avurdan-i iman va shinidan-i mantraha*).[90] In Rakhang, Muslims and followers of other religions "could become Buddhist by receiving and reciting the *Panj Tarani Mantra*" (*az giriftan va khvandan-i Mantra-yi Panj Tarani*).[91] The syncretic nature of religious practice and confessional belonging in Rakhang left the dividing lines between Buddhists and non-Buddhists fluid, challenging modern conceptions and definitions of organized and separate religious traditions.

In Rakhang, Shah 'Azizallah discovered shared cults and rituals across different but overlapping religious communities. The most pervasive of all these ritual worlds in Rakhang was that which surrounded the practice of Theravada Buddhism, as carried on by the way of the rawali. Shah 'Azizallah suggests the acceptance and syncretic appropriation of the "prophetic" figure of Gautama Buddha among the Muslims in Rakhang by noting the names attributed to Buddha by different confessional communities there: "'Gaudama' of the Pali language was known as 'Buddha Avatar' to the

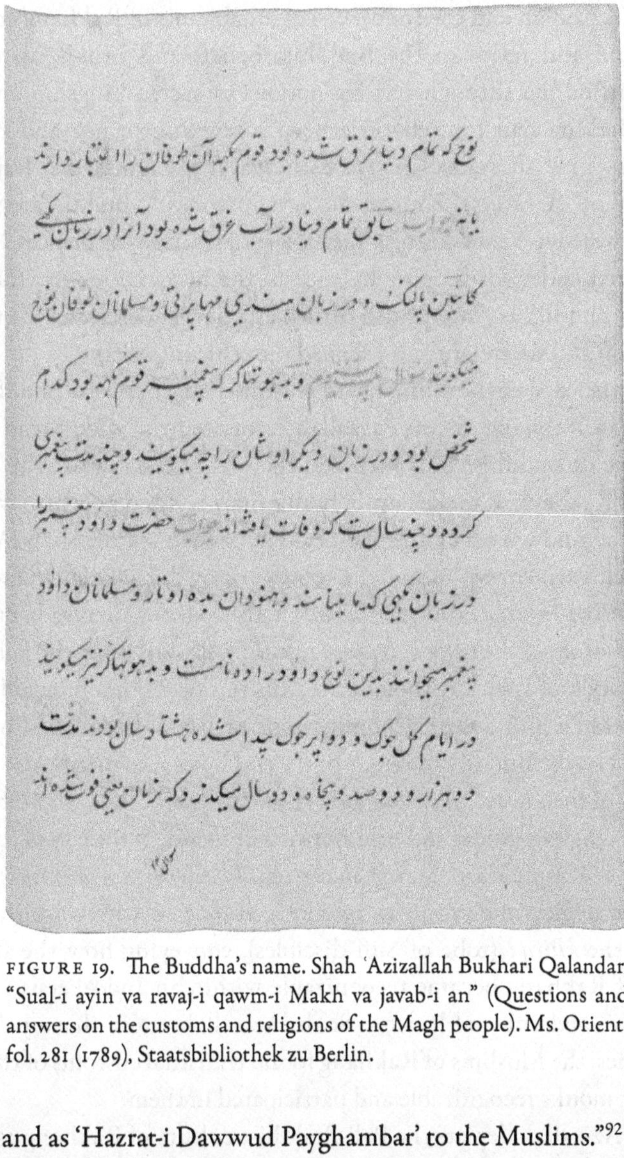

نوح که تمام دنیا غرق شده بود قوم مگه آن طوفان را اعتبار دارند
یا نه جواب سابق تمام دنیا در آب غرق شده بود آنرا در زبان مگهی
کانین پالنگ و در زبان هندی مهاپرلی و مسلمانان طوفان نوح
میگویند سوال پیشیم و بدهو تهاکر که پیغمبر قوم مگه بود کدام
شخص بود و در زبان دیگر اوشان را چه میگویند و چند مدت پیغمبری
کرده و چند سال است که وفات یافته اند جواب حضرت داود پیغمبر را
در زبان مگهی گدما بیاسند و هنودان بده اوتار و مسلمانان داود
پیغمبر میخوانند بدین نوع داود را ده نامست و بدهو تهاکر نیز میگویند
در ایام کل جوک و دواپر جوک پیدا شده هشتاد سال بودند مدت
دو هزار و دو صد و پنجاه و دو سال میگذرد که زمان یعنی فوت شده اند

FIGURE 19. The Buddha's name. Shah ʿAzizallah Bukhari Qalandar, "Sual-i ayin va ravaj-i qawm-i Makh va javab-i an" (Questions and answers on the customs and religions of the Magh people). Ms. Orient. fol. 281 (1789), Staatsbibliothek zu Berlin.

Hindus and as 'Hazrat-i Dawwud Payghambar' to the Muslims."[92] Muslims in Rakhang had thus appropriated Gautama Buddha into the sphere of Islam through association with the name of a known prophet—David. This commensurability of prophetic figures and prophethood between Buddhism and Islam moved in both directions, as Buddhists in Rakhang adopted Biblical and Islamic notions of the Flood of Noah, known in Arabic and Persian as *Tufan-i Nuh,* into their cosmographic views of the universe, referring to the world's great deluge in Pali as *Kahin Palank.*[93]

Shah 'Azizallah and the Indo-Persian inhabitants of Rakhang could also understand and relate to the Buddhist beliefs and rituals surrounding Gautama Buddha through relative notions of sacred kingship and sovereignty. Buddha had himself once been a reigning prince and universal sovereign—in Shah 'Azizallah's words, he was the "Chakravarty Raja" of the "Haft 'Iqlim" (Universal King of the Seven Climes).[94] Buddha's legend and teaching were wise council for kings, a sort of "mirror for princes," maxims that offered codes for keeping balance in the imperial realm. The way of Gautama Buddha as royal prince turned ascetic wanderer was the template of kingship and sovereignty and shaped the ethics of rulers.

In another sign of the mutuality of cult and ritual between Buddhists and Muslims in Rakhang, Shah 'Azizallah recounted the widespread Muslim acceptance of Buddhist holy men and the way of the rawali. The spiritual leaders of Rakhang were the rawali, Brahmin priests and holy men who "read the mantra" and wore a cloth robe as a sign of their status. Shah 'Azizallah likens their garment to "mean" the robe worn by Sufis (*az giriftan-i parcha ya'ni pushidan-i khirqa rawali mishavad*).[95] The codes of Theravada Buddhism and the "custom of the rawali" (*rasm-i rawali*) were written in the Pali *Kitab-i 'adalat* (Book of law).[96] Although the Muslims of Rakhang included those from the Shi'a and Sunni denominations of Islam, both Muslim groups (*firqa*) joined the Buddhist subjects of the empire in recognizing the spiritual authority of the rawali (*rawali ra buzurg midanand*). "The rawali," he wrote, "were the religious guides and held spiritual influence in the city of Rakhang" (*sardar-i din rawali ast va dar shahr-i Rakhang qiyam darand*).[97] Shah 'Azizallah depicts the rawali as ascetics and *darvish* who wore the mystic cloth of the *khirqa* (robe of Sufi disciples), conveying how the Buddhist monks of Rakhang became recognizable within an Indo-Persian Muslim perspective and cultural lexicon. Shah 'Azizallah wrote that in their Sufi sensibilities, the Muslims of Rakhang found the ritual customs of the mystic Buddhist monks recognizable and participated in them.

Shah 'Azizallah depicts the Pali-Buddhist culture of Rakhang as a world apart that Sufis could still find familiar, navigate, and translate to their own religious views. Indo-Persian Muslims in Rakhang found the recognizable in the strange. In the ritual practices and customs of Theravada Buddhism in the empire of Arakan, Muslims found elements they could relate to. To begin with, the Buddhists of Rakhang worshipped Gautama Buddha—his names, his relics, his idols—and were not devotees of a multifarious world of polytheistic gods like the Hindus. The vision of the prophetic Buddha was grafted onto the tree of Islamic beliefs by Shah 'Azizallah as it was by the Muslims resident in Rakhang, those who adapted to its Buddhist devotional landscape. Muslims in Rakhang connected with the Buddhist daily pattern of prayer, three times a day in the morning, afternoon, and night.[98] And just as Muslims made pilgrimage to the sacred shrine cities of Mecca and Medina, and the tombs of prophets and saints, so too did the Buddhists of Rakhang make pilgrimages (ziyarat) to designated sacred sites of pilgrimage (ziyarat-gah), the most hallowed place of all being Mahabudh Gahat (Mahabut) in the Indian region of Bihar, the site of the tree where Gautama Buddha reached enlightenment.[99]

While the practice of pilgrimage to the abodes of holy men would have been familiar to Muslims such as Shah 'Azizallah, the itineraries of Buddhist pilgrimage were set in an entirely different spiritual terrain and cosmographical world. According to these views, there existed limitless worlds, called *chakkawala* or *sakwala*. At the center of these worlds was a vast mountain named Sineru, alternately called Maha Meru, half submerged in a deep ocean known as the Great Sea. Four islands, called *deep*, radiated out from Sineru Mountain to the south, north, east, and west, each known for a species of tree that grew upon the island. Mrauk U, along with India and Ceylon, was located on the southern island called Jambudeep, thought to be sacred because in its center was the Mahabodhi tree of "golden leaves" and "ruby colored flowers."[100] This was the forested land where Buddha lived and attained nirvana, his relics and bones placed across temples on the distant corners of the island after his passing. This "universe" ('alam) or "world" (jahan), although comprised of "the known elements of earth, water, wind, and fire," was quite different from any Shah 'Azizallah had known.[101] But he strived to decode and restyle Buddhist concepts within an Indo-Persian, Sufi vocabulary and worldview. This effort to translate Arakanese Buddhism within an Indo-Persian and Islamic cultural sphere resulted in the production of a massive, nearly one-thousand-folio "Persian-Maghi Dictionary," written in the hand of a different munshi for Murray, now held in the British Library.[102] The unsigned and unfinished dictionary, most likely written by the munshi Mir Sadiq 'Ali, functioned as a sort of working practical glossary, still in draft form, for the purpose of translating Pali texts into Persian. The substance of the project, however, went beyond the lexicographic and entailed exchanges, conversions, and adaptations between the belief worlds of

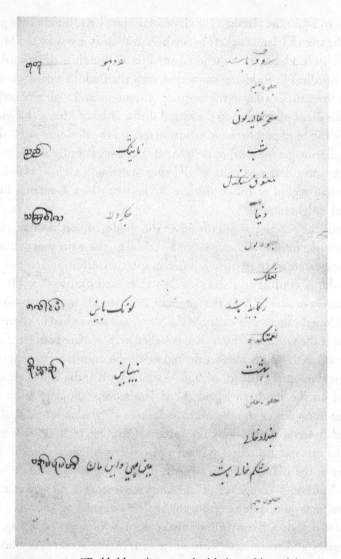

FIGURE 20. World (*dunya*) is a cycle (*chakrawala*), and heaven (*bihisht*) is nirvana (*niehban*). "Persian-Maghi Dictionary," Add. 12266 (ca. 1790), 207v, John Murray Collection, British Library, London.

Theravada Buddhism and Islam. It constituted a search for the possible connections between the tenets of Buddhism and Islam. Buddhist temples became *masjids,* or "mosques"; kyaung, or "monasteries," became *khana-yi Kaʿba,* or "houses of the Kaʿba"; the endless worlds of *chakkawala* became *dunya,* or the "world"; and nirvana rendered as *bihisht,* or "heaven."[103]

Around 1790, Shah 'Azizallah translated a Pali *jataka,* a book recounting the legends of the previous births of Gautama Buddha. Its manuscript exists at the Staatsbibliothek in Berlin under the title "Kitab-i kayfiyat-i pansad paydayish-i Buddha Thakur az zabani Buddha Thakur dar Maki bud tarjuma bi Farsi shud, dar Maki nam-i Sapapuram" (Book of the five hundred previous lives of Lord Buddha that was in the Magh language and was translated into Persian, called in Magh by the title Sapapuram).[104] The work is an adaptation of Buddhist jataka tales recast as Sufi *hikayat,* or parables, highlighted by a rendering of the story of Prince Vessantara, Buddha's last human rebirth before being born as Prince Siddartha. The tale of Prince Vessantara being sent into exile in the forest after giving away a magical rain-bringing white elephant and becoming an ascetic is a lesson on the merit of generosity and the most beloved of the jataka in Southeast Asia.[105] Through Shah 'Azizallah's translation, the Vessantara jataka becomes adapted into a Sufi allegory on renouncing the materiality of the earthly world, becoming a darvish, and retreating to the *khalvat* (solitude) of the wilderness, away from society, in order to be closer to the divine and supernatural.

Shah 'Azizallah's Persian translation of the jataka begins with a *bismallah,* an invocation of the name of God, and presents the teachings of Buddha and his past births through the language of Islamic asceticism. Framing the jataka tales, at the beginning of the manuscript, is a curious story of an encounter between a fisherman and a man who frequents prayerhouses that closely parallels the unorthodox and antinomian worldviews of Sufi vagabonds:

> *Naql ast.* . . . It is said that two men met one another in the street, one was a lifelong fisherman and the second passed his time saying and hearing prayers in a Buddhist temple [*masjid-i biku*], and thus giving praise to God [*hamd-i khuda*]. In passing each other by, they entered into a conversation and became acquainted with one another, learning about each other's lives. As a result of this meeting, the fisherman became forlorn and distraught because he did not think he had prayed enough in the *masjid-i biku* in order to merit earning his daily bread to feed his children, while the man who passed his days reciting and listening to prayers in the Buddhist temple regretted never having cast a net to catch fish. And in the end, the fisherman reached heaven and the man who frequented temples went to hell.[106]

Thus began Shah 'Azizallah's attempt to translate Magh folktales on the past rebirths of Buddha, known as *appadana* but styled in Persian as *paydayish,*

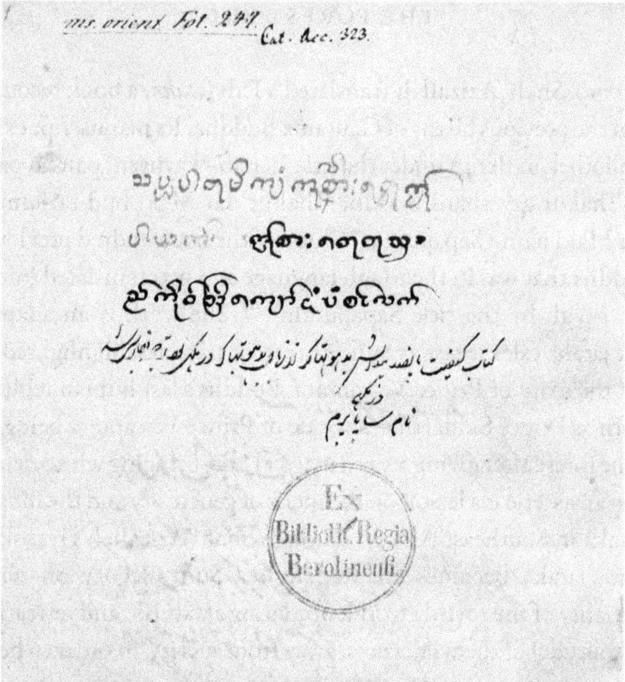

FIGURE 21. A Persian *jataka*, title page in Persian and Pali. Shah 'Azizallah Bukhari Qalandar, "Kitab-i kayfiyat-i pansad paydayish-i Buddha Thakur" (Book of the five hundred previous lives of Lord Buddha). Ms. Orient. fol. 247 (ca. 1790), Staatsbibliothek zu Berlin.

and Buddha's path to nirvana into the language and narratives of the Indo-Persian world.

The first jataka that Shah 'Azizallah recounts in the manuscript is the story of Prince Vessantara. Once, when a heavy rain was falling (*barish-i baran bisiyar shud*), Gautama Buddha said to his disciples that this was not the first time a great shower of rain had fallen on his followers: "I had once before seen this rain in one of my past births when I was born in the palace of a king and my name was Raja Vessantara" (*yak daf 'a paydayish-i man dar khana-yi raja bud va nam-i man Raja Vessantara bud va dar in paydayish yak ruz hamin qadr barish bud*). From the time of his birth, Vessantara was committed to the act of charity (*khayrat*) and to almsgiving. When he came of age, his father, King Sanjaya, made him the raja of the Sivi Empire. Vessantara spent his days performing acts of generosity and charity, giving *khayrat* to his subjects. One day, he gave away the empire's sacred rain-bringing white elephant (*fil-i safid*) to a neighboring land experiencing drought. The ministers in the court (*divan*) complained to Vessantara's father that such reckless acts of charity would lead the kingdom to ruin, and the prince was ordered to relinquish the throne, quit the kingdom, and retreat into the wilderness (*az mulk dast bardarad va dar biyaban biravad*). With his queen "Maddi," his son "Jali," and his daughter "Kanha," Vessantara "took the path of the wilderness" (*rah-i biyaban*). He gave up all ambitions of being a raja and devoted himself to "thoughts of God in the wilderness" (*dar biyaban rafta bi yad-i khuda khaham mand*). Living in the forest edge, away from crowds, Vessantara gave away his fortune, his children, and his wife in his quest to attain the perfection of generosity and to reach nirvana by becoming Buddha.[107]

In the hands of Shah 'Azizallah and his Persian translation, the jataka of Prince Vessantara is retold with a Sufi vocabulary and perspective. The jataka and its emphasis on the Buddhist virtue of boundless generosity and charity are adapted into a Persian Sufi allegorical tale. Shah 'Azizallah renders Prince Vessantara as an ascetic darvish seeking the spiritual silence (*khamush*) of the wilderness (*biyaban*). Vessantara's retreat to the forest edge becomes, in Shah 'Azizallah's telling, entwined with Sufi and Islamic notions of ritual and worship (*'ibadat*). Most prevalent of all in the translation is the theme of wilderness. In Sufi hikayat, the wilderness, connoting desert or forest, was a supernatural place where the darvish held mystic power. Sufi darvish, ascetics, and mendicants wandered the forest edge seeking truth. In stories of Sufis and their miracles, the forest was a domain of wonder and the realm of finding the divine soul.

Amid this process of literary and cultural translation, Shah 'Azizullah still manages to recover the essential narrative structure and thematics of the Vessantara jataka, detailing the Pali cosmography of Theravada Buddhism. Through the story of Prince Vessantara, Shah 'Azizallah perceived the forest worlds of Arakanese Buddhism. His Sufi-tinged telling of the Vessantara jataka encompassed the sacred signs and symbols of the wilderness environment in Theravada Buddhism, translating into Persian a space both familiar and strange. While Shah 'Azizallah's rendition of the story of Prince Vessantara becomes recognizable as a Sufi allegory of truth seeking in the wilderness, the forest setting of the tale is seen as a different and foreign environment and landscape, a wondrous nature with its own complex array of meanings, symbols, and signs. To this end, a Pali-Persian glossary appears following the narrative of the Vessantara jataka. In translating the jataka into Persian, Shah 'Azizallah vividly represented the Pali forest landscape and its plant and animal kingdoms, traceable in his representation of three elemental signs of the Pali forest: the lotus, the white elephant, and the lion.

## The Lotus

In his narrative sketches of the Pali forest, Shah 'Azizallah detailed its variety of flora and classified the properties of its plant life. The most pervasive and recurring of the plants he described was the lotus flower (*gul-i nilufar*), a symbol of Buddhist iconography in South and Southeast Asia. The lotus flower appears throughout the Vessantara jataka, most memorably when Vessantara's children hide in the leaves of lotus plants and become silent (*khamush*) after being given away by their father. In the glossary following the *jataka,* Shah 'Azizallah provides several variations of the Pali word that he transcribes as the lotus—*kirayi*. His affinity for the lotus is traceable in other manuscripts and narrative genres he left behind. He considers the lotus not only in the genre of Pali Buddhist literature he translated but also in scientific, medicinal, and natural history texts he compiled. In a botany of Bengal and surrounding lands written in 1792, titled *Tashrih al-ashjar* (A description of trees), he recounted the realm of wild and cultivated plants, detailing the wild (*barri*), garden (*bustani*), and mountain (*kuhi*) trees of the Indian Ocean world and their medicinal uses. He provided an illustrated account of the lotus, *nilufar* in Persian and *padma* in Hindi. The lotus was deemed "one of the famed

FIGURE 22. The wonders of the lotus. Shah 'Azizallah Bukhari Qalandar, "Tashrih al-ashjar" (A description of trees). Ms. Orient. fol. 171 (1792), Staatsbibliothek zu Berlin.

plants" (*az riyahin-i ma'ruf ast*) and grew in the "quiet" (*sida-yi kam*) of "warm places" (*mahhal-i garm*), flowering in purple, white, and sky blue colors. It was a flower of the tropical lands of "Hind"—India and the Indies. "During the spring season, the lotus is planted," Shah 'Azizallah wrote, with "its seeds being scattered whole into places where warm standing water is found, and there it thrives." Of the medicinal purposes of the lotus, Shah 'Azizallah wrote that it was "medicine for the heart" (*adviya-yi qalbi*) and taken mixed with saffron and cinnamon. Indian lotuses were "read" as fortunes (*fal khanand*), as sacred signs of the auspicious and the ominous.[108]

## The White Elephant

Shah ʿAzizallah's Persian translation of the jataka tales conveys the legends surrounding the animals of the Pali forest that Gautama Buddha encountered in the cycle of birth, death, and rebirth.[109] The charismatic megafauna of the Pali forest was the white elephant (*fil-i safid*), held sacred because it was one of Buddha's last rebirths before nirvana. It remained a symbol of sovereignty in Theravada Buddhism among sovereigns who took on the title of "Lord of the White Elephant" (Sahib-i Fil-i Safid).[110] Shah ʿAzizallah told the story of Prince Vessantara, who gave away the magical rain-bringing white elephant of his kingdom and was banished to the forest. In an ensuing jataka in the manuscript, Shah ʿAzizallah presented a tale of Buddha recounting once being born as a white elephant with six tusks that emitted magical rays. Living as "a raja of elephants" known as Jaha Dink Jahank, he dwelled in a marsh of lotus flowers on Silver Mountain in the Himalayas with his queens Mahasubhadda and Chullasubhadda:

> In one of my incarnations, I was a raja of elephants, and lived on Silver Mountain [*dar yak paydayish man raja-yi filan budam dar Kuh-i Nuqra*] and many elephants were my followers and companions on that mountain. I had two wives, one was Mahasubhadda and the other Chulasubhadda, and we were known as the Jaha Dink Jahank elephants and dwelled in a marsh full of trees and lotus plants [*dirakht-i nilufar*].[111]

One day, the raja of the elephants shook a flowering branch of a tree and the wind blew the petals in the direction of Mahasubhadda, on whom they fell. In her sorrow over not being the favorite, Chullasubhadda wasted away and died, and being reborn as the queen of the kingdom of Kasi, she told the king about the magical six-tusked Jaha Dink Jahank elephant of Silver Mountain. The king ordered the royal hunters (*sayyadan*) to kill the elephant chief and bring the magical tusks to his queen, but the hunters did not know where to search for such a rare species of elephant. Only one hunter set off for the forests of the Himalayas and Silver Mountain to search for the prized elephant. Following an arduous trek, the hunter reached Silver Mountain and found the Jaha Dink Jahank elephant, fatally wounding the creature with a poisoned arrow. Dressed in animal skins, the hunter approached the elephant as it lay dying, drew his sword, sawed off its tusks, and departed with the prized ivory, delivering it to the queen. Upon seeing the tusks, the queen remembered her previous life on Silver Mountain and died in sorrow.[112] This jataka of the of the six-tusked white elephant recounted the death of a rare and sacred fauna of the forest destined to be reborn as Buddha.

## The Lion

Shah 'Azizullah deemed the mythical winged lion known as "Singh" to be paramount among all the beasts in the Pali forest. He believed that the Singh, also called Chinthe in Arakan, was the most sacred and revered animal of the Pali wilderness (*Singh ra miyan-i janivaran buzurg mishumarand*).[113] The winged lion Singh is a recurrent image in Shah 'Azizallah's Persian translation of the jataka tales, a witness to the Buddha's past lives. He calls the Singh "the most powerful on Earth" (*aghni-yi zamin*) and "witness to the meaning" of the Buddha's past births (*shahid-i ma'ni hasti*).[114] In other instances, the Singh becomes linked with the planet, taking on the "meaning of Earth" (*yani zamin*).[115] In one instance, Shah 'Azizallah portrays Buddha sitting before two stone images of the Singh and recounting his former birth as a lion who roamed a forest habitat seeking to be reborn and to attain nirvana, a parallel to the story of Prince Vessantara, the ascetic king relinquishing the material world.[116] In Shah 'Azizallah's translation, lions appear as sacred symbols of sovereignty. As the Singh reigned over the animal kingdom, rajas reigned over human societies.[117] To be raja was to be "a reminder of the Singh among the people" (*man-and-i Singh dar marduman*), to be the raja of rajas.[118] By thus linking lions and sacred kingship, Shah 'Azizallah made sense of an encounter with a different but still recognizable cultural order, one akin to Persian symbols of kingship in the lion and the sun, as well as the Islamic name of 'Asadallah, "the lion of God," initially used for the Prophet Muhammad's kinsmen 'Ali and Hamza.

Shah 'Azizallah's translations of tales of the cosmic Pali wilderness recovered a forest landscape of Theravada Buddhism where natural phenomena were seen and understood as an array of sacred signs. Although it represented a different nature and belief system, this view of the environment as the divine and cosmic order of the universe meshed, in certain ways, with Muslim notions and framings of the wonders and marvels of existence. It was also in accord with Sufi accounts of finding truth in the wilderness in the hikayat, a didactic genre that detailed the journeys of ascetic Sufi saints relinquishing society for the solitude of the forest edge.

In translating Pali Buddhist literature into Persian, Shah ʿAzizallah Bukhari Qalandar traveled a strange and twisted path that looped back to itself. He began by investigating a supposedly far different world, a place, culture, and religion external to and distant from his own that he had to decipher. But in the end, Shah ʿAzizallah merged into the very realm he explored and reconnoitered. Under the auspices of the British East India Company, he set out into a foreign land beyond the frontiers of Islam, the domain of an Indian Ocean kingdom defined by perceptions of its geographical and cultural difference. But within an Orientalist project that sought out shared traditions across religions and cultures, he became enmeshed in beliefs, customs, and rituals that were mutual across the Bengal-Arakan borderland. Shah ʿAzizallah was employed by the company to use his fluent skills in Persian to decipher the Pali Buddhist laws and codes of the Kingdom of Arakan. Dispatched as part of an Orientalist quest to discover shared customs across "Eastern" kingdoms, languages, and religious systems, Shah ʿAzizallah came to find the traces of an old kinship with the Buddhist imaginary of Arakan through his sensibility as a Persianate Sufi wanderer, a qalandar who identified keenly with the asceticism of Buddha and his seeking of enlightenment in the wilderness. In more than a decade of compiling information and translating Buddhist tracts from Pali into Persian, he and the other munshis in the service of John Murray MacGregor created a rare archive of legal and cosmographical treatises, jatakas and other legendary tales, botanies and agricultural almanacs, and ethnographies and dictionaries. Taken together, the Pali-into-Persian manuscripts of Shah ʿAzizallah in the John Murray MacGregor archive contain microhistories of encounters between Buddhists and Muslims along the Indian Ocean borderlands of Mrauk U.

# Epilogue

THIS BOOK HAS EXAMINED microhistories of Indo-Persian contacts with Buddhist Southeast Asia through a corpus of late eighteenth- and early nineteenth-century Persian travel accounts. These inter-Asian encounters between the Mughal world and Southeast Asia, in particular the Burmese frontier, were facilitated through migration, trade, diplomacy, and the medium of the Persian language during the early colonial period. Despite the ruptures of the eighteenth century, Persian persisted as a language of literature and learning, court culture and diplomacy, and trade and commerce, Indo-Persian travelers and munshis connected to the East India Company and the Asiatic Society of Bengal encountered, described, and mapped the Burmese Empire and its littoral as a mythical forested realm "below the winds" of the Indian Ocean monsoons and at the far reaches of the Mughal world. Occurring within the context of a shifting imperial tide, as the Mughal Empire waned and the British East India Company ascended, these renewed Indo-Persian encounters on the Burmese frontier created interconnections as well as cultivating disconnections and notions of difference.

Indo-Persian accounts of the Burmese Empire and its littoral were written at the juncture of different imperial formations and epistemes. In these Persian narratives of travel and encounter in the Burmese Kingdom circa 1800, Mughal and British colonial perspectives were merged. Early modern Persian and Mughal views of space and sovereignty, of the wondrous landscapes and kingdoms on the edges of the Indian Ocean, which combined aspects of verisimilitude and empiricism with elements of the magical and the marvelous, became imbued with colonial perceptions of terrestrial surveying and the Oriental sublime in the "East." Indo-Persian theories of kingship and sovereignty over the rarities of nature across the spaces of the city and the wilderness became manifested and reworked in graphic projects of colonial mapping, botany, and ethnography concerning the Burmese frontier. Colonial Persian encounter narratives revealed a hidden kingdom's sovereignty and realm, its customs and religions, its flora, fauna, and landscapes.

Through construction of the geography of the far reaches of the Indian Ocean—its landscapes, kingdoms, customs, languages, and religions—Indo-Persian travelers, munshis, and intermediaries of the British East India Company perceived a place that was strangely familiar. Reaching the forest realm of a Buddhist raja and his subjects, they found it recognizable as a sovereign imperial domain on the far periphery of the Indo-Persian Mughal world. The Burmese Kingdom came to be constructed as the far edges of Indo-Persian networks of travel and trade. The microhistories of Indo-Persian encounters with the Burmese Empire detailed in this book capture a view of inter-Asian contact in times of change. Before Persian faded as a Mughal lingua franca, it brought a remote Indian Ocean empire into focus as a sovereign space at the geographical and cultural limits of India.

This late Mughal, early colonial moment of encounters through Persian with the Burmese Empire was fleeting, though, and looking back, seems to have been already in its twilight and demise. Even before the denouement of Persian in India in Thomas Macauley's "Minute on Education" in 1835, John Crawfurd, the British envoy on the embassy to Ava in 1827, deemed "the use of the Persian language in correspondence with some of the Asiatic Governments ... a great absurdity, and a compliance with the local usages of India." The Persian language, he continued, as far as the Burmese "could understand of its contents, might as well have been Hebrew."[1] In the three decades since Michael Symes's mission, the status of Persian as a contact language between Mughal India and the Burmese Empire had definitely been diminished.

The waning of Persian as a courtly language of correspondence, exchange, and diplomacy was also reflected in the nature of the protonationalist forms of Persian materials printed about the Burmese Empire in the mid- to late nineteenth century. Descriptions of the Burmese Empire featured in Qajar geographical treatises from the mid-nineteenth century, including Zayn al-'Abidin Shirvani's *Bustan al-Sayyahah* (The garden of journeys) and Farhad Mirza Mu'tamad al-Dawla's *Jam-i Jam* (The cup of Jamshid), as well as in a rare late nineteenth-century account of travels from Iran to Burma.[2] But these texts, which were closely based on "modern" European geographical knowledge of the world and its parts, with a perceptible focus on the nascent unit of the homeland or nation, belonged to a different time, one in which places and identities were becoming more fixed than before. Reports of the Burmese Kingdom appeared occasionally in Persian newsletters printed during the reign of the Qajar dynasty, such as *Ruznama-yi Iran* of Tehran and *Farhang* of Isfahan, which detailed the Southeast Asian country in sections classified as "foreign news" (*akhbar-i kharija*), from lands distinct and outside the "guarded domains" (*mamalik-i mahrusa*) of Iran.

Under the heading "Asia," an 1871 issue of *Ruznama-yi Iran* still invoked the "strangeness" (*gharibi*) of the Andaman Islands of the Burmese littoral through enduring tropes of "islands of cannibals" (*jazayir-i mardumkhur*). Although such legends were said to still strike fear in the hearts of seafarers, such fantastical perceptions were deemed the work of the imagination before the report transitioned into a quite different and rather civilizational and anthropological account of the islands' inhabitants and their savage way of life.[3] During the 1880s, during the final years of the Burmese Konbaung dynasty, letters from Iranian and Armenian merchants in Rangoon and Mandalay were printed in issues of the newspaper *Farhang* of Isfahan. The letters told of merchants from Iran residing for decades in the Burmese Kingdom, with names such as Hajji Mirza Muhammad ʿAli Isfahani, ʿAbd al-Husayn Isfahani, and Khwaja Balthazar of New Julfa, Isfahan, who encouraged the advancement of trade and wrote of their longing to again see Qajar Iran.[4] One letter, sent from the Burmese royal capital of Mandalay on the eve of its fall in early 1885 took on a protonational and anti-imperial tone in reporting in detail of the impending conflict between the Konbaung dynasty and the British Empire, which had already conquered Rangoon.[5] Likewise, late nineteenth-century Urdu texts reflect a parallel hardening of divisions, finding colonial precedents in their census-like outlook on Burma according to distinct religious economies and confessional identities.[6] These later Persian and Urdu encounters and travel narratives were produced in a period of enclosing frontiers and were vastly different than those of a century before.

The ruins of the stories told in this book and the fading signs of contacts between the Mughal and Burmese worlds can be found in the weathered temple-like stone mosques and dargah (tombs of Sufi saints) that mark the urban and forest landscape of Myanmar and Arakan. These spaces are the remains of Muslim merchants, saints, warriors, and princes from across the Indian Ocean world, whose migrations to the Buddhist kingdoms of

Myanmar between the sixteenth and nineteenth centuries formed remarkably varied and cosmopolitan Muslim societies. In our times, these faded traces of a forgotten past and plural society are threatened, endangered by the hardening divide between Buddhist and Muslim communities in Southeast Asia, as witnessed in the intercommunal violence that has decimated and displaced long-standing Muslim societies in Myanmar over the last decade.

These early modern Islamic Indo-Persian connections with Buddhist Southeast Asia seem impossible in our times. The prevailing attitude now finds Buddhism and Islam to be two distinct, incompatible religions, the former's relics and images an affront to the iconoclasm of the latter, with its purported penchant for broken idols and destroyed temples. There seems little time to consider the ways that such religious beliefs could be intertwined and share mutual worlds and middle grounds. The fading history of Indian Ocean and pan-Asian exchanges across regions and cultures is obscured by the current political landscape in an increasingly xenophobic and nationalist Myanmar. The inter-Asian crossings that once created the multiethnic and multiconfessional societies of early modern Buddhist kingdoms were forgotten—and came to be disconnected—during the colonial and nationalist periods of the nineteenth and twentieth centuries as Buddhists and Muslims, Burmese and non-Burmese, came to be rigidly divided into distinct religious and ethnic communities. As the nation of Myanmar crafted a rigidly Burmese and Theravada Buddhist identity, Indo-Persian Muslim communities in the country came to be labeled as foreigners and viewed as unwanted migrants from the days of British colonialism, becoming increasingly excluded and marginalized in society. The tragic fate of the Rohingya people, a stateless Muslim minority in Myanmar who have been dispossessed and driven from their homelands in Arakan due to intercommunal violence and religious persecution, is a grotesquely telling sign of just how much things have changed. Indo-Persian Muslim societies, once part of the cosmopolitan and syncretic fabric of the early modern Buddhist Kingdom of Mrauk U, became outcasts of the Burmese nation-state. The nation is a method to define and limit societies, cultures, and geographies, just as it is a method to write histories. By remembering a different time and place, an inter-Asian expanse less bounded and confined, it is hoped these microhistories of Indo-Persian encounters in Southeast Asia circa 1800 in some ways disrupt the bordered lens of region and nation in recounting the past.

Across Myanmar, the rubble and ruins of Muslim sacred spaces recall the once-flourishing Indo-Persian communities of Burmese empires. The material presence of Islam in Buddhist Southeast Asia can be measured through the landscape of ruined and endangered Muslim spaces. Many of these sites are in Rakhine State (Arakan) in northern Myanmar, where Muslim communities thrived during the Kingdom of Mrauk U, but they can also be found in the former royal capitals of the last Burmese Empire, the Konbaung dynasty, in the upper Irrawaddy River delta, and in the southern Mon Hanthawaddy Kingdom of Pegu. Through these endangered Muslim spaces and archaeological traces—hidden mosques, shrines, and tombs in overgrown forests and barbwired urban streets—the built environment and spatial worlds of the past in Myanmar become perceptible, even as they fade away.

Ruins are vestiges of lost worlds, remnants of lives, traces of cultures. The timeworn stone debris of lost empires are the material presence of fading histories. Built by empires, uncovered by archaeologists, and experienced by those who live in their detritus, ruins disappear, lost to natural disasters, destroyed by human violence, and ravaged by the passing of time. A recent collection edited by Ann Stoler, *Imperial Debris: On Ruins and Ruination*, calls for seeing ruins as durable corrosions and traces of colonial aftermaths on the material environment. Ruins are not dead and discursive relics of the past but rather the physical remains of a process of colonial "ruination," with critical effects on the present. In case studies of submerged villages in southern India, razed ancestral homes in Palestine, and the toxic terrains of oil refineries in Durban, South Africa, among other chapters on the theme of ruination around the globe, *Imperial Debris* examines how empire and colonial formations have marked present landscapes and lives.

As I traveled through the wastelands of Islamic Myanmar, I saw the "imperial debris" of the past, the spatial ruins and the fragments of earlier imperial patterns. But this was something older, a different imperial debris that transcends "colonial aftermaths"—these were the traces of precolonial Asian empires and kingdoms. These were the aftermaths of a forgotten *longue durée* of empire, signs that preceded the postcolonial experience and predicament. Although Myanmar has its share of colonial ruins, something in the country's artifacts of Islam harkens back to times before European colonialism, to an age of contact between the Indo-Persian Mughal world and the Buddhist kingdoms of Southeast Asia. The architecture and ruins of Islam in Myanmar bear the archaeological imprint of a deeper, almost forgotten past: a history of Islam in Myanmar that can be viewed and read through its spatial remains. Embedded in the material culture and archaeology of Muslim spaces in Myanmar—the crumbling walls of mosques and shrines—is a history of inter-Asian connections and how they fell apart.

The material presence and physical traces of Indo-Persian Muslims in Myanmar can be seen in the heart of its largest city, Rangoon. On "Mughal Street," now called Shwe Bon Tha Street in downtown Rangoon, in the core of the colonial district, one finds most of the city's Indo-Persian Muslim communities and their architectural traces.[7] Located in the western sector of Strand Road, near the banks of the Rangoon River, Mughal Street is in the center of the city's economic district. From its intersection with Merchant Street and all the way up to the bazaar of Bogyoke Aung San Market, Mughal Street is lined with the shops of Indian merchants. This Indo-Persian Muslim quarter of Rangoon was settled mostly by merchants from India, but it was also created by Iranian, Armenian, and Parsi traders who arrived beginning in the late eighteenth through the nineteenth centuries. All along Mughal Street and its surroundings are found the landmarks of Indo-Persian Muslim communities. At the corner of Mughal Street and Mahabandula Road, in the shadow of the gilded Sule Pagoda, stands the grand Surti Sunni Jama Masjid, built by merchants from Surat on the northwestern coast of India. The iconic white mosque, with its dome and grand minarets, was built in the nineteenth century and is prominently pictured in an old colonial painted postcard titled "The Mosque Rangoon," shown looming over a dirt road; but even now, crowded by concrete and pavement as the city has grown around it, the mosque still casts its presence.

The Surti Sunni Jama Masjid is part of a complex of mosques built by Muslim communities in the old colonial quarter of Rangoon and just two blocks from it, on Thirtieth Street, steps from Sule Pagoda, stands the Hyderabad-styled Mogul Shia Masjid. Inscriptions on the mosque name it the "Mogul Shia Masjid" and bear the names of migrants who established the mosque, from such Iranian and Afghan cities as Isfahan, Shiraz, and Kabul. During the holy month of Muharram, members of the mosque go into the streets bearing ornamental gilded tabernacles of the grave of the martyr, silver banners of the Hand of Fatima, and other religious relics in ta'ziya commemorations that reenact the martyrdom of the Shia saint Husayn ibn 'Ali. This trail of Indo-Persian mosques extends northward through the city, in the direction of the Dargah of Bahadur Shah Zafar, the tomb of the exiled last king of the Mughal Empire located at the foot of Shwe Dagon Pagoda, Myanmar's most sacred Buddhist shrine.

But Rangoon was a colonial city and its Muslim spaces were built within a colonial context. To see traces of Islam in the times of former Buddhist empires requires heading north to the former royal capitals of Ava, Amarapura, and Mandalay on the upper Irrawaddy River. The traces appear in the mosques in Amarapura and in the enclaves of the "Rakhine Quarter" on the outskirts of Mandalay, the neighborhood where the Kaman Muslim archers of the Mrauk U Empire of Arakan settled following its fall in 1784. Beneath the pillars of elegant Kaman mosques built during the reign of the Burmese King Bodawpaya, locals still speak about the existence of a most hallowed site, a sacred Sufi shrine in a garden of "Zagawa" trees in the former royal city of Amarapura.

The garden shrine is located down a shady lane not far from the famous teak bridge of Hajj U Bein. Almost hidden in a grove of trees, the multiarched brick shrine appears as a raw and striking piece of Indo-Persian architecture adapted to the Burmese soil. The structure dates to 1814 and is partially destroyed, having been set on fire in riots against Muslims in 1997. Its weathered and decaying brick walls shelter an inner hall completely exposed to the open air. Known to locals as the Dargah, the structure contained the tomb of the Sufi saint Hazrat-i Sayyid Muhammad Sharif 'Abid Shah Husayni. The partially destroyed dargah is a ruined space that holds the history of a Muslim Sufi saint who crossed the Indian Ocean from the Deccan of India to reach the Burmese Kingdom.

In 1795, a nineteen-year-old Sufi mendicant named Sayyid Muhammad Sharif 'Abid Shah Husayni from Aurangabad in the Deccan traveled to the royal city of Amarapura. The young saint possessed a noble saintly lineage and, as his name suggests, claimed descent from the second Shia imam, Husayn ibn 'Ali (625–80). According to his legend, he was born a prince in the city of Aurangabad in the Deccan in 1776 but became an ascetic Sufi saint, wandering from India to Amarapura in 1795, at the age of nineteen.

Inside the shrine, beneath a green, gilt silk covering and an array of flowers, lies the saint's grave inlaid with a mosaic of mirrors in floral patterns. An inscription etched on a stone pillar by his tomb, with the heading in Arabic and the narrative in Burmese, recounts the story of his life. It begins by detailing his origins in India and his belonging to the Naqshbandi, Qadiri, and Chishti Sufi brotherhoods, before his arrival in Amarapura:

Hazrat-i Sayyid Muhammad Sharif 'Abid Shah Husayni (1776–1814): The Master's name was Muhammad Sharif and his title 'Abid Shah, the "Submissive King." He was a descendant of Husayn ibn 'Ali, the grandson

FIGURE 23. The tomb of Hazrat-i Sayyid Muhammad Sharif 'Abid Shah Husayni (1776–1814), a Naqshbandi, Qadiri, and Chishti Sufi saint and descendant of Imam Husayn from the Deccan, in Amarapura. Photograph by Arash Khazeni.

of the Prophet Muhammad Rasul Allah and part of the lineage of Khwaja Baha al-Din Naqshbandi. His father was Sayyid Khwaja and his mother was the sister of the Nizam of Aurangabad. The Nizam had no descendants and sought to appoint his nephew as prince, but Muhammad Sharif had no interest in property and throne. Since the time of his childhood, he had committed the scriptures of the Qur'an to memory and sought to follow the way of saints. The Master belonged to the Hanafi school of Islam, and followed the path of the Qadiri, Chishti, and Naqshbandi Sufi brotherhoods, earning the titles of 'Abid Shah, the "Submissive King," and Murid-i Bayat, the "Old Student." He made the decision to live life-long in the role of a sweeper at the dargah of the saint Khwaja Mu'in al-Din Chishti in Ajmer in the Indian state of Rajasthan. In 1794, however, during the reign of King Bodawpaya, he arrived in the royal city of Amarapura. The Master was nineteen years old at the time.[8]

The inscription attests to 'Abid Shah Husayni's descent from the Shia saint Husayn ibn 'Ali, his belonging to the illustrious Sufi pedigrees of the Naqshbandi, Qadiri, and Chishti, and his kinship to Nizam 'Ali Khan Asaf Jah II of the Deccan (r. 1762–1803). Despite the prestige of his lineage, 'Abid Shah Husayni renounced the earthly world and took to a life of wandering—leaving the city of Aurangabad at a time when it was coming under the control of Maratha warriors and becoming a mendicant shrine sweeper in Ajmer before somehow wandering into the heart of the Burmese Kingdom.

One day, the inscription continues, after 'Abid Shah Husayni had gained followers through acts of charisma, he was brought to a royal audience with the Burmese king. Becoming aware of 'Abid Shah Husayni's descent from the nizam, King Bodawpaya ordered him to attend the royal audience permanently. Upon performing a series of apocryphal miracles (*karamat*) in the presence of the king, he was appointed as the first Islamic judge, or *qadi*, in the Burmese Konbaung Empire.[9] A decree recorded in the *The Royal Orders of Burma* reads, "An Order has already been issued that all Muslims in the Kingdom shall take 'Abid Shah Husayni as their leader in all matters of their religion and this Order is also meant for the Muslims living in Rakhine."[10] It was followed up by the command to "let the learned monks together with Brahmins of Amarapura and Benares who could do the translation, translate the works which 'Abid Shah Husayni had brought from India."[11]

The Sufi saint used to frequent a garden near the Red Pagoda, and when he died in 1814 he was buried there in a grove of Zagawa trees on the order of the king. His tomb became a dargah, a Sufi place of pilgrimage, and a *qabris-tan*, or graveyard, for local Muslims. The cemetery became known as Lin Zin Kone, and behind the shrine were the tombs of notable Muslims from the early Konbaung period. There is the carved white stone grave of Saya Gyi U Nu Muhammad Qasim (1762–1822), a Muslim scholar, poet, and travel writer in the Burmese court and confidante of King Bodawpaya, who traveled on missions to India to retrieve Buddhist, Sanskrit, and Persian texts and wrote a versified travelogue about his journey to Bengal, as well as works on the religion of Islam. Also buried in the graveyard, in a similar tomb, is Hajj U Bein, a courtier and governor of Amarapura during the reign of King Bodawpaya who sponsored construction of an eponymous teak bridge spanning Taungthaman Lake. All across the cemetery lay the stone graves of Muslims who had been buried there over the last two hundred years since the time of 'Abid Shah Husayni's death.

In January 2014, the graves were in a dilapidated state, and an order was pending by the Municipal Government of Mandalay to demolish the graveyard, under the pretext of creating a public park to serve as a vista point for the iconic U Bein Bridge. The graveyard was destroyed in March 2014, with only the shrine of 'Abid Shah Husayni and the graves of Saya Gyi U Nu and Hajj U Bein left standing. But the story of 'Abid Shah Husayni's tomb does not end there. The cemetery has subsequently become the site of an archaeological excavation of what is thought to be the tomb of the last Thai king, Udumbara, who along with thousands of slaves was brought to Amarapura from the Kingdom of Ayutthaya after its conquest by the Konbaung dynasty in 1767 and lived out the remainder of his days as a monk. When he died nearly thirty years later, his body was enshrined in a red-bricked tomb. This was the Buddhist Red Pagoda near the garden that 'Abid Shah Husayni used to frequent and was buried in and that, over time, was transformed into a Muslim cemetery. The fragile and fading layers of history that lie in debris at the site of the tomb of 'Abid Shah Husayni are the ruins of spaces of Buddhist-Islamic cross-cultural contact and Indo-Persian presence in the early modern kingdoms of Southeast Asia.[12]

The western state of Rakhine, once known as Arakan, is a densely forested region between a rugged range of mountains and the Bay of Bengal. Between the fifteenth and eighteenth centuries, Arakan was the site of the Kingdom of Mrauk U, known in Persian and Bengali as Rakhang or Roshang, a seaborne empire that was the hub of a trade network in slaves, rice, and spices that reached from South to Southeast Asia. Combining Indo-Persian Islamic court culture with Theravada Buddhist tradition, Mrauk U was a syncretic empire that maintained close relations with and shared much in common with the Mughal world. Due to these long-standing ties, there are more Muslims in Rakhine State than any other region of Myanmar.

To reach the ruins of the city of Mrauk U requires travel to Sittwe (formerly known as Akyab), a colonial port town that sits where the wide mouth of the tidal Kaladan River meets the Bay of Bengal. Along the banks of the undammed river, villagers survive through subsistence agriculture, fishing, and the herding of water buffalo. After one passes thatched villages and their wooden fleets of teak canoes, interspersed by mangrove forests that enclose the river, the hills of Mrauk U and the spires of its red brick temples come into view.[13] The city and its Bengali-influenced Buddhist temples, with their Islamicate domes, still exist nearly as they did centuries ago, with villagers living amid majestic five-hundred-year-old tombs.

But in Rakhine State one enters the wastelands of the Indo-Persian world in Southeast Asia. This is a place where the Indo-Persian past is broken, burned, and almost forgotten. It is a place that no longer exists. The traces of the former Indo-Persian populations and their spaces are gone from the capital city of Mrauk U. The oldest mosque in Mrauk U, the more than five-

FIGURE 24. The leaning spire of the cosmic Laungbanpyauk Paya in Mrauk U, fronted by its wall of fragments of turquoise and cobalt Persianate tilework. Photograph by Arash Khazeni.

century-old Santikan Mosque, built in the fifteenth century by Muslim soldiers who helped found the empire in honor of the Indo-Persian warrior Sindhi Khan, was destroyed in the 1990s.[14] Nineteenth-century archaeologist and professor of Pali, Emil Forchhammer, whose *Report on the Antiquities of Arakan* is an indispensable guide to the ruins of Rakhine State, described it as a simple rectangular structure akin to the Buddhist architecture of Mrauk U, with "a hemispherical low cupola constructed on the same principle as the domes of Shitthaung and Dukkanthein pagodas."[15] The mosque once stood in the outer city, southeast of the city walls amid rice paddies, but all that remains is a heap of broken and scattered stones. No signs are left today of the refuge of the Mughal prince Shah Shuja' and his fabled Kaman archers amid the creeks that wind through the old city. All that remains are fragments scattered here and there: broken *mihrab* prayer niches and Persian inscriptions inconspicuously displayed in the Palace Museum; handfuls of defunct and discarded bilingual Persian and Pali or Sanskrit coins; the crumbling turquoise blue Persian floral tilework adorning the walls of the cosmic temple Laungbanpyauk Paya. There are only scarce traces of this episode of the history of the golden city of Mrauk U and its cosmopolitan early modern past. Only the debris of these past places remain in this haunted landscape.

Rakhine State is of course the site of the devastating and tragic oppression and persecution of the Rohingya. The Rohingya are a stateless Muslim community with precolonial origins in Arakan, dating back to the reign of the Mrauk U Kingdom, when it ruled over Arakan and parts of Bengal. As recently as a decade ago, the Rohingya constituted nearly one-fifth of the population of Rakhine State, but their official status in Myanmar is that of "foreigner" and "Bengali," and they are denied citizenship. Dismissed in this way from society, with denials of centuries of their presence in Arakan, and thus the nation of Myanmar, the destitute and dispossessed Rohingya population has been the target of violent attacks by Buddhist mobs, sanctioned by the Burmese military. Hundreds of thousands of Rohingya have emigrated from Myanmar and taken to the sea in the uncertain search for shelter, with many ending up in dire and overpopulated refugee camps across the border in Bangladesh.[16]

In Sittwe, signs of the atrocities committed against the Rohingya can be seen in the charred and broken sacred spaces of Islam that were once found in the colonial port city. The majestic Friday Mosque, known as the Jama Mosque, lies abandoned in the heart of town in a state of disrepair, its windows shattered, its walls broken and covered by the creeping vines of its overgrown garden. Since the anti-Muslim riots of 2012 and 2013, the mosque has been strictly off-limits, surrounded by barbed wire and under military guard. Its broken stone minarets loom over town like an old gray ghost. Down the road from the Jama Mosque, toward the sea on the edge of town, the shrine of Shafi Khan is also in a ruinous state after having been set on fire. The charred white structure—with its turreted walls, four minarets, and intricate carved stone details—has been abandoned. The shrine to the legendary Sufi saint of Chittagong Badr al-Din Awliya, or Pir Badr, a domed structure with four minarets known as the Badr Maqam and also held sacred by Buddhists and Hindus, lies in ruins, enclosed within an inaccessible military garrison. The sacred and communal spaces of Islamic ritual and practice in Sittwe were closed down, as the city's desperate Rohingya were collected into isolated camps, before continuing violence and atrocities forced their community into exile.

The remaining Muslims in Rakhine State are mostly Kaman, descendants of royal Mughal archers of Afghan descent who took refuge in the Kingdom of Mrauk U during the seventeenth century, following the flight of the ill-fated Mughal prince Shah Shujaʿ. They are settled around the town of Thandwe in villages along the southern bank of the Thandwe River, where anti-Muslim riots spread in 2013. Thandwe is an old Arakanese town located

FIGURE 25. The burned and abandoned Shafi Khan Dargah, a nineteenth-century Rohingya shrine and mosque in the port town of Sittwe. Photograph by Arash Khazeni.

in a hilly valley above the Bay of Bengal. Its ancient history is attested to by the three gilded pagodas—Andaw Paya, Sandaw Paya, and Nandaw Paya— that stand upon hilltops along the river, like beacons to the Buddhist heritage of Arakan. But below these pagodas, often hidden in dense forest, lie a web of Muslim tombs, shrines, and mosques.

These sacred spaces were encountered and experienced by Muslim traders, mariners, and travelers approaching from the sea. Large boulders known to locals as the Sinjat Rocks mark the river mouth where it meets the Bay of Bengal, but to Muslim travelers of the past these rocks held meaning as markers of a Badr Maqam, a shrine to the Chittagonian Sufi saint Badr al-Din Awliya. Entering the stream of the tidal river, the traveler passes a string of Muslim villages and their Sufi landmarks on a pilgrimage route through a network of shrines and mosques. Passing by the fishing village of Singal, with its picturesque docked boats and gilded pagoda at the edge of the river mouth, the river winds its way until it reaches the Muslim village of Zadi Pyin, set deep within a lush forest . On a hill overlooking the river and a valley rice field, up a flight of ninety-nine stone steps, is the shrine of the Sufi saint Ashin Gyi Awliya Wali. It is marked only by three green, red, and yellow banners on a circular stone platform. Zadi Pyin was once a Buddhist

FIGURE 26. Shwe Kyaung Dargah. The more than four-hundred-year-old tomb of an unknown Qadiri saint in Shwe Kyaung Village, Thandwe. Photograph by Arash Khazeni.

village, the legend goes, until the sixteenth century, when an aged long-haired Sufi mystic wearing a white Burmese waist cloth, or *longyi,* appeared in the land of the Rakhine kings. Living on the hill for many years, the saint is said to have spoken only of Allah and spent his days in devotion. Ashin Gyi lived for many years atop the hill, descending to the village from time to time, and he helped the villagers find the best place to dig a well, before disappearing forever. No one remembers where he came from or where he went, what his real name was or whether he died in Rakhine or not. But the well he helped build in Zadi Pyin is called Ashin Gyi to this day. Over time, his followers built a mosque in the village next to the old well, known as Zadi Pyin Masjid, now in ruins and overgrown with vines.

Farther up the river, beneath the shadow of Nandaw Paya, with its reclining Buddha, stands an unusual wooden structure next to a Muslim graveyard. Situated in a prime location at a bend in the river, in the Muslim village of Shwe Kyaung, the spot is known by the names Mughal Hill or Masjid Hill. The white circular structure is a shrine known as Shwe Kyaung Dargah and houses the more than four-hundred-year-old tomb of a "Kaman Shaykh." It is the still-frequented sacred tomb of a Qadiri Sufi saint whose name has been lost. The grave lies in a candle-lit chamber in the center of the shrine, adorned

FIGURE 27. The interior of the destroyed mosque of Zadi Pyin Village, Thandwe. Photograph by Arash Khazeni.

by relics to the Panj Tan—the five sacred "bodies" of the Prophet Muhammad, Ali, Fatima, Husayn, and Hassan. Outside the structure are the stone graves of Kaman shaykhs buried there over the centuries, just below a pagoda said to enshrine a rib of the Buddha as a relic.

As the river winds through a landscape of villages set amid lush hills and rice fields, it reaches the gilded temple of Sandaw Paya, which enshrines a hair of the Buddha. In the woods, at the foot of the hill, are scattered a number of abandoned and ruined structures that have the appearance of Muslim shrines and graves. Nineteenth-century archaeologists likened one of the structures to a "Mahomedan burial monument."[17] A low and unusual rectangular shrine of white plaster seeming like a Muslim tomb contains a stone imprint of Buddha's foot set over the surface of a grave. The syncretic architecture of the edifice, an Islamic domed tomb adorned with Buddhist relics, is a physical representation, a spatial sign of the hybrid, mutual, and overlapping cultural worlds of Buddhists and Muslims that existed in early modern Arakan. On this lonely sloping field below Sandaw Paya lies the rubble of a now buried and almost irretrievable past.

The end point of this riverine Sufi pilgrimage trail arrives at Andaw Paya, a temple that houses a tooth relic on a hill where it was believed Buddha once

FIGURE 28. The Badr Maqam, also known as the Parahla, or the "Beautiful Pagoda," below Andaw Paya in Thandwe. Photograph by Arash Khazeni.

lived as a serpent king in a past life. The Sinjat Rocks at the meeting of the river mouth with the ocean were known as the markers of a Badr Maqam, a shrine dedicated to the Sufi saint Badr al-Din Awliya, or Pir Badr. Shrines known as Badr Maqam, replicas of the saint's actual tomb in Chittagong, are found along the coastline of mainland Southeast Asia from Myanmar to Thailand. Muslim mariners and merchants regarded Pir Badr as the patron saint of the sea, and his identity was at times blurred with that of Khwaja Khizr, with whom he was closely associated as an oceanic mystic dispensing baraka (blessings) before sea journeys. There are known to be two Badr Maqam shrines in Rakhine State, one cracked and in ruins under military surveillance in Sittwe, as noted above, and the other somewhere unknown along the Thandwe littoral and its tidal river.

Emil Forchhammer left important clues about the history of the Badr Maqam in his research on the shrine in Sittwe. The structures could be identified based on their common architectural style, which was "a mixture of the Burmese turreted pagoda the Mahomedan four-cornered minaret structure surmounted by a hemispherical cupola." The structures known as Badr Maqam embodied "the blending of the Indian mosque and the Burmese spire."[18] The spatial synthesis of temple and mosque architecture was attended by universal practices of worship between Muslims, Buddhists, and Hindus, with certain variations and differences. To Muslims the Badr Maqam was the dargah of a Sufi saint; to Buddhists it was the abode of a *nat,* a guardian spirit.; and to Hindus it was the place of a *deva,* a supernatural, divine being.[19] Buddhists pronounced "Badr Maqam" as the more familiar "Buddermokan" and "Buddhamaw," rendering it closer to the name of the ascetic sage Gautama Buddha.[20]

Down the hill from Andaw Paya, in a low grove of trees, stands an exquisite domed structure known as the Parahla, meaning the "Beautiful Pagoda." The Parahla is a small square shrine with a dome and four minarets built upon a low platform. Constructed of bricks covered with white plaster, its gilded dome and minarets echo the hue of the golden Andaw Paya perched above on the hill. Forchhammer identified it as "a small image house containing an image of Gotama" dating from the early nineteenth century, adding that "the shrine is peculiar; it represents a combination of the style of the Native-image house and the Mahomedan mosque."[21] Although called by a different name, this shrine is the famed but unknown Badr Maqam of Thandwe. It is still in use today and visited by devotees. Inside the chamber of the shrine, beneath its arched ceiling, are rows of small Buddha images and votive offerings, while in the prayer niche, or mihrab, stands a large painted Buddha image. Here, along a winding tidal river running through the Arakan mountains to the Bay of Bengal, remain the living ruins of the Badr Maqam, a place from an almost forgotten past of Indo-Persian contacts in Southeast Asia.

# NOTES

## INTRODUCTION

1. Recent studies have presented a view of Burma and its maritime borderlands as dynamic spaces of cross-cultural interactions. See Charney, "Where Jambudipa and Islamdom Converged"; Charney, "The Rise of a Mainland Trading State"; Charney, "Crisis and Reformation in a Maritime Kingdom of Southeast Asia"; Gommans and Leider, eds., *The Maritime Frontier of Burma*; Lieberman, *Strange Parallels*; Leider, *Le Royaume d'Arakan, Birmanie*; Willem van Schendel, *The Bengal Borderland*; Dijk, *Seventeenth-Century Burma and the Dutch East India Company*; van Galen, "Arakan and Bengal"; J.C. Scott, *The Art of Not Being Governed*; Mukherjee, ed., *Pelagic Passageways*; Amrith, *Crossing the Bay of Bengal;* and d'Hubert, *In the Shade of the Golden Palace.*

2. On this dialectical theme in early modern global encounters, see Subrahmanyam, "Connected Histories."

3. Hodgson, *The Venture of Islam,* 2:293–314.

4. Hodgson, 2:293–94; Hodgson, *Rethinking World History*, editor's introduction.

5. Hodgson, *The Venture of Islam,* 2:293–575.

6. The emerging body of work on the Persianate world is wide ranging; however, some key examples include Fragner, *Die "Persophonie"*; Spooner and Hanway, *Literacy in the Persianate World*; Micallef and Sharma, eds., *On the Wonders of Land and Sea*; Peacock and Tor, *Medieval Central Asia and the Persianate World*; Kia and Marashi, "After the Persianate" and Kia, *Persianate Selves.* The span of the Persianate world has also been traced through the lens of material culture and global commodity history. See Khazeni, *Sky Blue Stone.* The Persianate turn was also spurred by authors adopting an "Indo-Persian" frame. For an early example of this framework, see Islam, *Indo-Persian Relations.* For more recent studies adopting the Indo-Persian frame, see Alam and Subrahmanyam, *Indo-Persian Travels in the Age of Discoveries, 1400–1800*; Kinra, *Writing Self, Writing Empire*; Pello, *Tutiyan-i Hind.*

7. The two volumes of essays, which include some overlapping contributors, take different though complementary approaches to the Persianate world in the early modern period of empires, when it cohered before breaking apart during its nineteenth-century twilight and was superseded by the national languages of Farsi, Dari, Tajik, and Urdu. Whereas *The Persianate World: Rethinking a Shared Space*, edited by Abbas Amanat and Assef Ashraf, traces various literary and cultural networks that threaded together the Persianate "core" of Iran, India, and Central Asia, *The Persianate World: The Frontiers of a Eurasian Lingua Franca*, edited by Nile Green, zooms out the lens to examine "Persographia," the domain of written Persian as a lingua franca not in the core zones of India, Iran, and Central Asia, but rather in a broad, global, pan-Eurasian expanse of land stretching from China to the Balkans, often in places not under the cultural and political influence of Persian or Islam.

8. On the theme of travel and encounter, this project takes off from the work of Sanjay Subrahmanyam. See, for instance, Subrahmanyam, *Explorations in Connected History: From the Tagus to the Ganges*; Subrahmanyam, *Explorations in Connected History: Mughals and Franks*; Alam and Subrahmanyam, *Indo-Persian Travels in the Age of Discoveries*; Subrahmanyam, *Three Ways to Be Alien*; and Subrahmanyam, *Courtly Encounters*. The literature on encounters has been enriched and revitalized since interventions by Edward Said in *Orientalism*. It now includes studies of non-European encounters and representations, moral and political encounters, scientific and botanical encounters, and religious and linguistic encounters among its various strands. See Davis, *Trickster Travels*; Euben, *Journeys to the Other Shore*; Raj, *Relocating Modern Science*; Kinra, *Writing Self, Writing Empire*; and Truschke, *Culture of Encounters*.

9. Hodgson, *The Venture of Islam*, 2:542–43.

10. Hodgson, 2:546.

11. Hodgson, 2:548.

12. Hodgson, 2:543.

13. Hodgson, 2:547–48.

14. Even at the time Hodgson was writing, he could refer to some early scholarship on the subject of Islam in the Southeast Asian archipelago: Snouck-Hurgronje, *The Achehnese*; Vlekke, *Nusantara*; van Leur, *Indonesian Trade and Society*; and Meilink Roelofsz, *Asian Trade and European Influence in the Indonesian Archipelago between 1500 and about 1630*. See Hodgson, *The Venture of Islam*, 2:579.

15. Conversely, the Sanskrit cultural connections between South Asian and Southeast Asian kingdoms have been far more closely examined, from George Coedès's pioneering work on "Indianized states" to Sheldon Pollock's recent conception of the "Sanskrit cosmopolis." G. Coedès, *Les états hindouisés d'Indochine et d'Indonésie*, trans. Cowing as *The Indianized States of Southeast Asia*; Pollock, *The Language of the Gods in the World of Men*.

16. Ferrand, *Relations de voyages et textes géographiques arabes, persans et turks relatifs à l'Extrême-Orient du VIIIᵉ au XVIIIᵉ siècles*; Bausani, *Malesia*; Bausani, *Le letterature del sud-est asiatico*; Bausani, "Note su una antologia inedita di versi mistici persiani"; Bausani, "Un manoscritto persiano-malese di grammatica araba del XVI secolo"; Bausani, *Notes on the Structure of the Classical Malay Hikayat*.

17. Aubin, "Les Persans au Siam sous le règne de Narai, 1656–1688"; Lombard and Aubin, eds., *Marchands et hommes d'affaires asiatiques dans l'Océan Indien et la Mer de Chine*, trans. as *Asian Merchants and Businessmen in the Indian Ocean and the China Sea*.

18. Subrahmanyam, "Persianization and 'Mercantilism' in Bay of Bengal History, 1400–1700," and "Dutch Tribulations in Seventeenth-Century Mrauk U," in *Explorations in Connected History: From the Tagus to the Ganges*; Alam and Subrahmanyam, *Indo-Persian Travels in the Age of Discoveries, 1400–1800*; Subrahmanyam, "And a River Runs through It." See also Marcinkowski, *From Isfahan to Ayutthaya*; d'Hubert and Leider, "Traders and Poets at the Mrauk U Court"; and d'Hubert, *In the Shade of the Golden Palace*.

19. For some recent work on Islam in Malaysia and Indonesia (the Southeast Asian archipelago), based on Jawi sources, see Rickfels, *Jogjakarta under Sultan Mangkubumi, 1749–1792*; Rickfels, *Seen and Unseen Worlds in Java*; Rickfels, *Mystic Synthesis in Java*; Ho, *The Graves of Tarim*; Feener, *Muslim Legal Thought in Modern Indonesia*; Feener and Sevea, eds., *Islamic Connections*; Feener, Daly, and Reid, eds., *Mapping the Acehnese Past*; Laffan, *The Makings of Indonesian Islam*; Ricci, *Islam Translated*; Tagliacozzo, *The Longest Journey*; Peacock and Gallop, eds., *From Anatolia to Aceh*; and Formichi and Feener, eds., *Shi'ism in Southeast Asia*. For a translation of a classic Malay travel account to India from the late Mughal/early colonial period, see Rijaluddin, *Hikayat Perintah Negeri Benggala*.

20. Eaton, *The Rise of Islam and the Bengal Frontier, 1204–1760*; Eaton and Wagoner, *Power, Memory, Architecture*.

21. For some key works in this body of literature on Persian travel writing, see Wright, *The Persians amongst the English*; Cole, "Invisible Occidentalism"; Cole, "Mirror of the World"; Khan, *Indian Muslim Perceptions of the West during the Eighteenth Century*; Tavakoli-Targhi, *Refashioning Iran*; Tavakoli-Targhi, "Early Persianate Modernity"; Sohrabi, *Taken for Wonder*; Green, *Bombay Islam*; and Green, *The Love of Strangers*.

22. Building on studies predominantly concerned with Persian descriptions and perceptions of Europe and the West, a new wave of studies has turned toward analysis of Persianate travel writing on India, the Indian Ocean, and Central Asia. See Alam and Subrahmanyam, *Indo-Persian Travels in the Age of Discoveries*; Green, *Bombay Islam*; Khazeni, "Across the Black Sands and the Red"; Kia, "Limning the Land"; Kia, "Imagining Iran before Nationalism"; and Kia, *Persianate Selves*.

23. Bayly, *Empire and Information*; Fisher, *Counterflows to Colonialism*; Fisher, *The Travels of Dean Mahomet*; Jasanoff, *Edge of Empire*. See also Bayly, "Knowing the Country," Fisher, "The Office of Akhbār Nawīs," and other articles, all in *Modern Asian Studies* 27, no. 1 (1993).

24. Said, *Orientalism*.

25. See Bayly, *Empire and Information*. For an exception to this prevalent method and perspective on Persian in the encounter between Europe and India, focusing specifically on the Persian correspondence left behind by the

eighteenth-century Franco-Swiss Orientalist Antoine-Louis Henri Polier, see Alam and Alavi, eds. and trans., *A European Experience of the Mughal Orient.*

26. Bayly, *Imperial Meridian.*

27. See, for instance, Cohn, *Colonialism and Its Forms of Knowledge*; Bayly, *Empire and Information*; and Raman, *Document Raj.* By contrast, the literature on early modern scribal cultures has more deeply explored the words and worlds of Indo-Persian munshis. See, for instance, Kinra, *Writing Self, Writing Empire.*

28. For some explorations of inter-Asian connections and exchanges in the late nineteenth century and the context of colonialism, see Ho, *The Graves of Tarim*; Green, *Bombay Islam*; Amrith, *Crossing the Bay of Bengal*; and Alavi, *Muslim Cosmopolitanism in the Age of Empire.*

29. Qazi Ghulam Qasim Mihri, "Manzumat," Add. 26172 (1792), 54ff, Oriental and India Office Collections, British Library. Also see Rieu, *Catalogue of the Persian Manuscripts in the British Museum* 2:720–21.

30. Qazi Ghulam Qasim Mihri, "Manzumat," fol. 1r.

31. Qazi Ghulam Qasim Mihri, "Manzumat," fol. 5r, 23r.

32. For a poem in praise of "Sultan 'Abd al-Qadir" ('Abd al-Qadir al-Gilani), see Qazi Ghulam Qasim Mihri, "Manzumat," fols. 5v–6r. For verses in praise of "Shah Naqshband" (Baha-ud-Din Naqshband Bukhari), see Qazi Ghulam Qasim Mihri, "Manzumat," fols. 6r–6v.

33. Qazi Ghulam Qasim Mihri, "Manzumat," fol. 51r.

34. Qazi Ghulam Qasim Mihri, "Manzumat," fol. 52r–53r.

35. Qazi Ghulam Qasim Mihri, "Manzumat," fol. 52r.

36. See, for instance, Rangarajan, *Fencing the Forest*; Arnold and Guha, eds., *Nature, Culture, Imperialism*; Skaria, *Hybrid Histories*; and Arnold, *The Tropics and the Traveling Gaze.*

37. Eaton, *The Rise of Islam and the Bengal Frontier*; Eaton and Wagoner, *Power, Memory, Architecture.* On this theme more broadly within the context of world history, see Richards, *The Unending Frontier.*

38. An early work of this nature was Digby, *War-Horse and Elephant in the Delhi Sultanate.* More recently, on the Mughal hunt, see Allsen, *The Royal Hunt in Eurasian History*; Hughes, *Animal Kingdoms*; and Trautmann, *Elephants and Kings.* On Mughal gardens, see Westcoat and Wolschke-Bulmahn, eds., *Mughal Gardens*; Ali and Flatt, eds., *Garden and Landscape Practices in Pre-colonial India*; and Sharma, *Mughal Arcadia.*

39. Grove, *Green Imperialism*, 3, and chap. 2; Raj, *Relocating Modern Science.* See also Sivasundaram, *Islanded.* While still based predominantly on the European language sources that received, translated, and incorporated vernacular knowledge, these works have also, along the way, identified indigenous textual materials and genres, ranging from Indian botanies to Sri Lankan palm leaf manuscripts, which spurred the sciences of natural history, geography, and archaeology.

40. For some recent biographical approaches to South Asian and Indian Ocean history, see Ghosh, "The Slave of MS. H. 6"; Jasanoff, *Edge of Empire*; Eaton, *A Social*

History of the Deccan, *1300-1761*; Subrahmanyam, *Three Ways to Be Alien*; and C. Anderson, *Subaltern Lives;* and Green, *The Love of Strangers.*

CHAPTER ONE. OFFSHORE: MIRZA IʿTISAM AL-DIN AND
MIRZA ABU TALIB KHAN

1. This concept of "colonial Mughal" borrows from the work of Mohamad Tavakoli-Targhi and his notion of "homeless texts," with regard to the encounter between Iran and Europe and the mixture of Orientalist and Occidentalist knowledge in nineteenth-century Persian texts produced in Iran and India. See Tavakoli-Targhi, *Refashioning Iran.*

2. Wright, *The Persians amongst the English*; Digby, "An Eighteenth-Century Narrative of a Journey from Bengal to England"; Digby, "Beyond the Ocean"; Cole, "Invisible Occidentalism"; Cole, "Mirror of the World"; Fisher, *The Travels of Dean Mahomet*; Fisher, *Counterflows to Colonialism*; Khan, *Indian Muslim Perceptions of the West during the Eighteenth Century*; Tavakoli-Targhi, *Refashioning Iran.*

3. For the edited and translated text of Buzurg ibn Shahriyar's *ʿAjaʾib al-Hind,* see *The Book of Wonders of India*, trans. Freeman-Grenville. For the edited first part of Zakariya Qazvini's *ʿAjaʾib al-makhluqat wa gharaʾib al-mawjudat*, see *Zakarija Ben Muhammed Ben Mahmud el-Cazwini's Kosmographie*, ed. Wüstenfeld.

4. On this duality of tones in early modern Persian texts about Southeast Asia, see Subrahmanyam, *Europe's India*, 311.

5. On the theme of wonders, see Mottahedeh, "ʿAjaʾib in *The Thousand and One Nights*"; Digby, *Wonder-Tales of South Asia*; Alam and Subrahmanyam, *Indo-Persian Travels in the Age of Discoveries, 1400–1800*; Berlekamp, *Wonder, Image, and Cosmos in Medieval Islam*; and Sohrabi, *Taken for Wonder.*

6. For some studies and explorations on the identification of the islands of Waq Waq, see Ferrand, *Textes géographiques arabes, persans et turks relatifs a l'Extrême-Orient du VIIIᵉ au XVIIIᵉ siècles*; Le Strange, trans., *The Geographical Part of the Nuzhat al-Qulub*, 220-34; Qazvini, *The Book of Wonders of India*; Toorawa, "Waq al-Waq"; and Tibbetts et al., "Wakwak."

7. Zakariya ibn Muhammad Qazvini, "ʿAjaʾib al-makhluqat wa gharaʾib al-mawjudat," India, ca. 1168 Hijri (1755), 56a–56b, Islamic Manuscripts Collection, Firestone Library, Princeton University.

8. Qazvini, 56a–56b.

9. Qazvini, 56b.

10. Qazvini, 55a–55b, 56a.

11. For this seventeenth-century Persian travel account to Thailand, see Muhammad Ibrahim Rabi ibn Muhammad Ibrahim, *Safina-yi Sulaymani.* See also Aubin, "Les persans au Siam sous le règne de Narai, 1656–1688"; Subrahmanyam, "Iranians Abroad"; Alam and Subrahmanyam, *Indo-Persian Travels in the Age of Discoveries, 1400–1800*, chap. 4; and Marcinkowski, *From Isfahan to Ayutthaya.*

12. Alam and Subrahmanyam, *Writing the Mughal World*, 101–6. See also Alam and Subrahmanyam, *Indo-Persian Travels in the Age of Discoveries, 1400–1800*, chap. 4.

13. See Rafi' ud-Din Ibrahim bin Nur ud-Din Tawfiq Shirazi, "Tazkirat al-muluk," Add. 23883 (1611), fols. 303a–307b, Oriental and India Office Collections, British Library. See also Rieu, *Catalogue of the Persian Manuscripts in the British Museum*, 1:316; and Ferishta, *History of the Rise of the Mahomedan Power in India*, 1:lxv, 1–30, 193. Also see Elliott and Dowson, eds., *The History of India as Told by Its Own Historians*, 549. For a more recently edited Persian edition of the text, see Astarabadi, *Tarikh-i Firishta*.

14. See, for instance, Rafi' ud-Din Ibrahim bin Nur ud-Din Tawfiq Shirazi, "Tazkirat al-muluk," fols. 303a–307b. See also Rieu, *Catalogue of the Persian Manuscripts in the British Museum*, 1:i, 316.

15. Mirza I'tisam al-Din, "Shigarfnama-yi vilayat," Or. 200 (1812), Oriental and India Office Collections, British Library. The date of completion of the manuscript is given in the colophon, fol. 113r. This chapter is based on my translation of the original Persian manuscript in the British Library. There exist over a dozen other Persian manuscripts of the *Shigarfnama* in addition to the London text in archives in Aligarh, Cambridge, Chennai, Hyderabad, Kolkata, Lucknow, New Delhi, Oxford, and Patna as listed in Subrahmanyam, *Europe's India*, 379–80n53. Also see Storey, *Persian Literature*, 1143–44.

16. The abridged Urdu version and English translation were prepared by James Edward Alexander and his munshi, "Shumsher Khan." See Alexander, *Shigurf Namah-I-Velaët*. For a more recent translation, based on a later Bengali version of the text, which also omits original passages on the Indian Ocean and Southeast Asia, see Mirza Sheikh I'tesamuddin, *The Wonders of Vilayet*.

17. Mirza I'tisam al-Din, "Shigarfnama-yi vilayat," Or. 200 (1812), fols. 2v–3r.

18. Mirza I'tisam al-Din, "Shigarfnama," fols. 3r–3v. In Alexander's English translation of 1827, Swinton's name is given mysteriously as "Captain S." Alexander, *Shigurf Namah-I-Velaët*, 8–9.

19. Mirza I'tisam al-Din, "Shigarfnama," fol. 5r.

20. Mirza I'tisam al-Din, "Shigarfnama," fols. 6v–7r.

21. Mirza I'tisam al-Din, "Shigarfnama," fol. 8v.

22. Mirza I'tisam al-Din, "Shigarfnama," fols. 2r.

23. Mirza I'tisam al-Din, "Shigarfnama," fols. 8v–9r. The poem borrows a well-known phrase from the eleventh Sura of the Qur'an on the sailing of Noah's Ark. Its currency among mariners and seafarers in late eighteenth-century Bengal is suggested by its repeated recitation in 'Abd al-Latif's *Tuhfat al-'alam* (259).

24. Mirza I'tisam al-Din, "Shigarfnama-yi vilayat," Or. 200 (1812), fol. 9r.

25. Mirza I'tisam al-Din, "Shigarfnama," fol. 9r.

26. Mirza I'tisam al-Din, "Shigarfnama," fol. 9r.

27. Mirza I'tisam al-Din, "Shigarfnama," fols. 14r–14v.

28. Southgate, trans., *Iskandarnamah*; Mirsayyidov, ed., *Ayina-yi Iskandari*.

29. Sharma, *Amir Khusraw*, 56–57; Subrahmanyam, *Explorations in Connected History: From the Tagus to the Ganges*, 74–75; Piemontese, "Le submersible Alexandrin dans l'abysse, selon Amir Khusrau," 253–71.

30. Ho, *The Graves of Tarim*, 155–56. For the text of the *Malay Annals*, see Brown, trans., *Sejarah Melayu*. For an older, colonial-era translation, see Leyden, trans., *Malay Annals*.

31. Mirza I'tisam al-Din, "Shigarfnama," fols. 14v–15r.

32. Mirza I'tisam al-Din, "Shigarfnama," fols. 14v–15r.

33. Mirza I'tisam al-Din, "Shigarfnama," fol. 31r.

34. Mirza I'tisam al-Din, "Shigarfnama," fols. 24v–25r.

35. Mirza I'tisam al-Din, "Shigarfnama," fols. 32r–32v.

36. Mirza I'tisam al-Din, "Shigarfnama," fols. 32r–32v.

37. Mirza I'tisam al-Din, "Shigarfnama," fols. 23r–23v.

38. Mirza I'tisam al-Din, "Shigarfnama," fols. 23r–23v.

39. Mirza I'tisam al-Din, "Shigarfnama," fol. 25r.

40. Mirza I'tisam al-Din, "Shigarfnama," fol. 25r.

41. Mirza I'tisam al-Din, "Shigarfnama," fol. 25r.

42. Mirza I'tisam al-Din, "Shigarfnama," fol. 25r.

43. Mirza I'tisam al-Din, "Shigarfnama," fols. 25r–25v.

44. Mirza I'tisam al-Din, "Shigarfnama," fol. 25v.

45. Mirza I'tisam al-Din, "Shigarfnama," fol. 25v.

46. Mirza Abu Talib Khan, "Masir-i Talibi fi bilad-i Afranji," Add. 8145–47 (1806), Oriental and India Office Collections, British Library.

47. Stewart, trans., *Travels of Mirza Abu Taleb Khan in Asia, Africa, and Europe*, 1–2; Mirza Abu Talib Khan, *Masir-i Talibi fi bilad-i Afranji*, ed. Mirza Husayn 'Ali and Mir Qudrat 'Ali; Mirza Abu Talib Khan, *Masir-i Talibi (The Travels of Mirza Aboo Talib Khan)*. This chapter is based on the Persian text edited by Husayn Khadivjam and published in 1973 (Mirza Abu Talib Khan, *Masir-i Talibi ya Safarnama-yi Mirza Abu Talib Khan*) and Stewart's English translation.

48. Wright, *The Persians amongst the English*; Cole, "Invisible Occidentalism"; Cole, "Mirror of the World"; Fisher, *The Travels of Dean Mahomet*; Fisher, *Counterflows to Colonialism*; Khan, *Indian Muslim Perceptions of the West during the Eighteenth Century*; Tavakoli-Targhi, *Refashioning Iran*; Sohrabi, *Taken for Wonder*; Green, *The Love of Strangers*. Also see the essays by Bayly, Fisher, and others in the special issue of *Modern Asian Studies* 27, no. 1 (1993). For further references to Abu Talib's travels and travel account, see Kabir, *Mirza Abu Talib Khan*; Yusufi, *Farhang-i Khurasan*; Afshar, "Safarnamaha-yi Farsi ta Ruzgar-i Istiqrar-i Mashrutiyat"; Afshar, "Persian Travelogues"; Sankhdher, "Mirza Abu Talib Khan, His Life and Works"; and Llewellyn-Jones, "Indian Travellers in Nineteenth-Century England." For more recent works that explore Indo-Persian travels to India, see Tavakoli-Targhi, *Refashioning Iran*; Alam and Subrahmanyam, *Indo-Persian Travels in the Age of Discoveries, 1400–1800*; Kia, "Limning the Land; and Kia, "Imagining Iran before Nationalism."

49. Mirza Abu Talib Khan, *Masir-i Talibi* (1973), 3; Stewart, *Travels of Mirza Abu Taleb Khan in Asia, Africa, and Europe*, 1:1–2.

50. Mirza Abu Talib Khan, *Masir-i Talibi* (1973), 3; Stewart, *Travels of Mirza Abu Taleb Khan in Asia, Africa, and Europe*, 1:2.

51. Mirza Abu Talib Khan, *Masir-i Talibi* (1973), 4; Stewart, *Travels of Mirza Abu Taleb Khan in Asia, Africa, and Europe*, 1:3.

52. Mirza Abu Talib Khan, *Masir-i Talibi* (1973), 4-5; Stewart, *Travels of Mirza Abu Taleb Khan in Asia, Africa, and Europe*, 1:3-4.

53. Mirza Abu Talib Khan, *Masir-i Talibi* (1973), 7; Stewart, *Travels of Mirza Abu Taleb Khan in Asia, Africa, and Europe*, 1:11-13.

54. Mirza Abu Talib Khan, *Masir-i Talibi* (1973), 7-8; Stewart, *Travels of Mirza Abu Taleb Khan in Asia, Africa, and Europe*, 1:14-16.

55. Mirza Abu Talib Khan, *Masir-i Talibi* (1973), 9-10; Stewart, *Travels of Mirza Abu Taleb Khan in Asia, Africa, and Europe*, 1:20-23.

56. Mirza Abu Talib Khan, *Masir-i Talibi* (1973), 11; Stewart, *Travels of Mirza Abu Taleb Khan in Asia, Africa, and Europe*, 1:23-24.

57. Mirza Abu Talib Khan, *Masir-i Talibi* (1973), 12; Stewart, *Travels of Mirza Abu Taleb Khan in Asia, Africa, and Europe*, 1:24.

58. Mirza Abu Talib Khan, *Masir-i Talibi* (1973), 3-4.

59. Mirza Abu Talib Khan, *Masir-i Talibi* (1973), 12; Stewart, *Travels of Mirza Abu Taleb Khan in Asia, Africa, and Europe*, 1:27.

60. Mirza Abu Talib Khan, *Masir-i Talibi* (1973), 13-14; Stewart, *Travels of Mirza Abu Taleb Khan in Asia, Africa, and Europe*, 1:30-34.

61. Mirza Abu Talib Khan, *Masir-i Talibi*, 15; Stewart, *Travels of Mirza Abu Taleb Khan in Asia, Africa, and Europe*, 1:34.

62. Mirza Abu Talib Khan, *Masir-i Talibi* (1973), 21.

63. Mirza Abu Talib Khan, *Masir-i Talibi* (1973), 23.

64. Mirza Abu Talib Khan, *Masir-i Talibi* (1973), 15; Stewart, *Travels of Mirza Abu Taleb Khan in Asia, Africa, and Europe*, 1:36.

65. Mirza Abu Talib Khan, "Lubb al-siyar va jahan muma," Or. 1871 (1793), fol. 4a, Oriental and India Office Collections, British Library.

66. Mirza Abu Talib Khan, *Masir-i Talibi* (1973), 144-45; Stewart, *Travels of Mirza Abu Taleb Khan in Asia, Africa, and Europe*, 1:237-39.

67. Stewart, *Travels of Mirza Abu Taleb Khan in Asia, Africa, and Europe*, 3:256.

68. Mirza Abu Talib Khan, *Masir-i Talibi* (1973), 15; Stewart, *Travels of Mirza Abu Taleb Khan in Asia, Africa, and Europe*, 1:37-38.

69. Mirza Abu Talib Khan, *Masir-i Talibi* (1973), 15; Stewart, *Travels of Mirza Abu Taleb Khan in Asia, Africa, and Europe*, 1:36-37.

70. Mirza Abu Talib Khan, *Masir-i Talibi* (1973), 15-16; Stewart, *Travels of Mirza Abu Taleb Khan in Asia, Africa, and Europe*, 1:38-39.

71. Mirza Abu Talib Khan, *Masir-i Talibi* (1973), 16; Stewart, *Travels of Mirza Abu Taleb Khan in Asia, Africa, and Europe*, 1:39.

72. Mirza Abu Talib Khan, *Masir-i Talibi* (1973), 16; Stewart, *Travels of Mirza Abu Taleb Khan in Asia, Africa, and Europe*, 1:40-41.

73. On this dynamic in Burmese history, see J. C. Scott, *The Art of Not Being Governed*.

74. Mirza Abu Talib Khan, *Masir-i Talibi* (1973), 15–16; Stewart, *Travels of Mirza Abu Taleb Khan in Asia, Africa, and Europe*, 1:38–39.

75. Mirza Abu Talib Khan, *Masir-i Talibi* (1973), 15–16; Stewart, *Travels of Mirza Abu Taleb Khan in Asia, Africa, and Europe*, 1:38–39.

76. Temple, *Census of India*, 179–80.

77. Temple, 180.

78. Fontana, "On the Nicobar Islands and the Fruit of the Mellori," 149, 150.

79. Fontana, 150.

80. Haensel, *Letters on the Nicobar Islands*, 35–36.

81. Dillwyn, *A Descriptive Catalogue of Recent Shells*, 1:72–108; Mawe, *The Linnaean System of Conchology*, 23–27.

82. Dillwyn, *A Descriptive Catalogue of Recent Shells*, 1:109–31; Mawe, *The Linnaean System of Conchology*, 29–32.

83. Dillwyn, *A Descriptive Catalogue of Recent Shells*, 1:158–208; Mawe, *The Linnaean System of Conchology*, 41–46.

84. Dillwyn, *A Descriptive Catalogue of Recent Shells*, 1:247–84; Mawe, *The Linnaean System of Conchology*, 57–64.

85. Dillwyn, *A Descriptive Catalogue of Recent Shells*, 1:352–435; Mawe, *The Linnaean System of Conchology*, 85–92.

86. Dillwyn, *A Descriptive Catalogue of Recent Shells*, 2:815–73; Mawe, *The Linnaean System of Conchology*, 149–59.

87. Dillwyn, *A Descriptive Catalogue of Recent Shells*, 1:438–39; Mawe, *The Linnaean System of Conchology*, 93–97.

88. Dillwyn, *A Descriptive Catalogue of Recent Shells*, 1:458–59; Mawe, *The Linnaean System of Conchology*, 96.

89. Mirza Abu Talib Khan, *Masir-i Talibi* (1973), 17; Stewart, *Travels of Mirza Abu Taleb Khan in Asia, Africa, and Europe*, 1:44.

90. Mirza Abu Talib Khan, *Masir-i Talibi* (1973), 17–19; Stewart, *Travels of Mirza Abu Taleb Khan in Asia, Africa, and Europe*, 4:44–45, 47–48.

91. Mirza Abu Talib Khan, *Masir-i Talibi* (1973), 16; Stewart, *Travels of Mirza Abu Taleb Khan in Asia, Africa, and Europe*, 1:41.

92. Mirza Abu Talib Khan, *Masir-i Talibi* (1973), 16–17; Stewart, *Travels of Mirza Abu Taleb Khan in Asia, Africa, and Europe*, 1:41–43.

## CHAPTER TWO. OF ELEPHANTS, RUBIES, AND TEAK: MIR ʿABD AL-LATIF KHAN

1. Recent studies have presented a view of Burma and its maritime borderlands as dynamic spaces of cross-cultural interactions. See Gommans and Leider, *The Maritime Frontier of Burma*; Lieberman, *Strange Parallels*; Leider, *Le Royaume d'Arakan, Birmanie*; van Schendel, *The Bengal Borderland*; J. C. Scott, *The Art of Not Being Governed*; Mukherjee, *Pelagic Passageways*; and Amrith, *Crossing the Bay of Bengal*.

2. Mir ʿAbd al-Latif Khan Shushtari, "Tuhfat al-ʿAlam," Add. 23533 (1801), fols. 172a–177a, Oriental and India Office Collections, British Library; Mir ʿAbd al-Latif Khan Shushtari, *Tuhfat al-ʿalam* (1847). The page numbers cited in this chapter are from the 1847 edition. A version of the text edited by Samad Muvahhad was published in Tehran in 1984.

3. ʿAbd al-Latif Khan, *Tuhfat al-ʿalam* (1847), 100.

4. For existing discussions of ʿAbd al-Latif's life and writings, see Wright, *The Persians amongst the English*; Cole, "Invisible Occidentalism"; Cole, "Mirror of the World"; Tavakoli-Targhi, *Refashioning Iran*; Tavakoli-Targhi, "Early Persianate Modernity," 267–69; Dalrymple, *White Mughals*; and Amanat, "Through the Persian Eye." Building on these studies, which have been predominantly concerned with ʿAbd al-Latif's depiction of Europe, or "Farang," Mana Kia has turned toward an analysis of views of India in the work of ʿAbd al-Latif and other late eighteenth- and early nineteenth-century Persianate travel writers. See Kia, "Limning the Land"; and Kia, "Imagining Iran before Nationalism."

5. Mirza Abu Talib Khan, *Masir-i Talibi* (1973); Stewart, trans., *Travels of Mirza Abu Taleb Khan in Asia, Africa, and Europe*.

6. See the copies of the 1847 edition housed in the Near East Collection of the Firestone Library, Princeton University, and in the Middle Eastern Collection of the Widener Library, Harvard University. The existence of manuscripts of *Tuhfat al-ʿalam* from the early nineteenth century in archival collections in India, Britain, and Iran provides other possible clues to the readership of the book. See, for instance, ʿAbd al-Latif, "Tuhfat al-ʿalam" (1801), British Library; ʿAbd al-Latif Shustari, "Tuhfat al-ʿalam," Pers. Ms. Elliot 382 (1814), Bodleian Library; Mirza Muhammad Sadiq Vaqaʾiʿ Nigar, "Qavaʾid al-muluk," Ms. F/1757 (n.d.), Kitabkhana-yi Milli-yi Iran [National Library of Iran], Tehran

7. For the safarnama, see Afshar, "Persian Travelogues"; Tavakoli-Targhi, *Refashioning Iran*; Tavakoli-Targhi, "Early Persianate Modernity," 267–69; Alam and Subrahmanyam, *Indo-Persian Travels in the Age of Discoveries*; Sohrabi, *Taken for Wonder*; Micallef and Sharma, *On the Wonders of Land and Sea*; Kia, "Accounting for Difference"; Kia, "Limning the Land"; and Green, *The Love of Strangers*.

8. Thackston, ed. and trans, *Nasir-i Khusraw's Book of Travels*; Dankoff and Kim, ed. and trans., *An Ottoman Traveller*.

9. Sohrabi, *Taken for Wonder*, 15–16, 30, 36. For further discussion of ʿAbd al-Latif's views of Europe, see Tavakoli-Targhi, *Refashioning Iran*; Tavakoli-Targhi, "Early Persianate Modernity," 267–69; Dalrymple, *White Mughals*; and Amanat, "Through the Persian Eye."

10. Tavakoli-Targhi, "Early Persianate Modernity," 267–68. On the genre of axioms for kings during the nineteenth century, see Amanat, *Pivot of the Universe*.

11. These travel accounts include Muhammad ʿAli Hazin Lahiji, *Tarikh va safarnama-yi Hazin*, ed. Davvani; Belfour, trans., *The Life of Sheikh Mohammed Ali Hazin*; and Mirza Abu Talib Khan, *Masir-i Talibi* (1973).

12. ʿAbd al-Latif Khan, *Tuhfat al-ʿalam* (1847), 370.

13. Symes, *An Account of an Embassy to the Kingdom of Ava*. Symes was accompanied by a Persian "Moonshee . . . a Mussulman professor of language" during his mission, which conducted correspondence with Bodawpaya in Persian (126).

14. 'Abd al-Latif Khan, *Tuhfat al-'alam* (1847), 163–66.

15. 'Abd al-Latif Khan, 254–57, 259.

16. 'Abd al-Latif Khan, 259.

17. 'Abd al-Latif Khan, 263–64.

18. 'Abd al-Latif Khan, 11–12.

19. 'Abd al-Latif Khan, 263–64. For a discussion of Newtonian and Western science in *Tuhfat al-'alam* and other late eighteenth- and early nineteenth-century Persian texts, see Tavakoli-Targhi, *Refashioning Iran*; and Tavakoli-Targhi, "Early Persianate Modernity," 267.

20. 'Abd al-Latif Khan, *Tuhfat al-'alam* (1847), 260.

21. 'Abd al-Latif Khan, 260–61.

22. 'Abd al-Latif Khan, 261.

23. 'Abd al-Latif Khan, 260–62.

24. Mirza Abu Talib Khan, *Masir-i Talibi* (1973), 452–54.

25. See Dalrymple, *White Mughals*.

26. 'Abd al-Latif Khan, *Tuhfat al-'alam* (1847), 431, 473, 472; Yule and Burnell, eds., *Hobson-Jobson*, s.v. "teak," 693.

27. 'Abd al-Latif Khan, *Tuhfat al-'alam* (1847), 163–66, 472–73.

28. Hall, ed., *Michael Symes*, lxiii–lxvii.

29. It ought to be noted, however, that 'Abd al-Latif's descriptions of the peoples of Burma and their customs were at times imbued with a sense of discomfort. This often arose from the author's sense of different and unfamiliar gender relations and customs regarding women. For instance, according to 'Abd al-Latif, most of the people of the tropical kingdom, both women and men, were unclothed, covering only their private parts. 'Abd al-Latif also briefly discusses what he regarded as the strange customs and laws of Burma. In a passage in *Tuhfat al-'alam* on marriage customs and the rights of women, he writes:

> And in marriage, the parties involved conclude a contract according to a fixed manner and mutual consent, and the woman can stay as long as she wishes. Men send their daughters and wives to work in the service of foreigners who come to that land and after the foreigners have left, they take them back again. And if someone becomes acquainted with a woman and meets with her in secret and takes her to his house, the woman's husband or father—if she is a young girl—have the right to issue a complaint. The governor will then seek out the man and fine him 90 rupees and order the woman returned to her home. And if that woman goes back again to the same man's house for a second time, they fine him 60 rupees, and 30 rupees the third time. If this happens a fourth time, nothing is done and the couple is left together. (475)

For 'Abd al-Latif, Burma was a land on the peripheries of Bengal and a place of foreign and strange customs, including unusual interrelations between men and women.

30. 'Abd al-Latif Khan, *Tuhfat al-'alam* (1847), 434–35.

31. 'Abd al-Latif Khan, 472.

32. 'Abd al-Latif Khan, 471.

33. 'Abd al-Latif Khan, 472.

34. 'Abd al-Latif Khan, 471–72.

35. On elephants and empire, see I. T. Anderson, *The Dynasty of Abu*; Digby, *War-Horse and Elephant in the Delhi Sultanate*; Mikhail, *The Animal in Ottoman Egypt*; Hughes, *Animal Kingdoms*; and Trautmann, *Elephants and Kings*.

36. Abu'l-Fazl ibn Mubarak, *The Ain i Akbari*, i, 117.

37. Shway Yoe, *The Burman*, 480.

38. 'Abd al-Latif Khan, *Tuhfat al-'alam* (1847), 476–77.

39. 'Abd al-Latif Khan, 477.

40. 'Abd al-Latif Khan, 472.

41. Schimmel, *The Empire of the Great Mughals*, 66.

42. 'Abd al-Latif also wrote of precious mines of diamonds (*almas*), gold (*tala*), and silver (*nuqra*) in Burma. 'Abd al-Latif, *Tuhfat al-'alam* (1847), 473.

43. J. G. Scott, *Burma*, 237.

44. 'Abd al-Latif Khan, *Tuhfat al-'alam* (1847), 473.

45. 'Abd al-Latif Khan, 473–74.

46. Kirkpatrick, ed., *Select Letters of Tippoo Sultan to Various Public Functionaries*, 245–46.

47. National Archives of India, *Calendar of Persian Correspondence*; Kirkpatrick, *Select Letters of Tippoo Sultan to Various Public Functionaries*, 245–46; Jones, *The Works of Sir William Jones*, 2: ii, 111–15; Stewart, ed. and trans., *Original Persian Letters*, 12–15, 116–22.

48. 'Abd al-Latif Khan, *Tuhfat al-'alam* (1847), 432. This nomenclature, along with the knowledge that the tree grew plentifully in the Burmese Empire, circulated widely among Indo-Persian merchants and travelers. In *Hobson-Jobson* the name "teak" is said to derive from the Malayal *tekka* and the Tamil *tekku*, while the Sanskrit term *saka* is given as the root of the Hindi word *sagwan* and the Persian and Arabic word *saj*, referring to the tree and the timber used for shipbuilding, found in the Western Ghats and, more abundantly, in the upland forests of Burma, "the Kingdom of Martaban in the East Indies . . . in the tropical latitudes of Asia." Yule and Burnell, *Hobson-Jobson*, s.v. "teak," 910–11.

49. 'Abd al-Latif Khan, *Tuhfat al-'alam* (1847), 474.

50. On the Burmese teak trade in the Konbaung period, see Symes, *An Account of an Embassy to the Kingdom of Ava*, 121, 217, 235, 320, 419, 449, 457–58; Buchanan, "Journal of Progress and Observations during the Continuance of the Deputation from Bengal to Ava," 179–80, Ms. Eur. C 13 (1795), Oriental and India Office Collections, British Library; and Sangermano, *The Burmese Empire*, 219–20.

51. 'Abd al-Latif Khan, *Tuhfat al-'alam* (1847), 474, 476–77.

52. Sangermano, *The Burmese Empire*, 260–62.

53. 'Abd al-Latif Khan, *Tuhfat al-'alam* (1847), 474.

54. 'Abd al-Latif Khan, 474–75.

1. Symes, *An Account of an Embassy to the Kingdom of Ava*, 291, 344.

2. Buchanan Hamilton, "On the Religion and Literature of the Burmas," 264.

3. Buchanan Hamilton, 195. The scholars and scientists on the mission were familiar with the interests of the Asiatic Society in Indian astronomy and had read the essay on the subject by William Jones. See Jones, "On the Antiquity of the Indian Zodiac," in *The Works of Sir William Jones*, 4:71–92.

4. Cox, *Journal of a Residence in the Burmhan Empire;* Yule, *Narrative of the Mission Sent by the Governor-General of India to the Court of Ava in 1855;* J. G. Scott, *Burma: From the Earliest Times to the Present Day;* Harvey, *History of Burma from the Earliest Times to 10 March 1824.*

5. Hall, *Michael Symes*, xviii.

6. On this theme of the immersion of Europeans within the currents of Persianate and Mughal culture, see Alam and Alavi, ed. and trans., *A European Experience of the Mughal Orient;* and Jasanoff, *Edge of Empire.* More specifically in regard to travel and exploration, see Teltscher, *The High Road to China.*

7. On the Bengal-Arakan borderland, see van Schendel, *The Bengal Borderland.*

8. Lieutenant J. Brougham, the Second Battalion Sepoys, to the Honourable Sir John Shore, Governor-General, Ramoo, December 28, 1794, Magh Borderers and Marauders, India Office Records, IOR/F/4/71/1583, Oriental and India Office Collections, British Library.

9. Brougham to Shore, December 28, 1794.

10. Brougham to Shore, December 28, 1794.

11. Brougham to Shore, December 28, 1794

12. Letter from the magistrate of the Zillah of Chittagong, November 20, 1794, Magh Borderers and Marauders, India Office Records, IOR/F/4/71/1583.

13. Extract Bengal Political Considerations, October 10, 1794, Magh Borderers and Marauders. India Office Records, IOR/F/4/71/1583.

14. Extract Bengal Political Considerations, March 27, 1794, Magh Borderers and Marauders, India Office Records, IOR/F/4/71/1583.

15. Extract Bengal Political Considerations, August 11, 1794, Magh Borderers and Marauders, India Office Records, IOR/F/4/71/1583.

16. Extract Bengal Political Considerations, August 11, 1794.

17. Report of Captain Symes, January 23, 1797, India Office Records, IOR/L/PS/19/56, Oriental and India Office Collections, British Library.

18. Stewart, *Original Persian Letters*, 12–15.

19. Harvey, *Outline of Burmese History*, 122–23. On the prevalence of French shipbuilding techniques in Burma, also see Symes, *An Account of an Embassy to the Kingdom of Ava*, 218.

20. Hall, *Michael Symes*, xx–xxiii.

21. Leider, *King Alaungmintaya's Golden Letter to King George II.*

22. Harvey, *Outline of Burmese History*, 122–23.

23. J. G. Scott, *Burma: A Handbook of Practical Information*, 282.

24. Symes, *An Account of an Embassy to the Kingdom of Ava*, 293.

25. National Archives of India, *Calendar of Persian Correspondence*; Kirkpatrick, *Select Letters of Tippoo Sultan to Various Public Functionaries*, 245–46; Jones, *The Works of Sir William Jones*, 2:111–15; Stewart, *Original Persian Letters*, 12–15, 116–22.

26. Hall, *Michael Symes*, lxiii–lxvii.

27. National Archives of India, *Calendar of Persian Correspondence, 1794–1795*, 11:367. See also Bodawpaya's letter to John Shore, Governor-General of Bengal, dated 28 Shaban in the Hijri year of 1209 (March 21, 1795), in National Archives of India, 11:398–99; and letter to the collector of Chittagong, 1795, in Jones, *The Works of Sir William Jones*, 111–15.

28. On the upland peoples of Burma, see J. C. Scott, *The Art of Not Being Governed*. On Mughal political practices based on a shared and layered sovereignty, see Alam and Subrahmanyam, *The Mughal State, 1526–1750*.

29. Jones, *The Works of Sir William Jones*, 2:111–12.

30. Jones, 2:112–13.

31. Jones, 2:113–14.

32. Jones, 2:114.

33. Jones, 2:114–15.

34. "From Nandaw, Rajah of Pegu," January 8, 1788, in National Archives of India, *Calendar of Persian Correspondence, 1788–1789*, 8:23.

35. "From the Vazir of the King of Pegu," January 8, 1788, in National Archives of India, *Calendar of Persian Correspondence, 1788–1789*, 8:24.

36. Hunter, *A Concise Account of the Climate, Produce, Trade, Government, Manners of the Kingdom of Pegu*.

37. "From the minister of the King of Pegu," November 1, 1788, in National Archives of India, *Calendar of Persian Correspondence, 1788–1789*, 8:24, 332–33.

38. "To the King of Pegu," September 16, 1789, in National Archives of India, *Calendar of Persian Correspondence, 1788–1789*, 8:607.

39. "To the Minister of Pegu," September 17, 1793, in National Archives of India, *Calendar of Persian Correspondence, 1788–1789*, 10:342; "From the Minister of Ava," October 28, 1795, in National Archives of India, *Calendar of Persian Correspondence, 1794–1795*, 11:369; "From the King of Ava," October 28, 1795, in National Archives of India, *Calendar of Persian Correspondence, 1794–1795*, 11:369.

40. Hall, *Michael Symes*, xxxvi; Hall, *Burma*, 98; Banerjee, *The Eastern Frontier of British India, 1784–1826*, 117–23.

41. Hall, *Michael Symes*, xxxvii.

42. "From the Governor of Pegu," November 6, 1794, in National Archives of India, *Calendar of Persian Correspondence, 1794–1795*, 11:185.

43. Symes, *An Account of an Embassy to the Kingdom of Ava*, 121.

44. Hall, *Michael Symes*, lxii.

45. Symes, *An Account of an Embassy to the Kingdom of Ava*, 157, 293.

46. See National Archives of India, *Calendar of Persian Correspondence, 1794–1795*, 11:398–99.

47. John Shore, Governor-General, to Michael Symes, Agent to the Court of Ava, Fort William, June 17, 1795, India Office Records, IOR/L/PS/19/56.

48. See National Archives of India, *Calendar of Persian Correspondence, 1794–1795*, 11:398–99.

49. Symes, *An Account of an Embassy to the Kingdom of Ava*, 1.

50. Symes, 292.

51. Symes, 127–38.

52. Symes, 140; Michael Symes, Agent to the Court of Ava, Pegu, to the Honourable Sir John Shore, Governor-General, April 7, 1795, India Office Records, IOR/L/PS/19/56.

53. Symes, *An Account of an Embassy to the Kingdom of Ava*, 142–43.

54. Symes, 144–45.

55. Symes, 151–52.

56. Symes, 146.

57. Symes to Shore, April 7, 1795, India Office Records, IOR/L/PS/19/56.

58. Symes, *An Account of an Embassy to the Kingdom of Ava*, 146.

59. Symes, 147, 148, 150. Symes also noted that in his "conversations with Birmans," he was "seldom at a loss to find some person who understood" Hindustani (164).

60. Symes, 147–48.

61. Symes, 148–49.

62. Symes to Shore, April 25, 1795, India Office Records, IOR/L/PS/19/56.

63. Symes, *An Account of an Embassy to the Kingdom of Ava*, 155–56.

64. Symes, 157–58.

65. Symes, 182, 183.

66. Symes, 168–69.

67. Symes to Shore, April 7, 1795, India Office Records, IOR/L/PS/19/56.

68. Symes, *An Account of an Embassy to the Kingdom of Ava*, 187–89.

69. Symes, 188–89.

70. Symes, 172.

71. Symes, 172–74.

72. Symes, 177.

73. Symes, 178, 179, 180.

74. Symes, 174.

75. Symes, 208.

76. Symes to Shore, April 25, 1795, India Office Records, IOR/L/PS/19/56.

77. Symes to Shore, May 15, 1795.

78. Symes to Shore, May 15, 1795.

79. On the history of the presence of these Indo-Persian communities in Southeast Asia, see Marcinkowski, *From Isfahan to Ayutthaya*. On Indo-Persian Armenian trade networks in the Indian Ocean and Southeast Asia, see Herzig, "The Armenian Merchants of New Julfa"; Aslanian, *From the Indian Ocean to the Mediterranean*. On the history of Muslims in Burma, see Yegar, *The Muslims of Burma*; Sin, "The Coming of Islam to Burma, down to 1700"; and Green, "Buddhism, Islam and the Religious Economy of Colonial Burma."

80. Symes, *An Account of an Embassy to the Kingdom of Ava*, 215.

81. Symes, 160.

82. Symes, 160.

83. Hall, *Michael Symes*, 121.

84. Hall, *Michael Symes*, 198, 203; Symes, *An Account of an Embassy to the Kingdom of Ava*, 162.

85. Hall, *Michael Symes*, 235–36.

86. Hall, 235–36.

87. Myint U, *The Making of Modern Burma*, 17.

88. Tin, *The Royal Administration of Burma*, 318.

89. Hall, *Michael Symes*, lii, lxxii, 167, 251; Qazi Ghulam Qasim Mihri, "Manzumat."

90. On Indo-Persian Armenian trade networks in the Indian Ocean and Southeast Asia, see Aslanian, *From the Indian Ocean to the Mediterranean*. On the history of Muslims in Burma, see Yegar, *The Muslims of Burma*.

91. There was also once an Armenian cemetery outside the church, but the only remaining written sign of the community within the crumbling walls of the now ruined edifice is an inscription in Latin and Armenian etched in stone, recording the names of the Armenian merchant, "Nicolas de Aguilar and his wife Margarita." Hall, *Michael Symes*, lxvii.

92. Symes, *An Account of an Embassy to the Kingdom of Ava*, 292.

93. Symes, 408.

94. Symes, 161.

95. Buchanan Hamilton, "On the Religion and Literature of the Burmas," 171, 195–204.

96. Moses and Ignazio de Brito, *Pawtugi Yazawin*. In *The History of Burma from the Earliest Times to 1824*, G. E. Harvey speculates that the text "was probably written within a generation of De Brito's death (1613) by some Burmanized Portuguese captive" (xvi–xvii). See also Hall, *Michael Symes*, lxviii.

97. Hamilton, *A Geographical, Statistical, and Historical Description of Hindostan and the Adjacent Countries*, 2:796.

98. Buchanan Hamilton, "On the Religion and Literature of the Burmas," 171, 195–204.

99. Judson, *An Account of the American Baptist Mission to the Burman Empire*, 39. Also see Hall, *Michael Symes*, lxix.

100. Symes, *An Account of an Embassy to the Kingdom of Ava*, 291.

101. Symes to Shore, August 15, 1795, India Office Records, IOR/L/PS/19/56.

102. Buchanan Hamilton, "On the Religion and Literature of the Burmas," 264.

103. George Thomas, Commander of the Sea Horse, Rangoon, to the Honourable Sir John Shore, Governor-General, June 19, 1795, India Office Records, IOR/L/PS/19/56.

104. Symes to Shore, June 15, 1795, India Office Records, IOR/L/PS/19/56.

105. Symes, 265, 269.

106. Symes, 268–70.

107. Symes to Shore, August 15, 1795, India Office Records, IOR/L/PS/19/56.

108. Symes, *An Account of an Embassy to the Kingdom of Ava*, 281.

109. Symes to Shore, August 15, 1795, India Office Records, IOR/L/PS/19/56.

110. Sangermano, *The Burmese Empire*, 75.

111. Symes, to Shore, August 15, 1795, India Office Records, IOR/L/PS/19/56.

112. Symes, *An Account of an Embassy to the Kingdom of Ava*, 344. Also see Symes to Shore, August 15, 1795, India Office Records, IOR/L/PS/19/56.

113. Symes, *An Account of an Embassy to the Kingdom of Ava*, 344.

114. Symes, 352–55.

115. Symes, 358–62.

116. Symes, 360, 362.

117. Symes, 360.

118. National Archives of India, *Calendar of Persian Correspondence, 1794–1795*, 11:398–99.

119. Symes, *An Account of an Embassy to the Kingdom of Ava*, 364–65.

120. Symes, 367–68.

121. Symes, 400.

122. Symes, 398.

123. Symes, 150, 157.

124. Symes, 292.

125. Symes, xiii, 303.

126. To the Honourable John Shore, Governor-General, from Michael Symes, Agent on the part of the Bengal Government to the Court of Ava, Ummerapoorah/ Ava, July 2, 1795, India Office Records, IOR/L/PS/19/56.

127. Symes, *An Account of an Embassy to the Kingdom of Ava*, 484.

128. Symes, 411–14.

129. Symes, 414–15.

130. Symes, 415.

131. Symes, 487–88.

132. Symes, 488–89.

133. Symes, 491–92.

134. Symes, 493.

135. Symes, 409, 410; Michael Symes, Most Obedient and Faithful Humble Servant, on board the Sea Horse, to the Honourable Sir John Shore, Governor-General, December 18, 1795, India Office Records, IOR/L/PS/19/56.

136. Symes, *An Account of an Embassy to the Kingdom of Ava*, 428.

137. Copy of notification published in the *Calcutta Gazette* respecting trade with Pegu, Fort William, January 17, 1796, India Office Records, IOR/L/PS/19/56.


CHAPTER FOUR. FOREST WORLDS: SINGEY BEY

1. Symes, *An Account of an Embassy to the Kingdom of Ava*, xi, 126.

2. For examples of such studies in the history of science focused on European botany, botanical expeditions, and bioprospecting, see Schiebinger and Swan, eds.,

*Colonial Botany*; Schiebinger, *Plants and Empire*; and Bleichmar, *Visible Empire*. For a different take, focused on the botany of the African diaspora during the transatlantic slave trade, see Carney and Rosomoff, *In the Shadow of Slavery*.

3. For examples of the literature on colonial botany in South Asia, see Grove, *Green Imperialism*; Arnold, *The Tropics and the Traveling Gaze* Raj, *Relocating Modern Science*; and Kelley, *Clandestine Marriage*. These works are nevertheless focused on British and European explorers and botanists, although Raj shifts the discussion of scientific exchanges to encounters between Europe and its colonies and the colonial reception of local knowledge.

4. For some existing studies on colonial Burma, see Harvey, *History of Burma*; Hall, *Europe and Burma*; Hall, *Burma*; Hall, *A History of Southeast Asia*; Aung, *A History of Burma*; Aung, *Epistles Written on the Eve of the Anglo-Burmese War, 1824*; Myint U, *The Making of Modern Burma*; and Leider, *King Alaungmintaya's Golden Letter to King George II*.

5. Shway Yoe, *The Burman*, 520; J. G. Scott, *Burma: A Handbook of Practical Information*, 291.

6. Shway Yoe, *The Burman*, 520.

7. Sangermano, *The Burmese Empire*, 260–62.

8. Shway Yoe, *The Burman*, 362.

9. J. G. Scott, *Burma: A Handbook of Practical Information*, 284.

10. Harvey, *Outline of Burmese History*, 122–23. On the prevalence of French shipbuilding techniques in Burma, also see Symes, *An Account of an Embassy to the Kingdom of Ava*, 218.

11. Hall, *Michael Symes*, xx–xxiii.

12. On the economy of the teak trade in late eighteenth-century Burma, see Symes, *An Account of an Embassy to the Kingdom of Ava*, 121, 217–18, 235, 320, 419, 449, 457–58; Buchanan, "Journal of Progress and Observations during the Continuance of the Deputation from Bengal to Ava," 179–80, Ms. Eur. C 13, Oriental and India Office Collections, British Library; and Sangermano, *The Burmese Empire*, 219–20.

13. Sangermano, 219.

14. Symes, *An Account of an Embassy to the Kingdom of Ava*, 121, 458–59; Sangermano, *The Burmese Empire*, 219.

15. On this nineteenth-century economic shift and its connections with the divergence thesis, see Pomeranz, *The Great Divergence*.

16. Aung, *Epistles Written on the Eve of the Anglo-Burmese War, 1824*. Also see Aung, *A History of Burma*, 190–91.

17. Kelley, *Clandestine Marriage*, 197–207; Arnold, *The Tropics and the Traveling Gaze*, 184.

18. On colonial botany in India, see Arnold, *The Tropics and the Traveling Gaze*; and Grove, *Green Imperialism*. For examples of the literature on colonial botany, botanical expeditions, and bioprospecting more broadly, see Schiebinger and Swan, *Colonial Botany*; Schiebinger, *Plants and Empire*; and Bleichmar, *Visible Empire*.

19. Kelley, *Clandestine Marriage*, 192.

20. Kelley, 192–93, 197.

21. Prain, "A Sketch of the Life of Francis Hamilton (once Buchanan)," i–lxxv.

22. Symes, *An Account of an Embassy to the Kingdom of Ava*, 422.

23. Symes, xi–xii.

24. Symes, 267, 473.

25. Britten, "Buchanan's Avan Plants," 279–82.

26. Symes, *An Account of an Embassy to the Kingdom of Ava*, 473–80.

27. Symes, 475.

28. Symes, 269–70.

29. Buchanan Hamilton, "On the Religion and Literature of the Burmas."

30. During the mission, Buchanan collected palm-leaf manuscripts on Buddhism written in the Burmese language, which he presented to Scottish Orientalist and scholar of Buddhism John Murray MacGregor upon returning to Bengal. See Buchanan Hamilton, "On the Religion and Literature of the Burmas," 173, 303.

31. Buchanan Hamilton, 174.

32. Buchanan Hamilton, 180–81.

33. Buchanan Hamilton, 177.

34. Buchanan Hamilton, 177, 236.

35. Buchanan Hamilton, 295.

36. Symes, *An Account of an Embassy to the Kingdom of Ava*, 186–91, 247–48.

37. Buchanan Hamilton, "On the Religion and Literature of the Burmas," 293.

38. Symes, *An Account of an Embassy to the Kingdom of Ava*, 186–91, 247–48.

39. The scholarly literature on the history of teak in Burma is scarce and little explored apart from Raymond Bryant's more anthropological study, *The Political Ecology of Forestry in Burma, 1824–1994*. More pertinent here are studies such as Jennifer Anderson's recent history of mahogany in the Atlantic world, *Mahogany: The Costs of Luxury in Early America*.

40. Wallich, *Plantae asiaticae rariores*, 3:68.

41. Wallich, 3:68–69.

42. Buchanan, "Journal of Progress and Observations during the Continuance of the Deputation from Bengal to Ava," 179–80, Ms. Eur. C 13.

43. Symes, *An Account of an Embassy to the Kingdom of Ava*, 427.

44. Wallich, *Plantae asiaticae rariores*, 3:68–69, plate 294.

45. Buchanan, "On the Religion and Literature of the Burmas," 286–87.

46. Symes, *An Account of an Embassy to the Kingdom of Ava*, 387–88.

47. Symes, 423–24.

48. Symes, 267.

49. Symes, 344–46.

50. On Bodawpaya's white elephants, see Sangermano, *The Burmese Empire a Hundred Years Ago*, 73–80.

51. Symes, *Journal of his Second Embassy to the Court of Ava in 1802*, lxiii–lxvii.

52. Buchanan, "Journal of Progress and Observations during the Continuance of the Deputation from Bengal to Ava," 116, Ms. Eur. C 13.

53. "Method of Catching Wild Elephants in Ava," in Symes, *An Account of an Embassy to the Kingdom of Ava*, 346–47.

54. Collis, *She Was a Queen*, 71. On this roping method of capturing elephants, also see, Sangermano, *The Burmese Empire*, 206–7.

55. On the Mahamuni and the Mrauk U Kingdom, see Collis, *The Land of the Great Image*. For more recent investigations of the history of Mrauk U, see Leider, *Le Royaume d'Arakan, Birmanie*; Gommans and Leider, *The Maritime Frontier of Burma*; Charney, "Crisis and Reformation in a Maritime Kingdom of Southeast Asia"; Charney, "The Rise of a Mainland Trading State; Subrahmanyam, "Persianization and 'Mercantilism' in Bay of Bengal History, 1400–1700" and "Dutch Tribulations in Seventeenth-Century Mrauk U," in *Explorations in Connected History: From the Tagus to the Ganges*; d'Hubert and Leider, "Traders and Poets at the Mrauk U Court"; and d'Hubert, *In the Shade of the Golden Palace*.

56. On Bodawpaya, the Buddhist *sangha*, and the conquest of Arakan, see Leider, "Forging Buddhist Credentials as a Tool of Legitimacy and Ethnic Identity."

57. Harvey, *Outline of Burmese History*, 148; Harvey, *History of Burma*, 267.

58. Symes, *An Account of an Embassy to the Kingdom of Ava*, 103–11.

59. Symes, 391.

60. Symes, 346–47.

61. Symes, 391.

62. Symes, 346–47.

63. Symes, 352–55.

## CHAPTER FIVE. IN THE WILDERNESS OF PALI: SHAH ʿAZIZALLAH BUKHARI QALANDAR

1. On Arakan as the frontiers of Islam, see Eaton, *The Rise of Islam and the Bengal Frontier, 1204–1760*. On Arakan as a land in between Buddhism and Islam, see Charney, "Where Jambudipa and Islamdom Converged."

2. Gommans and Leider, *The Maritime Frontier of Burma*; Charney, "The Rise of a Mainland Trading State."

3. On the cultivation of rice paddy and state building in the river deltas of Southeast Asia, see J. C. Scott, *The Art of Not Being Governed*; Lieberman, *Strange Parallels*; Lieberman, *Burmese Administrative Cycles*; and Reid, *Southeast Asia in the Age of Commerce, 1450–1680*, vol. 1, *The Lands below the Winds*.

4. Subrahmanyam, *Improvising Empire*; Subrahmanyam, *Explorations in Connected History: From Tagus to the Ganges*.

5. d'Hubert and Leider, "Traders and Poets at the Mrauk U Court," 86.

6. Manrique, *Travels of Fray Sebastien Manrique, 1629–1643*, 1:379.

7. On the syncretism in South Asia between Persian and Indic cultural worlds and Islam and Hinduism, see Eaton and Wagoner, *Power, Memory, Architecture*; and Ernst, *Refractions of Islam in India*.

8. On Persian and the numismatic history of Mrauk U, see d'Hubert, "The Lord of the Elephant." On the Persian titles of Arakanese kings, see Phayre, "On the History of Arakan"; Phayre, "The Coins of Arakan"; Phayre, *Coins of Arakan, of Pegu, and of Burma*; Phayre, *History of Burma, Including Burma Proper, Pegu, Taungu, Tenasserim, and Arakan*; Harvey, *History of Burma*, 137–49, 371–72; Collis and Bu, "Arakan's Place in the Civilization of the Bay"; Collis, *The Land of the Great Image*; Sin, "The Coming of Islam to Burma, down to 1700"; and Leider, "These Buddhist Kings with Muslim Names."

9. On Indo-Persian poetics in Mrauk U, see d'Hubert, *In the Shade of the Golden Palace*; and d'Hubert and Leider, "Traders and Poets at the Mrauk U Court."

10. Gommans and Leider, *The Maritime Frontier of Burma*, 156–60, 226.

11. Myint U, *The Making of Modern Burma*, 13–14.

12. On these Persian "Magh manuscripts," see Pertsch, *Die Handschriften-Verzeichnisse der Königlichen Bibliothek zu Berlin*, 1036–43. On the Pali into Persian translations of another munshi employed by Murray, named Ray Jaganath Sahay, see d'Hubert, "A Persian Account of the Religious Customs of the Magh (Arakanese) from Early Colonial Bengal." Also see d'Hubert, "India beyond the Ganges"; d'Hubert, "Bayan-i 'ibadat-i mukh-ha ba-nam-i Takadiba"; and Ernst, "Muslim Studies of Hinduism?."

13. On the notion of the "Pali imaginary," see Collins, *Nirvana*.

14. On Sufi wanderings between wilderness and gardens, see Hutton, *Art of the Court of Bijapur*, 89–91.

15. Subrahmanyam, *Explorations in Connected History: From Tagus to the Ganges*; Subrahmanyam, "Connected Histories."

16. Phayre, *Coins of Arakan, of Pegu, and of Burma*; Phayre, *History of Burma, Including Burma Proper, Pegu, Tangu, Tenasserim, and Arakan*; Collis, *The Land of the Great Image*.

17. On commercial and interimperial interconnections between Mrauk U and the Persianate and Mughal worlds, see Subrahmanyam, *Improvising Empire*; Subrahmanyam, "Persianization and 'Mercantilism' in Bay of Bengal History, 1400–1700," and "Dutch Tribulations in Seventeenth-Century Mrauk U," in *Explorations in Connected History: From the Tagus to the Ganges*; and Subrahmanyam, "And a River Runs through It." For recent historiography focused on the political and religious history of the Kingdom of Mrauk U, see Charney, "Where Jambudipa and Islamdom Converged"; Charney, "The Rise of a Mainland Trading State"; Charney, "Crisis and Reformation in a Maritime Kingdom of Southeast Asia"; Leider, *Le Royaume d'Arakan, Birmanie*; and van Galen, "Arakan and Bengal." On the art and architecture of Arakan, see Gutman, *Burma's Lost Kingdoms*; and Fraser-Lu, *Buddhist Art of Myanmar*.

18. d'Hubert, *In the Shade of the Golden Palace*.

19. Rieu, *Catalogue of the Persian Manuscripts in the British Museum*, 1:405–6. The letters are classified as Sloane Mss. 3259 and 3260 in the Sloan Manuscripts Collection of the British Library: Persian decree from Raja Chandrawizaya of Arakan to Khwaja George in Chennaipattan, 14 Sha'ban 1090 Magh [1728], Ms.

3259; Persian letter from Arakan to the Grand Merchant George in Chennaipattan, 20 Sha'ban 1090 Magh [1728], Ms. 3260.

20. Herbert, "The Making of a Collection," 59–60. The Burmese palm leaf is Sloane Ms. 4098 in the British Library.

21. For a seventeenth-century Persian travel account detailing these connections to Thailand, see Muhammad Ibrahim Rabi ibn Muhammad Ibrahim, *Safina-yi Sulaymani*. For an English translation, see *The Ship of Sulaimān*, trans. John O'Kane. Also see Aubin, "Les persans au Siam sous le règne de Narai, 1656–1688"; Subrahmanyam, "Iranians Abroad"; Alam and Subrahmanyam, *Indo-Persian Travels in the Age of Discoveries, 1400–1800*, 130–74; and Marcinkowski, *From Isfahan to Ayutthaya*.

22. See, for instance, Charney, "Where Jambudipa and Islamdom Converged"; Charney, "The Rise of a Mainland Trading State"; Charney, "Crisis and Reformation in a Maritime Kingdom of Southeast Asia"; Subrahmanyam, "Persianization and 'Mercantilism' in Bay of Bengal History, 1400–1700," and "Dutch Tribulations in Seventeenth-Century Mrauk U," in *Explorations in Connected History: From the Tagus to the Ganges* ; Subrahmanyam, "And a River Runs through It"; d'Hubert and Leider, "Traders and Poets at the Mrauk U Court," 77–111; and d'Hubert, *In the Shade of the Golden Palace*.

23. The kings of Mrauk U who used the Persian title of "shah" included Narameikhla/Sulayman Shah (1404–34), Minkhari/'Ali Khan (1434–59), Basawpyu/Kalim Shah (1459–82), Dawlya/Mokhu Shah (1482–92), Basawnyo/Muhammad Shah (1492–94), Yanaung/Nuri Shah (1494), Salingathu/Sikandar Shah (1494–1501), Minraza/Ilyas Shah (1501–23), Kasabadi/Ilyas Shah (1523–25), Minsaw-U/Jalal Shah (1525), Thatasa/Sultan 'Ali Shah (1525–31), Minbin/Babak Shah (1531–53), Minpalaung/Sikandar Shah (1571–93), Minrazagri/Salim Shah (1593–1612), Minkhamaung/Husayn Shah (1612–22), and Thirithudhamma/Salim Shah (1622–38). These Persian titles are based on sources that draw upon numismatic evidence and Arakanese chronicles. See Phayre, "On the History of Arakan"; Phayre, "The Coins of Arakan"; Phayre, *Coins of Arakan, of Pegu, and of Burma*; Phayre, *History of Burma, Including Burma Proper, Pegu, Taungu, Tenasserim, and Arakan*; Harvey, *History of Burma*, 137–49, 371–72; Collis and Bu, "Arakan's Place in the Civilization of the Bay"; Collis, *The Land of the Great Image*; Sin, "The Coming of Islam to Burma, down to 1700"; and Leider, "These Buddhist Kings with Muslim Names."

24. On Persian and its usage in courtly exchanges and as a language of correspondence between Mrauk U and Mughal India, focusing on the letters exchanged circa 1688 between Thirithudhamma Raja of Mrauk U and Islam Khan Mashhadi, the Mughal governor of Bengal, see Syed Hasan Askari, "The Mughal-Magh Relations down to the Time of Islam Khan Mashhadi," *Proceedings of the Indian History Congress* 22 (1959), 201–13; and Subrahmanyam, "Persianization and 'Mercantilism' in Bay of Bengal History, 1400–1700," in *Explorations in Connected History: From the Tagus to the Ganges*.

25. For overviews of the farman document, see Fragner, "Farmān"; and Busse, "Farmān." For some specific studies of the farman in Indo-Persian contexts, see Aubin, "Archives Persanes Commentées 1"; Khan, ed., *Farmans and Sanads of the*

*Deccan Sultans*; 'Abd al-Husayn Nava'i, *Shah Isma'il Safavi*; 'Abd al-Husayn Nava'i, ed., *Shah Tahmasp Safavi*; 'Abd al-Husayn Nava'i, *Shah 'Abbas*; Mohiuddin, *The Chancellery and Persian Epistolography under the Mughals*; and Modarressi Tabataba'i, ed., *Farmanha-yi Turkomanan-i Qara Quyunlu va Aq Quyunlu*.

26. Persian decree from Raja Chandrawizaya of Arakan to Khwaja George in Chennaipattan, 14 Sha'ban 1090 Magh [1728], Ms. 3259, Sloane Manuscripts Collection, British Library.

27. For the translation of the Pali seal, see van Galen, "Arakan and Bengal," 211. Van Galen's thesis drew upon a rich trove of Dutch East India Company sources but did not translate the Persian farman and accepted Rieu's misdating and misidentification of it as from the court of Chandrasudhamma Raja in 1679.

28. During the seventeenth and eighteenth centuries, there was a proliferation of Mughal commercial farmans, including decrees granting trading privileges to the British East India Company. In 1717, the Mughal emperor Farrukhsiyar issued a farman that allowed the company to trade within the empire free of customs duties. King Chandrawizaya's decree, written a little more than a decade later, was certainly more circumscribed in its promise of allowing two ships to be sent every monsoon season from Armenian merchants in Madras. In permitting trading privileges and offering protection, however, it was a farman crafted within the same context and pattern of early modern global interactions and exchanges.

29. Annabel Teh Gallop, "Piagam Serampas," 276. Also see Gallop, *The Legacy of the Malay Letter*.

30. *Records of Fort St. George: Proceedings of the Mayor's Court, 1728*, 45.

31. *Records of Fort St. George: Proceedings of the Mayor's Court Minutes, 1736–1737*, 3:26, 29, 37, 69–70, 90, 93.

32. *Records of Fort St. George: Diary and Consultation Book of 1707*, 21.

33. *Records of Fort St. George: Diary and Consultation Book of 1732*, 62.

34. On Armenian trading networks in the early modern world, including transactions with Southeast Asia, see Aslanian, *From the Indian Ocean to the Mediterranean*, 55. Also see Herzig, "The Armenian Merchants of New Julfa, Isfahan."

35. For a counterpoint on the usage of Persian in diplomatic rivalries between Arakan and Mughal India in the more volatile context of Magh piracy and slave raiding in the Bay of Bengal, see Askari, "The Mughal-Magh Relations down to the Time of Islam Khan Mashhadi."

36. On elephants and sovereignty over the *longue durée* of South Asian history, see Trautmann, *Elephants and Kings*. On animals and other megafauna in early modern Islamicate empires, see Mikhail, *The Animal in Ottoman Egypt*.

37. For an analysis of elephants and sovereignty in early modern Arakan based on numismatic analysis of the royal title "Lord of the White Elephant" (Sahib-i Fil-i Safid), see d'Hubert, "The Lord of the Elephant."

38. Pal, *Elephants and Ivories in South Asia*, 18.

39. On the prevalence of such themes in the trade correspondence of Armenian merchants, see Aslanian, *From the Indian Ocean to the Mediterranean*, 86–120, 166–201.

40. Persian letter from Arakan to the Grand Merchant George in Chennaipattan, 20 Sha'ban 1090 Magh [1728], Ms. 3260, Sloane Manuscripts Collection, British Library.

41. Symes, *An Account of an Embassy to the Kingdom of Ava*, 487–89.

42. d'Hubert and Leider, "Traders and Poets at the Mrauk U Court," 86–89.

43. d'Hubert and Leider, 87.

44. Yule and Burnell, *Hobson-Jobson*, 594–95.

45. Such views persisted even in the contemporary chronicles of the late eighteenth century. In *Riyaz al-Salatin*, a provincial chronicle of Bengal completed in 1788, Ghulam Husayn Salim (d. 1817), a native of Awadh who held the office of Dak Munshi in Bengal under George Udny, the Commercial Resident of the East India Company's factory at Maldah, represented Arakan as an imperial borderland and zone of cultural difference:

> And between the south and east of Bengal, is situated a large tract called Arkhang (Arracan); Chittagong adjoins it. The male and female elephant abounds there.... Their religion is distinct from Islam and Hinduism.... And the people never remiss in their obeisance to the authority of their sovereign and chief whom they style 'Wali'.... And the military force of that country consists of an elephant-corps and infantry. White elephants are found in its jungles, and on its boundaries are mines of minerals and precious stones." (Ghulam Hussain Salim, *Riazu-s-Salatin*, 14–15)

46. Stewart, *The History of Bengal*, ii.

47. Stewart, ii–iii.

48. This chapter follows these texts through Stewart's *History of Bengal* in order to retrace how they were recovered and read in the colonial archive of late eighteenth- and early nineteenth-century Bengal. For published editions of these Mughal imperial histories, see Ferishta, *History of the Rise of Mahomedan Power in India till the Year A.D. 1612*; Muhammad Qasim Hindu Shah Astarabadi, *Tarikh-i Firishta*; Abu'l Fazl, *The History of Akbar*; Thackston, trans., *The Jahangirnama*; Begley and Desai, eds., *The Shah Jahan Nama of 'Inayat Khan*; Muhammad Kazim ibn-i Muhammad Amin Munshi, *The Alamgir Namah*; Maulavi Kabir al-Din Ahmad, ed., *The Muntakhab al-Lubab of Khafi Khan*. See also Stewart, *The History of Bengal*, xi–xiii.

49. Stewart, iii, iv.

50. Stewart, 215.

51. Stewart, 207, 211.

52. Stewart, 240.

53. Stewart, 277–82, 296, 297.

54. "Calcutta in the Olden Time—Its People," *The Calcutta Review*, vol. 35 (1860): 217.

55. "Calcutta in the Olden Time—Its People," *The Calcutta Review*, vol. 35 (1860): 217.

56. See, for instance, the files on Magh Borderers and Marauders, India Office Records, IOR/F/4, Oriental and India Office Collections, British Library.

57. On this theme, see Bayly, *Empire and Information*; and Stoler, *Along the Archival Grain*.

58. *Philosophical Transactions Giving Some Account of the Present Undertakings, Studies, and Labours of the Ingenious, in Many Considerable Parts of the World*, 53:132.

59. *Philosophical Transactions Giving Some Account of the Present Undertakings, Studies, and Labours of the Ingenious, in Many Considerable Parts of the World*, 53:137.

60. *Philosophical Transactions Giving Some Account of the Present Undertakings, Studies, and Labours of the Ingenious, in Many Considerable Parts of the World*, 53:138.

61. *Philosophical Transactions Giving Some Account of the Present Undertakings, Studies, and Labours of the Ingenious, in Many Considerable Parts of the World*, 53:132.

62. Halhed, *A Code of Gentoo Laws*. On Halhed, see Rocher, *Orientalism, Poetry, and Millenium*. Also see Ernst, "Muslim Studies of Hinduism?," 187–95; Ernst, *Refractions of Islam in India*, 249–60; and Raj, *Relocating Modern Science*, 95–138.

63. *Asiatick Researches: or, Transactions of the Society Instituted in Bengal for Inquiring into the History and Antiquities, the Arts, Sciences, and Literature, of Asia*, vol. 1 (1788).

64. Raj, *Relocating Modern Science*, 125–26.

65. Jones, trans., *Al Sirajiyya*; Jones, trans., *The Institutes of Hindu Law*.

66. Raj, *Relocating Modern Science*, 130.

67. Jones, "On the Hindus," in *The Works of Sir William Jones*, 3:46.

68. Lopez, *From Stone to Flesh*, 150, 159–60.

69. On John Murray, see d'Hubert, "A Persian Account of the Religious Customs of the Magh (Arakanese) from Early Colonial Bengal"; d'Hubert, "Bayan-i 'ibadat-i mukh-ha ba-nam-i Takadiba"; and Herbert, "The Making of a Collection," 62.

70. Magh Manuscripts, Add. Mss. 12253–58, Oriental and India Office Collections: John Murray Collection, British Library. See also Herbert, "The Making of a Collection"; Lammerts, "The Murray Manuscripts and Buddhist Dhammasattha Literature Transmitted in Chittagong and Arakan."

71. Murray's Persian manuscripts were acquired for the Prussian Royal Library in 1829. See Pertsch, *Die Handschriften-Verzeichnisse der Königlichen Bibliothek zu Berlin*; d'Hubert, "A Persian Account of the Religious Customs of the Magh (Arakanese) from Early Colonial Bengal"; and d'Hubert, "Bayan-i 'ibadat-i mukh-ha ba-nam-i Takadiba."

72. I am grateful to Thibaut d'Hubert for making the draft and edited manuscripts of Shah 'Azizallah's travel account available to me. See Sayyid Shah 'Azizallah, "Safarnama," Ms. Orient. quart. 252–53 (1784–90), Orientabteilung–Persischen Handschriften: John Murray MacGregor Collection, Staatsbibliothek, Berlin. See also Pertsch, *Die Handschriften-Verzeichnisse der Königlichen Bibliothek zu Berlin*, 379–80.

73. See Sayyid Shah 'Azizallah, "Safarnama," Ms. Orient. fol. 281 (1789), Orientabteilung–Persischen Handschriften: John Murray MacGregor Collection,

Staatsbibliothek, Berlin; and Pertsch, *Die Handschriften-Verzeichnisse der Königlichen Bibliothek zu Berlin*, 52–53.

74. Pertsch, *Die Handschriften-Verzeichnisse der Königlichen Bibliothek zu Berlin*, passim; d'Hubert, "A Persian Account of the Religious Customs of the Magh (Arakanese) from Early Colonial Bengal"; d'Hubert, "Bayan-i 'ibadat-i mukh-ha ba-nam-i Takadiba."

75. Mir Sadiq 'Ali, "Kitab-i Buddha Thakur," Ms. Orient. fol. 179 (1779), fol. 251r, Orientabteilung–Persischen Handschriften: John Murray MacGregor Collection, Staatsbibliothek, Berlin; Pertsch, *Die Handschriften-Verzeichnisse der Königlichen Bibliothek zu Berlin*, 1039–41.

76. "Purnindu," Ms. Orient. fol. 255 (1781), fol. 214, Orientabteilung–Persischen Handschriften: John Murray MacGregor Collection, Staatsbibliothek, Berlin. Also see, Pertsch, *Die Handschriften-Verzeichnisse der Königlichen Bibliothek zu Berlin*, 1042–43.

77. Buchanan, "Journal of Progress and Observations during the Continuance of the Deputation from Bengal to Ava," 172, 176, Ms. Eur. C 13, Oriental and India Office Collections, British Library.

78. Shah 'Azizullah Bukhari Qalandar, "Sual-i ayin va ravaj-i qawm-i Makh va javab-i an," Ms. Orient. fol. 281 (1789), fols. 125v, 128v, Orientabteilung–Persischen Handschriften: John Murray MacGregor Collection, Staatsbibliothek, Berlin.

79. Shah 'Azizullah Bukhari Qalandar, fol. 125v.

80. Shah 'Azizullah Bukhari Qalandar, fol. 126v.

81. Shah 'Azizullah Bukhari Qalandar, fol. 127v.

82. Shah 'Azizullah Bukhari Qalandar, fol. 128r.

83. Shah 'Azizullah Bukhari Qalandar, "Sual-i ayin va ravaj-i qawm-i Makh va javab-i an." Also see Pertsch, *Die Handschriften-Verzeichnisse der Königlichen Bibliothek zu Berlin*, 52–55.

84. Shah 'Azizullah Bukhari Qalandar, fol. 131r.

85. Shah 'Azizullah Bukhari Qalandar, fol. 125r.

86. Shah 'Azizullah Bukhari Qalandar, fols. 125r, 131v.

87. Mir Sadiq 'Ali, "Kitab-i Buddha Thakur," Ms. Orient. fol. 179 (1779), fol. 65v, Orientabteilung–Persischen Handschriften: John Murray MacGregor Collection, Staatsbibliothek, Berlin.

88. Mir Sadiq 'Ali, fol. 66v.

89. Mir Sadiq 'Ali, fols. 67v–67r.

90. Shah 'Azizullah Bukhari Qalandar, "Sual-i ayin va ravaj-i qawm-i Makh va javab-i an," Ms. Orient. fol. 281 (1789), fol. 126r.

91. Shah 'Azizullah Bukhari Qalandar, fol. 126r.

92. Shah 'Azizullah Bukhari Qalandar, fol. 129r.

93. Shah 'Azizullah Bukhari Qalandar, fol. 129r.

94. Shah 'Azizullah Bukhari Qalandar, fol. 129v.

95. Shah 'Azizullah Bukhari Qalandar, fol. 127v.

96. Shah 'Azizullah Bukhari Qalandar, fol. 127v.

97. Shah 'Azizullah Bukhari Qalandar, fol. 128v.

98. Shah 'Azizullah Bukhari Qalandar, fol. 130r.

99. Shah 'Azizullah Bukhari Qalandar, fol. 130v. For accounts of Buddhist cosmographies of the world and its parts prevalent in Burma at the time, see Buchanan Hamilton, "On the Religion and Literature of the Burmas"; Sangermano, *The Burmese Empire*, 4–24; Hardy, *A Manual of Buddhism in Its Modern Development*, 1–35; and Hardy, *The Legends and Theories of the Buddhists Compared with History and Science*, 80–96. Also see Bigandet, *The Life or Legend of Gaudama*.

100. Mir Sadiq 'Ali, "Kitab-i Buddha Thakur," Ms. Orient. fol. 179 (1779), fol. 96r.

101. Mir Sadiq 'Ali, fols. 109v–109r.

102. Mir Sadiq 'Ali, "Persian-Maghi Dictionary," Add. 12266 (ca. 1790), Oriental and India Office Collections: John Murray Collection, British Library.

103. Mir Sadiq 'Ali, "Persian-Maghi Dictionary."

104. Shah 'Azizallah Bukhari Qalandar, "Kitab-i kayfiyat-i pansad·paydayish-i Buddha Thakur az zaban-i Buddha Thakur dar Maki bud tarjuma bi Farsi shud, dar Maki nam-i Sapapuram," Ms. Orient. fol. 247 (ca. 1790), Orientabteilung–Persischen Handschriften: John Murray MacGregor Collection, Staatsbibliothek, Berlin.

105. On the Vessantara jataka, see Collins, ed., *Readings of the Vessantara Jataka*. For an English translation from the Pali text of the Vessantara jataka, see Cowell and Rouse, trans., *The Jataka or Stories of the Buddha's Former Births*, 246–305.

106. Shah 'Azizallah Bukhari Qalandar, "Kitab-i kayfiyat-i pansad paydayish-i Buddha Thakur," Ms. Orient. fol. 247 (ca. 1790), fols. 1r–2v.

107. The Vesssantara jataka, followed by a glossary of pertinent Pali and Persian terms, appears on folios 7v–46v of Shah 'Azizallah Bukhari Qalandar, "Kitab-i kayfiyat-i pansad paydayish-i Buddha Thakur."

108. Shah 'Abd al-'Aziz Bukhari Qalandar, "Tashrih al-ashjar," Ms. Orient. fol. 171 (1792), fol. 108b, Orientabteilung–Persischen Handschriften: John Murray MacGregor Collection, Staatsbibliothek, Berlin.

109. On the history of Mughal animals, see Trautmann, *Elephants and Kings*.

110. On numismatic analysis of the early modern royal Arakanese title Sahib-i Fil-i Safid, see d'Hubert, "The Lord of the Elephant."

111. Shah 'Azizallah Bukhari Qalandar, "Kitab-i kayfiyat-i pansad paydayish-i Buddha Thakur," Ms. Orient. fol. 247 (1790), fol. 128r. The tale of the Buddha's previous incarnation as a raja of elephants appears in folios 128r–132r. The tale is recounted and translated into English in Francis and Thomas, *Jataka Tales*, 395–409. It is also referenced in Pal, *Elephants and Ivories in South Asia*, 33–34.

112. Shah 'Azizallah Bukhari Qalandar, "Kitab-i kayfiyat-i pansad paydayish-i Buddha Thakur," Ms. Orient. fol. 247 (ca. 1790), fols. 128r–132r.

113. Shah 'Azizullah Bukhari Qalandar, "Sual-i ayin va ravaj-i qawm-i Makh va javab-i an," Ms. Orient. fol. 281 (1789), fols. 127r–28v.

114. Shah 'Azizullah Bukhari Qalandar, "Kitab-i kayfiyat-i pansad paydayish-i Buddha Thakur," Ms. Orient. fol. 247 (ca. 1790), passim, but see for instance, fols. 63r, 65r, 73r, 123v, 125r.

115. Shah 'Azizullah Bukhari Qalandar, passim, but see for instance, fols. 80v, 83v, 91v, 100r, 104v, 105v, 108r, 116r, 123r, 124v, 127v, 136r, 148v.

116. Shah 'Azizullah Bukhari Qalandar, fols. 76v–77v.

117. Shah 'Azizullah Bukhari Qalandar, fol. 161r.

118. Shah 'Azizullah Bukhari Qalandar, fol. 163r.

## EPILOGUE

1. Crawfurd, *Journal of an Embassy from the Governor-General of India to the Court of Ava*, 109, 344

2. See the description of "Pegu" in Zayn al-Abidin Shirvani, *Bustan al-Sayyahah*, 182–83; and the description of "Barma" in Farhad Mirza Mu'tamad al-Dawla, *Jam-i Jam*. For a Qajar travel account to India, Kashmir, and Burma from the 1870s, see Fazlullah Husayni, "Safarnama-yi Hind, Kashmir u Barma," 709–81.

3. "Jazira-yi Andaman," *Ruznama-yi Iran*, 3 Sha'ban 1288 Hijri [October 18, 1871], Tehran, no. 47, 4, Near East Periodicals Collection, Firestone Library, Princeton University. I thank Farzin Vejdani for bringing these references to the Bumese Empire in late-Qajar-era newsprint to my attention.

4. See, for instance, "Surat-i maktubi az shahr-i Rangoon," *Farhang*, 20 Rajab 1298 Hijri [June 18, 1881], Isfahan, no. 103, 3; and "Az Bandar-i Rangoon," *Farhang*, 9 Jamadi al-Akhar 1299 [April 27, 1882], Isfahan, no. 148, 2, both in the Near East Periodicals Collection, Firestone Library, Princeton University.

5. "Maktubi az Mandalay pay-i takht-i dawlat-i Barma," *Farhang*, 14 Rabi' al-Avval 1302 [January 1, 1885], Isfahan, no. 288, 1-2, Near East Periodicals Collection, Firestone Library, Princeton University.

6. See, for instance, Nazir Ahmad Sahib Barelvi, *Vaqa'at-i Barhama*.

7. On the architectural traces of Mughal Street, see Henderson and Webster, *Yangon Echoes*. On Islam in colonial Burma, see Yegar, *The Muslims of Burma*; and Green, "Buddhism, Islam and the Religious Economy of Colonial Burma."

8. Inscription at the tomb of Hazrat-i Sayyid Muhammad Sharif Abid Shah Husayni, Amarapura, Myanmar. I am grateful to Ei Phyu Theint for the English translation of the Burmese script.

9. Myint U, *The Making of Modern Burma*; Tun, ed., *The Royal Orders of Burma, A.D. 1598–1885*, November 17, 1807, December 16, 1807, 6:101, 115.

10. Tun, *The Royal Orders of Burma, A.D. 1598–1885*, November 17, 1807, 6:101.

11. Tun, December 16, 1807, 6:115. The Muslim saint seems to have carried out his duties earnestly. In a strange case from 1806 recorded in *The Royal Orders of Burma*, 'Abid Shah Husayni alleged "that some foreigners were found playing a forbidden game of cards," and following an investigation an order was given to "execute the foreigners Mirzam, Nga Pu, and Piduraman." Tun, March 18 and 29, 1806, 5:212, 218.

12. On this theme of the genealogical landscape of Sufi graves and tombs, and their destruction, see Ho, *The Graves of Tarim*.

13. Amitav Ghosh has noted the symmetry between the temples and the hills, between "built form and landscape," while approaching Mrauk U, referring to the monuments as "forests of stone." Ghosh, *The Great Derangement*, 81–82.

14. On the Santikan Mosque, see Gutman, *Burma's Lost Kingdoms*, 135. According to a Burmese guide to Mrauk U published in 1992, the Santikan Mosque was still standing. See Khine, *A Guide to Mrauk-U*, 76. However, a different, updated guide book written five years later, in 1997, makes no mention of the mosque or the history of the presence of Muslims in Mrauk U. See Zan, *The Golden Mrauk-U*.

15. Forchhammer, *Report on the Antiquities of Arakan*, 39.

16. On the history and dispossession of the Rohingya people in Myanmar, see Yegar, *The Muslims of Burma*; Defert, *Le Rohingya de Birmanie*; Imtiaz Ahmed, *The Plight of the Stateless Rohingyas*; Ibrahim, *The Rohingyas*; and Ware and Laoutides, *Myanmar's "Rohingya" Conflict*.

17. Forchhammer, *Report on the Antiquities of Arakan*, 63.

18. Forchhammer, 60–61.

19. Temple, "A Burmese Saint," 575.

20. Forchhammer, *Report on the Antiquities of Arakan*, 60.

21. Forchhammer, 62.

# BIBLIOGRAPHY

## ARCHIVES

### British Library

*Oriental and India Office Collections*
Buchanan, Francis. "Journal of Progress and Observations during the Continuance of the Deputation from Bengal to Ava in 1795 in the Dominions of the Barma Monarch, by Dr. F. Buchanan." Ms. Eur 13 (1795).

Magh Borderers and Marauders. India Office Records, IOR/F/4 (1794–1815).

Mir 'Abd al-Latif Khan Shushtari. "Tuhfat al-'alam" [Rarity of the world]. Add. 23533 (1801).

Mirza Abu Talib Khan Isfahani. "Lubb al-siyar va jahan numa" [Edge of travels and view of the world]. Or. 1871 (1793).

———. "Masir-i Talibi fi balad-i Afranji" [Book of travels for learning in the lands of the Franks]. Add. 8145–47 (1806).

Mirza I'tisam al-Din. "Shigarfnama-yi vilayat" [Wonder book of provinces]. Or. 200 (1812).

Qazi Ghulam Qasim Mihri. "Manzumat" [Poems]. Add. 26172 (1792).

Rafi' ud-Din Ibrahim bin Nur ud-Din Tawfiq Shirazi. "Tazkirat al-muluk" [Biographies of kings]. Add. 23883 (1611).

Symes, Michael. Correspondence with and records of Captain Symes, Agent to the Court of Ava. India Office Records, IOR/L/PS/19/56 (1795–96).

*Oriental and India Office Collections: John Murray Collection*
Magh Manuscripts. Pali script palm leaf manuscripts with wooden coverboards and titles in Persian. Add. 12253–58 (ca. 1780–1800).

Mir Sadiq 'Ali. "Persian-Maghi Dictionary." Add. 12266 (ca. 1790).

Miscellaneous Papers. Add. 19502–4 (1788–1796).

*Oriental Manuscripts: Sloane Manuscripts Collection*
Persian decree from Raja Chandrawizaya of Arakan to Khwajeh George in Chennaipattan. Ms. 3259 (1728).
Persian letter from Arakan to the Grand Merchant George in Chennaipattan. Ms. 3260 (1728).


*Princeton University, Firestone Library*

*Islamic Manuscripts Collection*
Zakariya ibn Muhammad Qazvini. "'Aja'ib al-makhluqat wa ghara'ib al-mawjudat" [The wonders of creation and the strange things existing], India, ca. 1168 Hijri (1755).


*Near East Periodicals Collection*
"Jazira-yi Andaman" [Andaman Islands], *Ruznama-yi Iran,* 3 Sha'ban 1288 Hijri [October 18, 1871], Tehran, no. 47, 4.
"Maktubi az Mandalay pay-i takht-i dawlat-i Burma" [A letter from Mandalay the royal seat of the empire of Burma], *Farhang,* 14 Rabi' al-Avval 1302 [January 1, 1885], Isfahan, no. 288, 1–2.
"Az Bandar-i Rangoon" [From the Port of Rangoon], *Farhang,* 9 Jamadi al-Akhar 1299 [April 27, 1882], Isfahan, no. 148, 2.
"Surat-i maktubi az shahr-i Rangoon" [A letter written from the city of Rangoon] *Farhang,* 20 Rajab 1298 Hijri [June 18, 1881], Isfahan, no. 103, 3.


*Staatsbibliothek zu Berlin*

*Orientabteilung–Persischen Handschriften: John Murray MacGregor Collection*
Mir Sadiq 'Ali. "Kitab-i Buddha Thakur" [Book of the Lord Buddha]. Ms. Orient. fol. 179 (1779).
"Purnindu" [The full moon]. Ms. Orient. fol. 255 (1781).
Sayyid Shah 'Azizallah. "Safarnama" [Book of travels]. Ms. Orient. fol. 281 (1789).
———. "Safarnama" [Book of travels] Ms. Orient. quart. 252–53 (1784–90).
Shah 'Azizullah Bukhari Qalandar. "Kitab-i kayfiyat-i pansad paydayish-i Buddha Thakur az zaban-i Buddha Thakur dar Maki bud tarjuma bi Farsi shud, dar Maki nam-i Sapapuram" [Book of the five hundred previous lives of Lord Buddha that was in the Magh language and was translated into Persian, called in Magh by the title Sapapuram]. Ms. Orient. fol. 247 (ca. 1790).
———. "Sual-i ayin va ravaj-i qawm-i Makh va javab-i an" [Questions and answers on the customs and religions of the Magh people]. Ms. Orient. fol. 281 (1789).
———. "Tashrih al-ashjar" [A description of trees]. Ms. Orient. fol. 171 (1792).

'Abd al-Husayn Nava'i, ed. *Shah 'Abbas: Majmu'a-yi Asnad va Mukatibat-i Tarikhi Hamrah ba Yaddashtha-yi Tafsili.* 2 vols. Tehran: Intisharat-i Bunyad-i Farhang-i Iran, 1973.

———, ed. *Shah Isma'il Safavi: Asnad va Mukatibat-i Tarikhi Hamrah ba Yaddashtha-yi Tafsili.* Tehran: Intesharat-i Bunyad-i Farhang-i Iran, 1969.

———, ed. *Shah Tahmasp Safavi: Majmu'a-yi Asnad va Mukatibat-i Tarikhi Hamrah ba Yaddashtha-yi Tafsili.* Tehran: Intesharat-i Bunyad-i Farhang-i Iran, 1971.

Abu'l-Fazl ibn Mubarak. *The Ain i Akbari.* Trans. H. Blochman. 2 vols. Calcutta, 1867–73.

———. *The Akbar Nama of Abu-l-Fazl: History of the Reign of Akbar Including an Account of His Predecessors.* Trans. H. Beveridge. 2 vols. Calcutta: Asiatic Society of Bengal, 1902.

———. *The History of Akbar.* Trans. Wheeler M. Thackston. 5 vols. Cambridge, MA: Harvard University Press, 2015–19.

Alexander, James Edward, trans. *Shigurf Namah I Velaët; or, Excellent Intelligence Concerning Europe: Being the Travels of Mirza Itesa Modeen in Great Britain and France.* London: Parbury, Allen, and Company, 1827.

Begley, W. E., and Z. A. Desai, eds. and trans. *The Shah Jahan Nama of 'Inayat Khan: An Abridged History of the Mughal Emperor Shah Jahan, Compiled by His Royal Librarian.* New Delhi: Oxford University Press, 1990.

Belfour, F. C., trans. *The Life of Sheikh Mohammed Ali Hazin: Written by Himself, Edited from Two Persian Manuscripts, and Noted with Their Various Readings.* London, 1831.

Bigandet, P. *The Life or Legend of Gaudama, the Budha of the Burmese, with Annotations: The Ways to Neibban and Notice on the Phongyies or Burmese Monks.* Rangoon: American Mission Press, 1866.

Brown, C. C., trans. *Sejarah Melayu; or, Malay Annals.* Kuala Lumpur: Oxford University Press, 1970.

Buchanan Hamilton, Francis. "Account of a Map by a Slave of the Heir-apparent of Ava." *Edinburgh Philosophical Journal, Exhibiting a View of the Progress of Discovery in Natural Philosophy, Chemistry, Natural History, Practical Mechanics, Geography, Navigation, Statistics, Antiquities, and the Fine and Useful Arts,* vol. 6 (1822): 270–73.

———. "Account of a Map of the Countries Subject to the King of Ava, Drawn by a Slave of the King's Eldest Son." *Edinburgh Philosophical Journal, Exhibiting a View of the Progress of Discovery in Natural Philosophy, Chemistry, Natural History, Practical Mechanics, Geography, Navigation, Statistics, Antiquities, and the Fine and Useful Arts,* vol. 2 (1820): 262–71.

———. "Account of a Map of the Country between the Erawadi and Khiaenduaen Rivers." *Edinburgh Philosophical Journal, Exhibiting a View of the Progress of Discovery in Natural Philosophy, Chemistry, Natural History, Practical Mechanics,*

*Geography, Navigation, Statistics, Antiquities, and the Fine and Useful Arts,* vol. 6 (1822): 107–11.

———. "Account of a Map of the Country North from Ava." *Edinburgh Philosophical Journal, Exhibiting a View of the Progress of Discovery in Natural Philosophy, Chemistry, Natural History, Practical Mechanics, Geography, Navigation, Statistics, Antiquities, and the Fine and Useful Arts,* vol. 4 (1821): 76–87.

———. "Account of the Frontier between Ava and the Part of Bengal Adjacent to the Karnapuli River." *Edinburgh Journal of Science Exhibiting a View of the Progress of Discovery in Natural Philosophy, Chemistry, Mineralogy, Geology, Botany, Zoology, Comparative Anatomy, Practical Mechanics, Geography, Navigation, Statistics, Antiquities, and the Fine and Useful Arts,* vol. 3 (1826): 32–44.

———. "Account of Two Maps of Zaenmae or Yangoma." *Edinburgh Philosophical Journal, Exhibiting a View of the Progress of Discovery in Natural Philosophy, Chemistry, Natural History, Practical Mechanics, Geography, Navigation, Statistics, Antiquities, and the Fine and Useful Arts,* vol. 10 (1824): 59–67.

———. "A Comparative Vocabulary of Some of the Languages Spoken in the Burma Empire." *Asiatick Researches; or, Transactions of the Society Instituted in Bengal, for Enquiring into the History and Antiquities, the Arts, Sciences, and Literature, of Asia,* vol. 5 (1800): 219–40.

———. "On the Religion and Literature of the Burmas." *Asiatick Researches; or, Transactions of the Society Instituted in Bengal, for Enquiring into the History and Antiquities, the Arts, Sciences, and Literature, of Asia,* vol. 6 (1801): 163–308.

"Calcutta in the Olden Time—Its People," *The Calcutta Review* vol. 35 (1860): 164–227.

Cowell, E. B., and W. H. D. Rouse, trans. *The Jataka; or, Stories of the Buddha's Former Births. Translated from the Pali by Various Hands.* Cambridge: Cambridge University Press, 1907.

Cox, Hiram. *Journal of a Residence in the Burmhàn Empire, and More Particularly at the Court of Amarapoorah.* London: John Warren, Old Bond Street, 1821.

Crawfurd, John. *Journal of an Embassy from the Governor-General of India to the Court of Ava, in the Year 1827.* London: Henry Colburn, 1829.

Dankoff, Robert, and Sooyong Kim, eds. and trans. *An Ottoman Traveller: Selections from the Book of Travels of Evliya Çelebi.* London: Eland, 2011.

Dillwyn, Lewis Weston. *A Descriptive Catalogue of Recent Shells, Arranged According to the Linnaean Method.* Vols. 1–2. London: John and Arthur Arch, 1817.

Elliott, H. M., and John Dowson, eds. *The History of India as Told by Its Own Historians: The Muhammadan Period.* Vol. 6. London: Trübner and Company, 1875.

Farhad Mirza Mu'tamad al-Dawla. *Jam-i Jam.* Tehran: Chapkhana-yi Ustad 'Allah Quli Khan Qajar, 1856.

Fazlullah Husayni. "Safarnama-yi Hind, Kashmir va Barma (Guzarish-i Safar-i Navisanda bi Hind va Barma ta Salha-yi 1290–1294 Q.)." Ed. Firishta Kushki. *Payam-i Baharistan* (Fall 2011): 709–81.

Ferishta, Mahomed Kasim. *History of the Rise of Mahomedan Power in India till the Year A.D. 1612*. Trans. John Briggs with the assistance of Mir Khairat 'Ali Khan Akbarabadi "Mushtaq." 4 vols. London: Longman, Rees, Orme, Brown, and Green, 1829.

Fontana, Nicolas. "On the Nicobar Islands and the Fruit of the Mellori." *Asiatick Researches; or, Transactions of the Society, Instituted in Bengal, for Inquiring in the History and Antiquities, the Arts, Sciences, and Literature of Asia*, vol. 3 (1794):149–62.

Forchhammer, Emil. *Report on the Antiquities of Arakan*. Rangoon: Superintendent Government Printing, 1891.

Ghulam Hussain Salim. *Riazu-s-Salatin (A History of Bengal)*. Trans. Abdus Salam. Delhi: Idarah-i Adabiyat-i Delli, 1903.

Haensel, John Gottfreid. *Letters on the Nicobar Islands, Their Natural Productions, and The Manners, Customs, and Superstitions of the Natives: With an Account of an Attempt Made by the Church of the United Brethren, to Convert Them to Christianity*. London, 1812.

Halhed, Nathaniel. *A Code of Gentoo Laws; or, Ordinations of the Pundits, from a Persian Translation, Made from the Original, Written in the Shanscrit Language*. London, 1776.

Hall, D. G. E., ed. *Michael Symes: Journal of His Second Embassy to the Court of Ava in 1802*. London: George Allen and Unwin, 1955.

Hamilton, Walter. *A Geographical, Statistical, and Historical Description of Hindostan and the Adjacent Countries*. Vol. 2. London: John Murray, 1820.

Hardy, R. Spence. *The Legends and Theories of the Buddhists Compared with History and Science: With Introductory Notices of the Life and System of Gotama Buddha*. London: Frederic Norgate, 1881.

———. *A Manual of Buddhism in Its Modern Development*. London: Partridge and Oakey, 1853.

Hunter, William. *A Concise Account of the Climate, Produce, Trade, Government, Manners of the Kingdom of Pegu, Interspersed with Remarks Moral and Political*. London: J. Sewell, Cornhill; and J. Debrett, Piccadilly, 1789.

Jones, Sir William., trans. *Al Sirajiyya; or, The Mohammedan Law of Inheritance*. Calcutta: Joseph Cooper, 1792.

———, trans. *The Institutes of Hindu Law; or, The Ordinances of Menu*. Calcutta: Order of the Government, 1793.

———. *The Works of Sir William Jones, with the Life of the Author*. Ed. Lord Teignmouth. 13 vols. London: John Stockdale and John Walker, 1807.

Judson, Ann H. *An Account of the American Baptist Mission to the Burman Empire, in a Series of Letters Addressed to a Gentleman in London*. London: Joseph Butterworth and Son, 1827.

Kirkpatrick, William, ed. *Select Letters of Tippoo Sultan to Various Public Functionaries: Including His Principal Military Commanders, Governors of Forts and Provinces, Diplomatic and Commercial Agents &c &c &c. Together with Some*

*Addressed to the Tributary Chieftains of Shanoor, Kurnool, and Cannanore, and Other Sundry Persons.* London: Black, Parry, and Kingsbury, 1811.

Leyden, John, trans. *Malay Annals: Translated from the Malay Language.* London: Longman, Hurst, Rees, Orme, and Brown, 1821.

Manrique, Sebastien. *Travels of Fray Sebastien Manrique, 1629–1643.* 2 vols. Trans. C. E. Luard and H. Hosten. Oxford: Hakluyt Society, 1927.

Mawe, John. *The Linnaean System of Conchology, Describing the Orders, Genera, and Species of Shells, Arranged into Divisions and Families.* London: Longman, Hurst, Rees, Orme, and Brown, 1823.

Mir 'Abd al-Latif Khan Shushtari. *Tuhfat al-'alam: Va risala-yi zayl al-tuhfah.* Bombay: Mirza Zinal Abideen Kermany, 1847.

———. *Tuhfat al-'alam va zayl al-tuhfa.* Ed. Samad Muvahhad. 1801. Tehran: Tahuri, 1984.

Mirsayyidov, J., ed. *Ayina-yi Iskandari.* Moscow: Khavar, 1977.

Mirza Abu Talib Khan. *Masir-i Talibi fi bilad-i Afranji.* Ed. Mirza Husayn 'Ali and Mir Qudrat 'Ali. Calcutta: Fort William College, 1812.

———. *Masir-i Talibi: Mushtamil bar Ahval-i Sayr-i Mirza Abu Talib Khan (The Travels of Mirza Aboo Talib Khan in the Persian Language).* Abridged by David MacFarlane. Calcutta: Baptist Mission Press, 1836.

———. *Masir-i Talibi ya Safarnama-yi Mirza Abu Talib Khan.* Ed. Husayn Khadivjam. Tehran: Shirkat-i Sahami, 1973.

Mirza Sheikh I'tesamuddin. *The Wonders of Vilayet: Being the Memoir, Originally in Persian, of a Visit to France and Britain.* Trans. Kaiser Haq. Leeds: Peepal Tree, 2002.

Maulavi Kabir al-Din Ahmad, ed. *The Muntakhab al-Lubab of Khafi Khan.* 2 parts. Calcutta: College Press, 1869–74.

Modarressi Tabataba'i, Hossein, ed. *Farmanha-yi Turkmanan-i Qara Quyunlu va Aq Quyunlu.* Qum: Chapkhana-yi Hikmat, 1973.

Moses, Johannes, and Father Ignazio de Brito. *Pawtugi Yazawin* [History of the Portuguese]. Rangoon: Sun Press, 1918.

Muhammad 'Ali Hazin Lahiji. *Tarikh va safarnama-yi Hazin.* Ed. 'Ali Davvani. Tehran: Markaz-i Asnad, 1996.

Muhammad Ibrahim Rabi ibn Muhammad Ibrahim. *Safina-yi Sulaymani: Safarnama-yi safir-i Iran bih Siyam.* Ed. 'Abbas Faruqi. Tehran: University of Tehran, 1977.

———. *The Ship of Sulaimān.* Trans. John O'Kane. London: Routledge and Kegan Paul, 1972.

Muhammad Kazim ibn-i Muhammad Amin Munshi. *The Alamgir Namah.* Ed. Mawlawis Khadim Husain and Abd al-Hai. Calcutta: College Press, 1868.

Muhammad Qasim Hindu Shah Astarabadi. *Tarikh-i Firishta.* Ed. Muhammad Riza Nasiri. 2 vols. Tehran: Anjuman-i Asar va Mafakhir-i Farhangi, 2009–11.

National Archives of India. *Calendar of Persian Correspondence: Being Letters, Referring Mainly to Affairs in Bengal, Which Passed between Some of the Company's Servants and Indian Rulers and Notables.* Vols. 8–11 (1788–95). New Delhi: Government of India Press, 1940–69.

Nazir Ahmad Sahib Barelvi. *Vaqa'at-i Barhama: Jis Min Mulk-i Barhama.* Lahore: Matba'a Khadimulta'lim, 1901.

*Papers Relating to East India Affairs: Discussions with the Burmese Government.* London: House of Commons, 1825.

*Records of Fort St. George: Diary and Consultation Book of 1707.* Madras: Government Press, 1929.

*Records of Fort St. George: Diary and Consultation Book of 1732.* Madras: Government Press, 1930.

*Records of Fort St. George: Proceedings of the Mayor's Court, 1728.* Madras: Government Press, 1952.

*Records of Fort St. George: Proceedings of the Mayor's Court Minutes, 1736–1737.* Vol. 3. Madras: Government Press, 1937.

Sangermano, Father. *The Burmese Empire a Hundred Years Ago.* Westminster: Archibald Constable and Company, 1893.

Scott, James George. *Burma: A Handbook of Practical Information.* London: Alexander Moring, 1906.

———. *Burma: From the Earliest Times to the Present Day.* London: T. Fisher Unwin, 1924.

Shway Yoe (pseud. for James George Scott). *The Burman: His Life and Notions.* London, 1882.

Southgate, Minoo, trans. *Iskandarnamah.* New York: Columbia University Press, 1978.

Stewart, Charles. *The History of Bengal: From the First Mohammedan Invasion until the Virtual Conquest of That Country by the English.* London: Black, Parry, and Company, 1813.

———, ed. and trans. *Original Persian Letters, and Other Documents, with Facsimiles.* London, 1825.

———, trans. *Travels of Mirza Abu Taleb Khan in Asia, Africa, and Europe during the Years 1799, 1800, 1801, 1802, and 1803.* 3 vols. London: Longman, Hurst, Rees, Orme, and Brown, 1810.

Symes, Michael. *An Account of an Embassy to the Kingdom of Ava, Sent by the Governor-General of India in the Year 1795.* London: W. Bulmer and Company, 1800.

Thackston, Wheeler M., trans. *The Jahangirnama: Memoirs of Jahangir, Emperor of India.* Oxford: Oxford University Press, 1999.

———, ed. and trans. *Nasir-i Khusraw's Book of Travels.* Albany: SUNY Press, 1986.

Temple, Richard C. "A Burmese Saint." *Journal of the Royal Asiatic Society of Great Britain and Ireland* (1894): 565–66.

———. *Census of India.* Vol. 3, *The Andaman and Nicobar Islands.* Calcutta: Superintendent Government Printing, 1908.

Tun, Than, ed. *The Royal Orders of Burma, A.D. 1598–1885.* 10 vols. Kyoto: Center for Southeast Asian Studies, 1987.

Wallich, Nathaniel. *Plantae asiaticae rariores.* Vol. 3. London: Treuttel and Wurtz, 1832.

Yule, Henry. *Narrative of the Mission Sent by the Governor-General of India to the Court of Ava in 1855, with Notices of the Country, Government, and People*. London: Smith, Elder, and Company, 1858.

Yule, Henry, and A. C. Burnell, eds. *Hobson-Jobson: A Glossary of Colloquial Anglo-Indian Words and Phrases, and of Kindred Terms, Etymological, Historical, Geographical and Discursive*. London, 1886.

Zakariya Qazvini (Zakariya ibn Muhammad Qazvini). *'Aja'ib al-makhluqat wa ghara'ib al-mawjudat*. Ed. Ferdinand Wüstenfeld as *Zakarija Ben Muhammed Ben Mahmud el-Cazwini's Kosmographie*, 2 vols. Göttingen, 1848–49.

———. *The Book of Wonders of India: Mainland, Sea, and Islands*. Trans. Greville Stewart Parker Freeman-Grenville. London: East-West Publications, 1981.

Zayn al-Abidin Shirvani. *Bustan al-Sayyahah*. Tehran: Karkhana-yi Habib Allah, 1897.

### SECONDARY MATERIALS

Afshar, Iraj. "Persian Travelogues: A Description and Bibliography." In *Society and Culture in Qajar Iran: Studies in Honor of Hafez Farmayan*,145–62. Costa Mesa, CA: Mazda, 2002.

———. "Safarnamaha-yi Farsi ta Ruzgar-i Istiqrar-i Mashrutiyat." In *Jashnama-yi Ustad Zabih Allah Safa*, ed. Muhammad Turabi, 45–82. Tehran: Shahhab, 1998.

Ahmed, Imtiaz. *The Plight of the Stateless Rohingyas: Responses of the State, Society and the International Community*. Dhaka: University Press, 2010.

Alam, Muzaffar, and Sanjay Subrahmanyam. *Indo-Persian Travels in the Age of Discoveries, 1400–1800*. Cambridge: Cambridge University Press, 2007.

———. *The Mughal State, 1526–1750*. Delhi: Oxford University Press, 1998.

———. *Writing the Mughal World: Studies on Culture and Politics*. New York: Columbia University Press, 2012.

Alam, Muzaffar, and Seema Alavi, eds. and trans. *A European Experience of the Mughal Orient: The I'jāz-i Arsalānī (Persian Letters, 1773–1779) of Antoine-Louis Henri Polier*. Delhi: Oxford University Press, 2001.

Alavi, Seema. *Muslim Cosmopolitanism in the Age of Empire*. Cambridge, MA: Harvard University Press, 2015.Ali, Daud, and Emma J. Flatt, eds. *Garden and Landscape Practices in Pre-colonial India: Histories from the Deccan*. London: Routledge, 2012.

Allsen, Thomas T. *The Royal Hunt in Eurasian History*. Philadelphia: University of Pennsylvania Press, 2006.

Amanat, Abbas. *Pivot of the Universe: Nasir al-Din Shah Qajar and the Iranian Monarchy, 1831–1896*. Berkeley: University of California Press, 1997.

———. "Through the Persian Eye: Anglophilia and Anglophobia in Modern Iranian History." In Abbas Amanat and Farzin Vejdani, eds., *Iran Facing Others: Identity Boundaries in a Historical Perspective*, 127–52. New York: Palgrave Macmillan, 2012.

Amanat, Abbas, and Assef Ashraf, eds., *The Persianate World: Rethinking a Shared Space*. Leiden: Brill, 2018.

Amrith, Sunil S. *Crossing the Bay of Bengal: The Furies of Nature and the Fortunes of Migrants*. Cambridge, MA: Harvard University Press, 2013.

Anderson, Clare. *Subaltern Lives: Biographies of Colonialism in the Indian Ocean World*. Cambridge: Cambridge University Press, 2012.

Anderson, Ivan T. *The Dynasty of Abu: A History and Natural History of the Elephants and Their Relatives, Past and Present*. New York: Alfred Knopf, 1962.

Anderson, Jennifer. *Mahogany: The Costs of Luxury in Early America*. Cambridge, MA: Harvard University Press, 2012.

Arnold, David. *The Tropics and the Traveling Gaze: India, Landscape, and Science, 1800–1856*. Seattle: University of Washington Press, 2006.

Arnold, David, and Ramchandra Guha, eds. *Nature, Culture, Imperialism: Essays on the Environmental History of South Asia*. Delhi: Oxford University Press, 1997.

Aslanian, Sebouh. *From the Indian Ocean to the Mediterranean: The Global Trade Networks of Armenian Merchants from New Julfa*. Berkeley: University of California Press, 2011.

Aubin, Jean. "Archives Persanes Commentées 1: Note sur quelques documents Āq Qoyunlu." In *Mélanges Louis Massignon*, vol. 1, 123–47. Damascus: Institut Francais de Damas, 1956.

———. "Les persans au Siam sous le règne de Narai, 1656–1688." *Mare Luso-Indicum* 4 (1980): 95–126.

Aung, Maung Htin. *Epistles Written on the Eve of the Anglo-Burmese War, 1824*. The Hague: Martinus Nijhoff, 1967.

———. *A History of Burma*. New York: Columbia University Press, 1967.

Banerjee, Anil Chandra. *The Eastern Frontier of British India, 1784–1826*. Calcutta: Mukherjee and Company, 1964.

Bausani, Alessandro. *Le letterature del sud-est asiatico: Birmana, siamese, laotiana, cambogiana, viêtnamita, giavanese, malese-indonesiana, filippina*. Florence: Sansoni, 1970.

———. *Malesia: Poesie e leggende*. Milan: Nuova Accademia Editrice, 1963.

———. *Notes on the Structure of the Classical Malay Hikayat*. Trans. Lode Brakel. Clayton, Victoria: Monash University, Centre of Southeast Asian Studies, 1979.

———. "Note su una antologia inedita di versi mistici persiani con versione interlineare malese." *Annali dell'Istituto Orientale di Napoli* 18 (1968): 39–66.

———. "Un manoscritto persiano-malese di grammatica arabe del XVI secolo." *Annali dell'Istituto Orientale di Napoli* 19 (1969): 69–98.

Bayly, C. A. *Empire and Information: Intelligence Gathering and Social Communication in India, 1780–1870*. Cambridge: Cambridge University Press, 1996.

———. *Imperial Meridian: The British Empire and the World, 1780–1830*. London: Longman, 1989.

———. "Knowing the Country: Empire and Information in India." *Modern Asian Studies*, 27, no. 1 (1993): 3–43.

Berlekamp, Persis. *Wonder, Image, and Cosmos in Medieval Islam*. New Haven, CT: Yale University Press, 2011.

Bleichmar, Daniela. *Visible Empire: Botanical Expeditions and Visual Culture in the Hispanic Enlightenment*. Chicago: University of Chicago Press, 2012.

Britten, James. "Buchanan's Avan Plants." *Journal of Botany, British and Foreign* 40 (1902): 279–82.

Bryant, Raymond. *The Political Ecology of Forestry in Burma, 1824–1994*. Honolulu: University of Hawai'i Press, 1996.

Busse, Heribert. "Farmān." In *Encyclopaedia of Islam,* 2nd ed., vol. 2., 802–4. Leiden: Brill, 1965.

Carney, Judith, and Richard Nicholas Rosomoff. *In the Shadow of Slavery: Africa's Botanical Legacy in the Atlantic World*. Berkeley: University of California Press, 2009.

Charney, Michael. "Crisis and Reformation in a Maritime Kingdom of Southeast Asia: Forces of Instability and Political Disintegration in Western Burma (Arakan): 1603–1701." *Journal of the Economic and Social History of the Orient* 41, no. 2 (1998): 185–219.

———. "The Rise of a Mainland Trading State: Rakhaing under the Early Mrauk-U Kings, c. 1430–1603." *Journal of Burma Studies* 3, no. 1 (1998): 1–33.

———. "Where Jambudipa and Islamdom Converged: Religious Change and the Emergence of Buddhist Communalism in Early Modern Arakan (Fifteenth to Nineteenth Centuries)." PhD dissertation, University of Michigan, 1998.

Coedès, G. *Les états hindouisés d'Indochine et d'Indonésie*. 1948. Ed. Walter F. Vella and trans. Susan Brown Cowing as *The Indianized States of Southeast Asia*. Honolulu: University of Hawai'i Press, 1968.

Cohn, Bernard S. *Colonialism and Its Forms of Knowledge: The British in India*. Princeton, NJ: Princeton University Press, 1997.

Cole, Juan R. I. "Invisible Occidentalism: Eighteenth-Century Indo-Persian Constructions of the West." *Iranian Studies* 25, nos. 3–4 (1992): 3–16.

———. "Mirror of the World: Iranian 'Orientalism' in Early Nineteenth-Century India." *Critique* 8 (Spring 1996): 41–60.

Collins, Steven. *Nirvana: Concept, Imagery, Narrative*. Cambridge: Cambridge University Press, 2010.

———, ed. *Readings of the Vessantara Jataka*. Chicago: University of Chicago Press, 2016.

Collis, Maurice. *The Land of the Great Image: Being Experiences of Friar Manrique in Arakan*. London: Faber and Faber, 1943.

———. *She Was a Queen*. London: Faber and Faber, 1937.

Collis, M. S., and San Shwe Bu. "Arakan's Place in the Civilization of the Bay: A Study of Coinage and Foreign Relations." *Journal of the Burma Research Society* 15, no. 1 (1925): 34–52.

Dalrymple, William. *White Mughals: Love and Betrayal in Eighteenth-Century India*. London: Penguin, 2002.

Davis, Natalie Zemon. *Trickster Travels: A Sixteenth-Century Muslim Between Worlds.* New York: Hill and Wang, 2006.

Defert, Gabriel. *Le Rohingya de Birmanie: Arakanais, musulmans et apatrides.* Montreuil, France: Aux lieux d'être, 2007.

d'Hubert, Thibaut. "Bayan-i 'ibadat-i mukh-ha ba-nam-i Takadiba." In Fabrizio Speziale and Carl W. Ernst, eds., *Perso-Indica: An Analytical Survey of Persian Works on Indian Learned Traditions,* 1–6. Paris: Perso-Indica, 2013.

———. "India beyond the Ganges: Defining Arakanese Buddhism in Persianate Colonial Bengal." *Indian Economic and Social History Review* 56, no. 1 (2019): 1–31.

———. *In the Shade of the Golden Palace: Ālāol and Middle Bengali Poetics in Arakan.* Oxford: Oxford University Press, 2018.

———. "The Lord of the Elephant: Interpreting the Islamicate Epigraphic, Numismatic, and Literary Material from the Mrauk U Period of Arakan (c. 1430–1784)." *Journal of Burma Studies* 19, no. 2 (2015): 341–70.

———. "A Persian Account of the Religious Customs of the Magh (Arakanese) from Early Colonial Bengal." *Iranian Studies* 51, no. 6 (2018): 947–59.

d'Hubert, Thibaut, and Jacques P. Leider. "Traders and Poets at the Mrauk U Court: Commerce and Cultural Links in Seventeenth-Century Arakan." In Rila Mukherjee, ed., *Pelagic Passageways: The Northern Bay of Bengal before Colonialism,* 345–79. Delhi: Primus Books, 2011.

Digby, Simon. "Beyond the Ocean: Perceptions of Overseas in Indo-Persian Sources of the Mughal Period." *Studies in History* 15, no. 2 (1999): 247–60.

———. "An Eighteenth-Century Narrative of a Journey from Bengal to England: Munshi Ismail's New History." In *Urdu and Muslim South Asia: Studies in Honor of Ralph Russell,* 49–65. New Delhi: Oxford University Press, 1991.

———. *War-Horse and Elephant in the Delhi Sultanate: A Study of Military Supplies.* Oxford: Orient Monographs, 1971.

———. *Wonder-Tales of South Asia: Translated from Hindi, Urdu, Nepali, and Persian.* New Delhi: Oxford University Press, 2006.

Dijk, Wil O. *Seventeenth-Century Burma and the Dutch East India Company, 1634–1680.* Singapore: Singapore University Press, 2006.

Eaton, Richard M. *The Rise of Islam and the Bengal Frontier, 1204–1760.* Berkeley: University of California Press, 1993.

———. *A Social History of the Deccan, 1300–1761: Eight Indian Lives.* Cambridge: Cambridge University Press, 2008.

Eaton, Richard M., and Phillip B. Wagoner. *Power, Memory, Architecture: Contested Sites on India's Deccan Plateau, 1300–1600.* Delhi: Oxford University Press, 2014.

Ernst, Carl. "Muslim Studies of Hinduism? A Reconsideration of Arabic and Persian Translations from Indian Languages." *Iranian Studies* 36, no. 2 (2003): 173–95.

———. *Refractions of Islam in India: Situating Sufism and Yoga.* New Delhi: Sage, 2016.

Euben, Roxanne, *Journeys to the Other Shore: Muslim and Western Travelers in Search of Knowledge*. Princeton, NJ: Princeton University Press, 2008.

Feener, Michael. *Muslim Legal Thought in Modern Indonesia*. Cambridge: Cambridge University Press, 2007.

Feener, Michael, Patrick Daly, and Anthony Reid, eds. *Mapping the Acehnese Past*. Leiden: KITLV Press, 2011.

Feener, Michael, and Terenjit Sevea, eds. *Islamic Connections: Muslim Societies in South and Southeast Asia*. Singapore: ISEAS Press, 2009.

Ferrand, Gabriel, ed. *Relations de voyages et textes géographiques arabes, persans et turks relatifs à l'Extrême-Orient du VIIIᵉ au XVIIIᵉ siècles*. 2 vols. Paris: Ernest Leroux, 1913.

Fisher, Michael H. *Counterflows to Colonialism: Indian Travellers and Settlers in Britain, 1600–1857*. Delhi: Permanent Black, 2004.

———. "The Office of Akhbār Nawīs: The Transition from Mughal to British Forms" and other articles. *Modern Asian Studies* 27, no. 1 (1993).

———. *The Travels of Dean Mahomet: An Eighteenth-Century Journey through India*. Berkeley: University of California Press, 1997.

Formichi, Chiara, and Michael Feener, eds. *Shi'ism in Southeast Asia: 'Alid Piety and Sectarian Constructions*. London: Hurst and Company, 2015.

Fragner, Bert. *Die "Persophonie": Regionalitat, Identitat und Sprachkontakt in der Geschichte Asiens*. Berlin: Das Arabische Buch, 1999.

———. "Farmān." In *Enclyclopaedia Iranica*, vol. 9, 802–4. New York: Bibliotheca Persica, 1999.

Francis, H. T., and E. J. Thomas. *Jataka Tales*. Cambridge: Cambridge University Press, 1916.

Fraser-Lu, Sylvia. *Buddhist Art of Myanmar*. New Haven, CT: Yale University Press, 2015.

Gallop, Annabel Teh. *The Legacy of the Malay Letter*. London: British Library, 1994.

———. "Piagam Serampas: Malay Documents from Highland Jambi." In Dominik Bonatz, John Miksic, J. David Neidel, Mai Lin Tjoa-Bonatz, eds.; *Distant Tales: Archaeology and Ethnohistory in the Highlands of Sumatra*, 272–322. Newcastle: Cambridge Scholars Press, 2009.

Ghosh, Amitav. *The Great Derangement: Climate Change and the Unthinkable*. Chicago: University of Chicago Press, 2016.

———. "The Slave of MS. H. 6." *Subaltern Studies* 7 (1992): 157–220.

Gommans, Jos, and Jacques Leider, eds. *The Maritime Frontier of Burma: Exploring Political, Cultural, and Commercial Interaction in the Indian Ocean World, 1200–1800*. Leiden: KITLV Press, 2002.

Green, Nile. *Bombay Islam: The Religious Economy of the West Indian Ocean, 1840–1915*. Cambridge: Cambridge University Press, 2011.

———. "Buddhism, Islam and the Religious Economy of Colonial Burma." *Journal of Southeast Asian Studies* 46, no. 2 (2015): 175–204.

———. *The Love of Strangers: What Six Muslim Students Learned in Jane Austen's London*. Princeton, NJ: Princeton University Press, 2016.

———. *The Persianate World: The Frontiers of a Eurasian Lingua Franca.* Berkeley: University of California Press, 2019.

Grove, Richard H. *Green Imperialism: Colonial Expansion, Tropical Island Edens and the Origins of Environmentalism, 1600–1860.* Cambridge: Cambridge University Press, 1996.

Gutman, Pamela. *Burma's Lost Kingdoms: Splendours of Arakan.* Bangkok: Orchid Press, 2001.

Hall, D. G. E. *Burma.* London: Hutchinson University Library, 1960.

———. *Europe and Burma: A Study of European Relations with Burma to the Annexation of Thibaw's Kingdom, 1886.* London: Oxford University Press, 1945.

———. *A History of Southeast Asia.* London: Macmillan, 1955.

Harvey, G. E. *History of Burma from the Earliest Times to 10 March 1824, the Beginning of the British Conquest.* London: Longmans, Green, and Co., 1925.

———. *Outline of Burmese History.* Bombay: Longmans, Green, and Co., 1926.

Henderson, Virginia, and Tim Webster. *Yangon Echoes.* Bangkok: River Books, 2015.

Herbert, Patricia. "The Making of a Collection: Burmese Manuscripts in the British Library." *British Library Journal* 15, no. 1 (1989): 59–70.

Herzig, Edmund. "The Armenian Merchants of New Julfa, Isfahan: A Study in Pre-modern Asian Trade." DPhil. thesis, Oxford University, 1991.

Ho, Engseng. *The Graves of Tarim: Genealogy and Mobility across the Indian Ocean.* Berkeley: University of California Press, 2006.

Hodgson, Marshall G. S. *The Venture of Islam: Conscience and History in a World Civilization.* 3 vols. Chicago: University of Chicago Press, 1974–77.

Hughes, Julie E. *Animal Kingdoms: Hunting, the Environment, and Power in the Indian Princely States.* Cambridge, MA: Harvard University Press, 2013.

Hutton, Deborah. *Art of the Court of Bijapur.* Bloomington: University of Indiana Press, 2006.

Ibrahim, Azeem. *The Rohingyas: Inside Myanmar's Genocide.* London: Hurst and Company, 2018.

Islam, Riazul. *Indo-Persian Relations: A Study of the Political and Diplomatic Relations between the Mughul Empire and Iran.* Tehran: Iranian Culture Foundation, 1970.

Jasanoff, Maya. *Edge of Empire: Lives, Culture, and Conquest in the East, 1750–1850.* New York: Vintage, 2005.

Kabir, Humayun. *Mirza Abu Talib Khan.* Patna: Patna University, 1961.

Kelley, Theresa M. *Clandestine Marriage: Botany and Romantic Culture.* Baltimore: Johns Hopkins University Press, 2012.

Khan, Gulfishan. *Indian Muslim Perceptions of the West during the Eighteenth Century.* Karachi: Oxford University Press, 1998.

Khan, Yusuf Husain, ed. *Farmans and Sanads of the Deccan Sultans.* Hyderabad: The State Archives, 1963.

Khazeni, Arash. "Across the Black Sands and the Red: Travel Writing, Nature, and the Reclamation of the Eurasian Steppe Circa 1850." *International Journal of Middle East Studies* 42, no. 4 (2010): 591–614.

——. *Sky Blue Stone: The Turquoise Trade in World History*. Berkeley: University of California Press, 2014.

Khine, Tun Shwe. *A Guide to Mrauk-U: An Ancient City of Rakhine, Myanmar*. Yangon: Nine Nines Press, 1992.

Kia, Mana. "Accounting for Difference: A Comparative Look at the Autobiographical Travel Narratives of Muhammad 'Ali Hazin Lahiji and 'Abd al-Karim Kashmiri." *Journal of Persianate Studies* 2 (2009): 210–36.

——. "Imagining Iran before Nationalism: Geocultural Meanings of Land in Azar's *Atashkadeh*." In Kamran Scot Aghaie and Afshin Marashi, eds., *Rethinking Iranian Nationalism and Modernity*, 89–112. Austin: University of Texas Press, 2014.

——. "Limning the Land: Social Encounters and Historical Meaning in Early Nineteenth-Century Travelogues between Iran and India." In Roberta Micallef and Sunil Sharma, eds., *On the Wonders of Land and Sea: Persianate Travel Writing*, 44–67. Cambridge, MA: Ilex Foundation, 2013.

——. *Persianate Selves: Memories of Place and Origin Before Nationalism*. Stanford, CA: Stanford University Press, forthcoming.

Kia, Mana, and Afshin Marashi. "After the Persianate." *Comparative Studies of South Asia, Africa and the Middle East* 36, no. 3 (2016): 379–83.

Kinra, Rajeev. *Writing Self, Writing Empire: Chandar Bhan Brahman and the Cultural World of the Indo-Persian State Secretary*. Berkeley: University of California Press, 2015.

Laffan, Michael. *The Makings of Indonesian Islam: Orientalism and the Narration of a Sufi Past*. Princeton: Princeton University Press, 2011.

Lammerts, Christian. "The Murray Manuscripts and Buddhist Dhammasattha Literature Transmitted in Chittagong and Arakan." *Journal of Burma Studies* 19, no. 2 (2015): 407–44.

Leider, Jacques P. "Forging Buddhist Credentials as a Tool of Legitimacy and Ethnic Identity: A Study of Arakan's Subjection in Nineteenth-Century Burma." *Journal of the Economic and Social History of the Orient* 51, no. 3 (2008): 409–59.

——. *King Aulangmintaya's Golden Letter to King George II (7 May 1756): The Story of an Exceptional Manuscript and the Failure of a Diplomatic Overture*. Hannover: Gottfried Wilhelm Leibniz Bibliothek, 2009.

——. *Le Royaume d'Arakan, Birmanie: Son histoire politique entre le début du XV<sup>e</sup> et la fin du XVII<sup>e</sup> siècle*. Paris: Ecole française d'Extrême-Orient, 2004.

——. "These Buddhist Kings with Muslim Names: A Discussion of Muslim Influence in the Mrauk U Period." In *Études birmanes en hommage à Denise Bernot*, 189–215. Paris: EFEO, 1998.

Le Strange, Guy, trans. *The Geographical Part of the Nuzhat al-Qulub, Composed by Hamdallah Mustawfi of Qazwin*. Leiden: Brill, 1919.

Llewellyn-Jones, Rosie. "Indian Travellers in Nineteenth-Century England." *Indo-British Review* 18 (1990): 137–41.

Lieberman, Victor. *Burmese Administrative Cycles: Anarchy and Conquest, c. 1580–1760*. Princeton, NJ: Princeton University Press, 1984.

———. *Strange Parallels: Southeast Asia in Global Context, c. 800–1830*. 2 vols. Cambridge: Cambridge University Press, 2003–9.

Lombard, Denys, and Jean Aubin, eds. *Marchands et hommes d'affaires asiatiques dans l'Océan Indien et la Mer de Chine, XIIIᵉ–XXᵉ siècles*. Paris: EHESS, 1988. Trans. as *Asian Merchants and Businessmen in the Indian Ocean and the China Sea*. Delhi: Oxford University Press, 2000.

Lopez, Donald. *From Stone to Flesh: A Short History of the Buddha*. Chicago: University of Chicago Press, 2013.

Marcinkowski, M. Ismail. *From Isfahan to Ayutthaya: Contacts between Iran and Siam in the Seventeenth Century*. Singapore: Pustaka Nasional, 2005.

Meilink Roelofsz, Marie A. P. *Asian Trade and European Influence in the Indonesian Archipelago between 1500 and about 1630*. The Hague: Nijhoff, 1962.

Micallef, Roberta, and Sunil Sharma, eds. *On the Wonders of Land and Sea: Persianate Travel Writing*. Cambridge, MA: Ilex Foundation, 2013.

Mikhail, Alan. *The Animal in Ottoman Egypt*. Oxford: Oxford University Press, 2013.

Mohiuddin, Momin. *The Chancellery and Persian Epistolography under the Mughals*. Calcutta: Iran Society, 1971.

Moreton, Timothy. *Dark Ecology: For a Logic of Future Coexistence*. New York: Columbia University Press, 2016.

Mottahedeh, Roy. "'Aja'ib in *The Thousand and One Nights*." In Richard Hovanisian, Georges Sabagh, and Fedwa Malti-Douglas, eds., *The Thousand and One Nights in Arabic Literature and Society*, 29–39. Cambridge: Cambridge University Press, 1996.

Mukherjee, Rila, ed. *Pelagic Passageways: The Northern Bay of Bengal before Colonialism*. Delhi: Primus Books, 2011.

Myint U, Thant. *The Making of Modern Burma*. Cambridge: Cambridge University Press, 2001.

Pal, Pratapaditya. *Elephants and Ivories in South Asia*. Los Angeles: Los Angeles County Museum of Art, 1981.

Peacock, A. C. S., and Annabel Teh Gallop, eds. *From Anatolia to Aceh: Ottomans, Turks, and Southeast Asia*. Oxford: Oxford University Press, 2015.

Peacock, A. C. S., and D. G. Tor. *Medieval Central Asia and the Persianate World: Iranian Tradition and Islamic Civilisation*. London: I. B. Tauris, 2017.

Pello, Stefano. *Tutiyan-i Hind: Specchi identitari e proiezioni cosmopolite indo-persiane (1650–1856)*. Florence: Società editrice fiorentina, 2012.

Pertsch, Wilhelm. *Die Handschriften-Verzeichnisse der Königlichen Bibliothek zu Berlin*. Berlin: A. Asher and Co., 1888.

Phayre, Arthur P. "The Coins of Arakan." *Journal of the Asiatic Society of Bengal* 15 (1846): 232–40.

———. *Coins of Arakan, of Pegu, and of Burma*. London: Trubner and Company, 1882.

———. *History of Burma, Including Burma Proper, Pegu, Taungu, Tenasserim, and Arakan*. London: Trubner and Company, 1883.

———. "On the History of Arakan." *Journal of the Asiatic Society of Bengal* 1 (1844): 23–52.

*Philosophical Transactions Giving Some Account of the Present Undertakings, Studies, and Labours of the Ingenious, in Many Considerable Parts of the World.* Vol. 53. London: Royal Society, 1764.

Piemontese, A. M. "Le submersible Alexandrin dans l'abysse, selon Amir Khusrau." In Laurence Harf-Lancner et al., eds., *Alexandre le Grand dans les littératures occidentales et proche-orientales*, 253–71. Nanterre: Centre des sciences de la littérature de l'université Paris X, 1999.

Pollock, Sheldon. *The Language of the Gods in the World of Men: Sanskrit, Culture, and Power in Premodern India.* Berkeley: University of California Press, 2006.

Pomeranz, Kenneth. *The Great Divergence: China, Europe, and the Making of the Modern World Economy.* Princeton, NJ: Princeton University Press, 2000.

Prain, D. "A Sketch of the Life of Francis Hamilton (Once Buchanan), Some Time Superintendent of the Honourable Company's Botanic Gardens at Calcutta." *Annals of the Royal Botanic Garden* 10, no, 2 (1905): i–lxxv.

Raj, Kapil. *Relocating Modern Science: Circulation and the Construction of Knowledge in South Asia and Europe, 1650–1900.* London: Palgrave, 2007.

Raman, Bhavani. *Document Raj: Writing and Scribes in Early Colonial South India.* Chicago: University of Chicago Press, 2012.

Rangarajan, Mahesh. *Fencing the Forest: Conservation and Ecological Change in India's Central Provinces, 1860–1914.* Delhi: Oxford University Press, 1996.

Reid, Anthony. *Southeast Asia in the Age of Commerce, 1450–1680.* Vol. 1, *The Lands below the Winds.* New Haven, CT: Yale University Press, 1988.

Ricci, Ronit. *Islam Translated: Literature, Conversion, and the Arabic Cosmopolis of South and Southeast Asia.* Chicago: University of Chicago Press, 2011.

Richards, John F. *The Unending Frontier: An Environmental History of the Early Modern World.* Berkeley: University of California Press, 2003.

Rickfels, M. C. *Jogjakarta under Sultan Mangkubumi, 1749–1792.* Oxford: Oxford University Press, 1974.

———. *Mystic Synthesis in Java: A History of Islamization from the Fourteenth to the Early Nineteenth Centuries.* Norwalk, CT: East Bridge, 2006.

———. *Seen and Unseen Worlds in Java: History, Literature, and Islam in the Court of Pakubuwana II, 1726–1749.* Honolulu: University of Hawai'i Press, 1998.

Rieu, Charles. *Catalogue of the Persian Manuscripts in the British Museum.* 3 vols. London: Longmans and Co., 1879–83.

Rocher, Rosanne. *Orientalism, Poetry, and Millenium: The Checkered Life of Nathaniel Brassey Halhed, 1751–1830.* Delhi: Motilal Banarsidass, 1983.

Said, Edward. *Orientalism.* New York: Vintage, 1978.

Sankhdher, B. M. "Mirza Abu Talib Khan, His Life and Works." *Islamic Culture* 44 (1970): 245–48.

Schiebinger, Londa. *Plants and Empire: Colonial Bioprospecting in the Atlantic World.* Cambridge, MA: Harvard University Press, 2007.

Schiebinger, Londa, and Claudia Swan, eds. *Colonial Botany: Science, Commerce, and Politics in the Early Modern World.* Philadelphia: University of Pennsylvania Press, 2004.

Schimmel, Annemarie. *The Empire of the Great Mughals: History, Art, and Culture.* London: Reaktion Books, 2004.

Scott, James C. *The Art of Not Being Governed: An Anarchist History of Upland Southeast Asia.* New Haven, CT: Yale University Press, 2009.

Sharma, Sunil. *Amir Khusraw: The Poet of Sufis and Sultans.* Oxford: Oneworld, 2005.

———. *Mughal Arcadia: Persian Literature in an Indian Court.* Cambridge, MA: Harvard University Press, 2017.

Sin, Ba. "The Coming of Islam to Burma, down to 1700." *Bulletin of the Burma Historical Commission* 1 (1963): 1–19.

Sivasundaram, Sujit. *Islanded: Britain, Sri Lanka and the Bounds of an Indian Ocean Colony.* Chicago: University of Chicago Press, 2013.

Skaria, Ajay. *Hybrid Histories: Forests, Frontiers and Wildness in Western India.* Delhi: Oxford University Press, 1998.

Skinner, C., ed. and trans. *Hikayat Perintah Negeri Benggala,* by Ahmad Rijaluddin. The Hague: Nijhoff, 1982.

Snouck-Hurgronje, Christiaan. *The Achehnese.* Trans. A. W. S. O'Sullivan. 2 vols. 1893–94. Leiden: Brill, 1906.

Sohrabi, Naghmeh. *Taken for Wonder: Nineteenth-Century Travel Accounts from Iran to Europe.* Oxford: Oxford University Press, 2012.

Spooner, Brian, and William Hanway. *Literacy in the Persianate World: Writing and the Social Order.* Philadelphia: University of Pennsylvania Museum of Anthropology and Archaeology, 2012.

Stoler, Ann Laura. *Along the Archival Grain: Epistemic Anxieties and Colonial Common Sense.* Princeton, NJ: Princeton University Press, 2008.

———, ed. *Imperial Debris: On Ruins and Ruination.* Durham: Duke University Press, 2013.

Storey, C .A. *Persian Literature: A Bio-Bibliographical Survey.* Vol. 1, part 2. London: Luzac and Company, 1972.

Subrahmanyam, Sanjay. "And a River Runs through It: The Mrauk U Kingdom and Its Bay of Bengal Context." In Jos Gommans and Jacques Leider, eds., *The Maritime Frontier of Burma: Exploring Political, Cultural, and Commercial Interaction in the Indian Ocean World, 1200–1800,* 107–26. Amsterdam: KITLV Press, 2002.

———. "Connected Histories: Notes towards a Reconfiguration of Early Modern Eurasia." *Modern Asian Studies* 31, no. 3 (1997): 735–62.

———. *Courtly Encounters: Translating Courtliness and Violence in Early Modern Eurasia.* Cambridge, MA: Harvard University Press, 2012.

————. *Europe's India: Words, People, Empires, 1500–1800*. Cambridge, MA: Harvard University Press, 2017.

————. *Explorations in Connected History: From the Tagus to the Ganges*. Oxford: Oxford University Press, 2005.

————. *Explorations in Connected History: Mughals and Franks*. Oxford: Oxford University Press, 2005.

————. *Improvising Empire: Portuguese Trade and Settlement in the Bay of Bengal, 1500–1700*. Delhi: Oxford University Press, 1990.

————. "Iranians Abroad: Intra-Asian Elite Migration and Early Modern State Formation." *Journal of Asian Studies* 51, no. 2 (1992).

————. *Three Ways to Be Alien: Travails and Encounters in the Early Modern World*. Waltham, MA: Brandeis University Press, 2011.

Tagliacozzo, Eric. *The Longest Journey: Southeast Asians and the Pilgrimage to Mecca*. Oxford: Oxford University Press, 2013.

Tavakoli-Targhi, Mohamad. "Early Persianate Modernity." In Sheldon Pollock, ed., *Forms of Knowledge in Early Modern Asia: Explorations in the Intellectual History of India and Tibet, 1500–1800*, 257–87. Durham, NC: Duke University Press, 2011.

————. *Refashioning Iran: Orientalism, Occidentalism and Historiography*. Basingstoke: Palgrave, 2001.

Teltscher, Kate. *The High Road to China: George Bogle, the Panchen Lama, and the First British Expedition to Tibet*. New York: Farrar, Straus and Giroux, 2007.

Tibbetts, G. R., Shawkat Toorawa, G. Ferrand, G. S. P. Freeman-Grenville, and F. Vire. "Wakwak." In *Encyclopaedia of Islam*, 2nd ed., vol. 11, 103–9. Leiden: Brill, 2013.

Tin, U. *The Royal Administration of Burma*. Trans. Euan Bagshawe. Bangkok: Ava Publishing House, 2001.

Toorawa, Shawkat. "Waq al-Waq: Fabulous, Fabular, Indian Ocean (?) Islands." *Emergences* 10, no. 2 (2000): 387–402.

Trautmann, Thomas R. *Elephants and Kings: An Environmental History*. Chicago: University of Chicago Press, 2015.

Truschke, Audrey. *Culture of Encounters: Sanskrit at the Mughal Court*. New York: Columbia University Press, 2016.

van Galen, Stephan. "Arakan and Bengal: The Rise and Decline of the Mrauk-U Kingdom (Burma) from the Fifteenth to the Seventeenth Century." PhD dissertation, Leiden University, 2008.

van Leur, Jacob C. *Indonesian Trade and Society*. The Hague: Van Hoeve, 1955.

van Schendel, Willem. *The Bengal Borderland: Beyond State and Nation in South Asia*. London: Anthem Press, 2005.

Vlekke, Bernard H. M. *Nusantara: A History of Indonesia*. 1943. The Hague: Van Hoeve, 1960.

Ware, Anthony, and Costas Laoutides. *Myanmar's "Rohingya" Conflict*. Oxford: Oxford University Press, 2018.

Westcoat, James L., Jr., and Joachim Wolschke-Bulmahn, eds. *Mughal Gardens:*

*Sources, Places, Representations, and Prospects.* Washington, DC: Dumbarton Oaks Research Library and Collection, 1996.

Wright, Denis. *The Persians amongst the English: Episodes in Anglo-Persian History.* London: I. B. Tauris, 1985.

Yegar, Moshe. *The Muslims of Burma: The Study of a Minority Group.* Wiesbaden: Otto Harrassowitz, 1972.

Yusufi, Ghulam Husayn. *Farhang-i Khurasan.* Mashhad: Idara-yi Farhang Daftar-i Nashriya-yi Farhang, 1964.

Zan, U Shwe. *The Golden Mrauk-U: An Ancient Capital of Rakhine.* Yangon: Nine Nines Press, 1997.

# INDEX

Dukkanthein Paya, xi-xii, 179
Dupleix, Joseph, 115-116, 78-79

East India Company (British): and Asiatic
  Society of Bengal, 2, 6, 8, 13, 17, 24, 51,
  53, 55, 117, 120, 134, 151-153, 169; conquest of Bengal, 6, 28, 151; embassy to
  the Burmese Kingdom, 15-16, 73-76,
  85-111; *munshis* and scribes, 2, 8-9,
  13-14, 17, 25-27, 49, 55, 105, 134, 137,
  146, 150-154, 159, 168-170; origins and
  rule in India, 7, 15; rivalries with French
  East India Company, 42-43, 66-67,
  78-79, 84, 95-96, 104-105-106, 114-
  116; wars against Tipu Sultan and the
  Kingdom of Mysore, 10, 15, 42, 55, 60,
  79, 95-96, 104
eclipses, 73, 99, 101-102
elephants: and kingship and sovereignty, 12,
  15, 24, 62-64, 68, 80-81, 84, 102, 108,
  127-128, 144-145, 161, 163, 166-167; in
  the Burmese Kingdom, 51, 62-64, 81,
  108, 127-128, 145; in Theravada Buddhism, 63-64, 80, 122, 127, 161, 163-164,
  166-167; in the teak trade, 66, 112 ; ivory,
  77, 83, 93, 109, 133, 141, 144-145, 167;
  forest habitat, 24, 51, 62-64, 68, 127-128,
  144-145; "Lord of the White Elephant,"
  60, 62, 64, 80, 127, 166; *mahouts*, 63, 128;
  methods of capturing, 63, 126-128,
  127*fig.*; royal processions, 90, 102-103 ;
  white elephant, 24, 60, 62-64, 80, 108,
  127, 161, 163-164, 166-167

Farang, 7, 36, 38-40, 54
*Farhang* of Isfahan, 171
Farhad Mirza Muʿtamad al-Dawla, 170
*farman:* 140, 142-143; of Bodawpaya,
  108-109; of King Chandrawizaya Raja,
  xiii, 137-146, 138-139*figs.*; trade and
  commercial *farman*, 143, 209n28
Fath ʿAli Khan Qajar, 54
Forchhammer, Emil, 179, 184-185
Fort William College, 147

Ganges River, 41, 50, 85-86, 132, 148-149, 153
Gautama Buddha: asceticism and attain-
  ment of nirvana, 122, 135, 158-159;

Buddha Thakur, 155-156, 161-162;
  footprint 122-123, 123*fig.*; Hazrat-i
  Dawwud Payghambar, 157; images and
  idols of, 16, 102, 120, 129-30, 155; in
  Persian translations of Pali texts, 151-
  168; legend of flight to Arakan, 82, 129
  132, 155 ; past lives and incarnations, 17,
  127, 135, 161-167; Mahamuni image, 102,
  129-30, 130*fig.*, 132, 134, 155-156; names
  for, 155-157, 161-162; relics of, 92, 122-
  124, 129, 132, 155, 183; Vessantara jataka,
  161, 163-164, 166-167
*Glass Palace Chronicle*, 128

Hafiz, 43
Haft ʿIqlim/Seven Climes, 158
Hajj U Bein, 175, 177
Hajji Mirza Muhammad ʿAli Isfahani, 171
Halhed, Nathaniel, 151
Haydar ʿAli, 79
Hazrat-i Dawwud Payghambar, 157
*hikayat*, 25, 31, 34, 135, 161, 163, 167
*Hikayat Iskandar Zulkarnain*, 31
Hodgson, Marshall, 2-4
Hope, John, 86, 118
*hti*, 90-93, 90*fig.*
Hughli River, 29, 42, 84, 149
Hyderabad, 7, 15, 51-52, 54, 56, 59-60,174

Indian Ocean: boundaries of, xvi*map*, 2,
  4-5, 8, 10-11, 13, 22-25; cowries, 32,
  46-48, 133; described in *Shigarfnama*,
  28-36; described in *Masir-i Talibi*,42-48; described in *Tuhfat al-ʿAlam*,
  56-60; historiography and Southeast
  Asia, 5; in Indo-Persian travel writing, 2,
  8-11, 13-15, 21-28, 42-50, 56-60; islands
  and archipelagos, 21-50; monsoons, 14,
  16, 22, 45, 51, 59, 62, 66-67, 73, 76, 91, 93,
  99, 112-115, 124, 119, 141-143, 169;
  Southeast Asian littorals and kingdoms
  of, 6, 8, 14, 16, 22-25; wonders of, 2, 8,
  22-25; *zirbad*/"lands below the winds,"
  14, 22, 33, 51, 59, 62, 169
Indonesian Archipelago, 2, 5, 35, 78, 138
Indo-Persian: Indo-Persian world, 2-7,
  9-10, 23, 33, 60-62, 144, 163; Persian
  language, 2-7, 10, 23, 49, 53, 66, 74, 80,

157–161; in the Bengal borderlands, 76, 108, 134, 137–140, 150; manuscripts, 135, 137, 153, 164, 168; piracy, 149–150

Mahamuni image, 102, 129–30, 130*fig.*, 132, 134, 155–156

mahouts, 63, 128

Malay Archipelago, 4–5, 14, 31, 33–36, 43, 45, 47–49, 133

Maldives, 29, 32, 133

Mandalay, 117, 171, 175, 177

Manrique, Sebastien, 133

Marathas, 79, 96, 153, 177

*Masir-i Talibi*, 14–15, 21, 37–49

*masjid-i biku*, 161

Mecca, 54, 149, 159

Melaka, 31, 33–36, 43, 45

microhistory, 11, 13–14, 16, 114, 170

Mingun, 80, 101

Min Saw Mon Narameikhla/Sulayman Shah, 132–133, 140

Mir 'Abd al-Latif Khan, 15, 51–69, 57*fig. See also Tuhfat al-'alam*

Mir 'Alam, 52, 59–60

Mir Ja'far 'Ali Khan, 27

"mirrors for princes," 54

Mir Sadiq 'Ali, 159–160

Mirza Abu Talib Khan, 14–15, 21–22, 36–50, 39*fig.*, 53, 55, 60, 147. *See also Masir-i Talibi*

Mirza I'tisam al-Din, 14, 22, 25–36, 27*fig.*, 38. *See also Shigarfnama-yi vilayet*

Mirza Zinal Abideen Kermany, 52–53

Moguls, 1, 80, 94, 96, 174

Mogul Shia Masjid, 174

Mogul Street, 174

Mon Hanthawaddy Kingdom, 7, 24, 46, 50, 62, 78–80, 89–90, 92–93, 101, 119, 134, 173

monsoons: climate, 45, 62, 67, 115; "lands below the winds," 14, 22, 51, 59, 169; monsoon forests, 16, 112–114, 119; rice harvest and, 91; seasons, 45, 66, 73, 76, 91, 93, 99, 112, 114, 124, 141–143; teak and, 114–115

Mrauk U: Bay of Bengal and, 16, 133–134; Buddhist temples, 133, 179*fig.*; Burmese conquest of, 7, 16, 76–78, 80–84, 101, 121, 129, 132, 134, 136, 146; Bengal bor-

derlands, 76–78, 105, 108, 111, 134, 137, 150–151; cultural and religious heterogeneity, 152–153; East India Company reconnaissance on, 146–154; *farman* of Chandrawizaya Raja, 137–146, 138–139*figs.*; historiography of, 136; Indo-Persian culture in, 23, 132–137, 152–153; Indian Ocean connections, 133–134; in Mughal travel writing and chronicles, 24, 62, 146–149; Kaladan River, 132, 147, 151; Mahamuni image, 129–130, 130*fig.*,134; mosques in, xi, 133, 179, 215n14; Murray's *munshis* and, 134–137, 151–168; Persian usage in the court of, 23, 137–146; royal city and Kingdom of, 5, 16, 23, 132–137, 154–155; ruins of, 178–185; Theravada Buddhism and syncretism in, 17, 134–136, 151–168. *See also* Arakan

Mughal Empire: and the Indo-Persian world, 3; contacts with Mrauk U Kingdom, 16, 133–134, 140, 142, 144, 147–148; disintegration and waning of, 2, 6, 15, 28, 51, 55, 69, 169, 174; Indian Ocean frontiers of, 13, 15–16, 22, 49–50, 52, 69, 147–148; Mughal imperium, 7, 80; Persian as courtly language of, 23, 53, 74, 80, 138, 152, 170

Muhammad 'Ali Hazin Lahiji, 55

Muhammad Baqir Majlisi, 52

Muhammad ibn Rabi, 23–24

Muhammad Qasim Hindu Shah "Firishta," 24, 148

munshis: of the Burmese Empire, 6–7, 55, 78–85, 94–96, 98, 146; of the East India Company and Asiatic Society, 9, 13–14, 17, 25–27, 49, 55, 105, 134, 137, 146, 150–154, 159, 168–170

Murshidabad, 40

Mysore Kingdom, 10, 42, 55, 65–66, 79, 95–96, 104, 147

Nadir Shah Afshar, 40

Naf River, 76

*nakhuda*, 84, 142, 144

Nandaw Paya, 181–182

Naqshbandi, 10, 96, 153, 175–176

Narai, 5, 23, 138

Negrais, 78–79
Nicobar Islands, 10, 14, 21, 43–49
Nile to Oxus Zone, 3–4
nirvana, 16, 121–122, 135, 156, 159–160, 163, 166–167
Nizami, 30
nizam of Hyderabad, 7, 52, 56, 60
Noah's Flood, 56, 58, 152, 157,

Orientalism: in Indo-Persian writings on Southeast Asia, 2, 13, 15, 17, 21, 24, 51, 69, 134, 151, 168; in the East India Company and Asiatic Society of Bengal, 2, 13, 17, 24, 37, 51, 74, 85, 134, 146–147, 151–152, 168
Ottoman Empire, 3, 54, 149

padishah: Indo-Persian notions of kingship and sovereignty, 52; raja and, 15, 52, 62; kings of Mrauk U, 132–133, 208n23; title of Southeast Asian sovereigns, 15, 23, 32, 34, 52, 62, 64, 67, 141, 155
*Padmavati*, 134
Pagan, 7, 99–100, 129
Pali: and Buddhism, 121–122, 134–137, 151–168; into Persian, 16–17, 134–137, 151–168; language, script, and texts, 74, 122, 133, 135, 137, 139, 142,146, 153–156, 158–159, 161–162, 164, 168
*Panj Tarani Mantra*, 156
*parabeik*, 97, 137, 142
Parahla, 184–185, 184*fig.*
Parsi merchants, 94–95, 98, 105, 174
Pegu: arrival of Islam to, 34, 36; Indian Ocean littorals, islands, and *zirbad*, 29, 33–34, 45–46; in Indo-Persian literature 10, 23–24, 34, 36, 45–46, 51–69; in the Konbaung dynasty, 44, 62–65, 77–81, 83–84, 89–90, 92–93, 101–102, 109–110, 116, 130 ; royal city of Mon Hantha-waddy Kingdom, 7, 24, 50, 62, 78–80, 101, 119, 133, 141, 143, 173; Shwe Mawdaw Paya, 65, 90, 90*fig.*, 91, 124
Persian language: and Southeast Asia, 1–7, 10, 49, 66, 74, 80, 84–85, 87–89, 103–105, 138–139; and the Mughal Empire, 23, 53, 74, 80, 138, 152, 170; as an inter-Asian language, 1–7, 10, 66, 74, 80,

84–85, 87–89, 103–105, 138–139; Pali translations, 134–135, 151–152, 154, 161, 169–170
Persianate and Persianate world, 3–4; 187–188nn6,7; conceptions of kingship and sovereignty in, 52, 140; Southeast Asia Qazi and, 4–6, 10, 14, 75–76, 144–146; views of Buddhism, 135, 168
Persian Gulf: and the Indian Ocean world, xvi*map*, 15, 23, 52–53, 58, 60; port and shrine cities of, 52, 54, 56
piracy, 106, 146, 148–151
Pir Badr/Badr al-Din Awliya, 180–181, 184. *See also* Badr Maqam
*Plantae asiaticae rariores*, 125
Pondicherry, 78–79, 115
Portuguese traders, 78, 94–95, 98, 110, 133, 147–149
pundits, 15, 81, 87, 94, 151

Qadiri, 10, 175–176, 182
Qaf, 30
Qajar dynasty, 54, 60, 64, 171
*qasida*, 10, 96
Qazi Ghulam Qasim Mihri, 9–10, 96

Rakhang/Roshang, 152, 154–155
Rakhine State (Arakan), xi-xii, 5, 135, 178; Muslims in, 178; "Rakhine Quarter" of Mandalay, 175; ruins of mosques and shrines in, 173, 178–185. *See also* Arakan
Ramni, 23
Rangoon: Armenian merchants in, 88–89, 94–99, 104–105, 171, 174; Dagon formerly, 79, 92; dargah of Bahadur Shah Zafar, 1, 174; East India Company Embassy's arrival in, 87–89; English resident in, 109–111; in the early Konbaung period, 92–99; government of, 88–89; merchant communities in, 94–99; Moguls, 1, 80, 94, 96, 174; Mogul Shia Masjid, 174; Mogul Street, 174; Shwe Dagon Paya, 1, 65, 87, 92–93, 174; Sule Pagoda, 174; Surti Sunni Jama Masjid, 174; trade of 83–84, 93–97
Rangoon River, 67, 87
*rawali*, 153–154, 156, 158
*Rawzat al-Tahirin*, 24, 33–34

rhinoceros, 24, 62–63

Richardson, David, 41–42

Rohingya Muslims: persecution, stateless-
ness, and migration, xi, 172, 180, 215n16;
historical connections to the city of
Rakhang/Roshang and Persian etymol-
ogy, 152, 154–155; in Sittwe, 180–181;
Rohingya mosques and shrines, 180–181

Roxburgh, William, 118

*Ruznama-yi Iran*, 171


*safarnama* genre, 6, 14, 53–54, 111

Safavid Empire, 3, 23–24, 52, 138

*Safina-yi Sulaymani*, 23–24

Said, Edward, 9

*sajda*, 65

Sandaw Paya, 181, 183

Sangermano, Vincentius, 101, 116

Sanskrit, 47, 55, 87, 117, 122, 151–152, 155, 177,
179

Santikan Mosque, xi, 133, 179, 215n14

Saya Gyi U Nu Muhammad Qasim, 177

Sayyid ʿAbdallah Shushtari, 55

Sayyid Nimatallah Jazayiri, 52

Sayyid Pak, 34

Sayyid Riza Shushtari, 52

"Sea Gypsies," 87

*Sea Horse*, 85, 87–89, 110, 131

Seringapatam, 10, 42, 55, 60, 96

Shafi Khan Dargah, 180–181, 181*fig.*

Shah ʿAlam II, xii, 27–28

Shah ʿAzizallah Bukhari Qalandar, 17,
132–137, 151–168

Shah Shujaʿ, xi, 149, 179

Shaista Khan, 149

Shan Hills, xii, 65, 75, 81, 114

*Shigarfnama-yi vilayet*, 14, 22, 25–36,
192n15

*shiko*, 64–65, 106–107

Shwe Dagon Paya, 1, 65, 87, 92–93, 174

Shwe Kyaung, 182, 182*fig.*

Shwe Mawdaw Paya, 65, 90, 90*fig.*, 91, 124

*Shwepandawgyi*, 125–126, 126*fig.*

Shittaung Paya,179

Shore, Sir John, 73, 81, 83, 85, 105

Shushtar, 52, 54

Sindhi Khan, 179

Sinero/Maha Meru, 159

Singey Bey, 16, 87, 90, 90*fig.*, 102, 106, 107
*fig.*, 110, 110*fig.*, 112–131, 120–121*figs.*,
123*fig.*, 126–127*figs.*, 130*fig.*

Singh (mythical winged lion), 167

Sittwe, 178, 180–181, 184

Sorrel, George, 84

Stewart, Charles, 37, 44, 78, 147–148

Sufism: and Theravada Buddhism in
Arakan, 17, 135, 137, 151–168,184–185;
brotherhoods and networks, 10, 96, 153,
175–176; dargah, 1, 17, 171, 174–178,
180–185; Sufi saints and conversion in
Southeast Asia, 4, 34–36; Shah
ʿAzizallah Bukhari Qalandar, 17, 132–
137, 151–168; wandering and asceticism
in the wilderness, 11, 135, 161–164,
167–168

Sule Pagoda, 174

Sumatra, 4–5, 10, 23, 29, 31, 96, 133

sumptuary laws, 67, 114

Surti Sunni Jama Masjid, 174

Symes, Michael, 15–16, 43–44, 55, 73–76,
85–111, 110*fig.*, 119, 122, 129, 146. *See also
Account of an Embassy to the Kingdom of
Ava*

Syriam, 78–79, 97–98, 115

Swinton, Archibald, 27–28


Tahir Muhammad Sabzavari, 24, 33. *See
also Rawzat al-Tahirin*

*Tarikh-i Firishta*, 24, 148

teak trade, 66–67, 112, 114–117, 146

Thailand: Ayutthaya Kingdom, 5–7, 23–24,
80, 101, 138; relation to the Burmese
Kingdom, 43, 77, 80, 101, 138, 184

Thandwe, 180, 182–185

Theravada Buddhism: and Southeast Asian
empires, 3, 129, 133, 138; customs and
rituals, 152–160; elephants and 63–64,
80, 122, 127, 161, 163–164, 166–167; in
Arakan, 17, 129, 133, 139, 151–168; Indo-
Persian perceptions of, 151–168; Mahamuni image, 102, 129–30, 130*fig.*, 132,
134, 155–156; *jataka*, 17, 135, 161–168;
nirvana, 16, 121–122, 135, 156, 159–160,
163, 166–167; past lives and incarnations
of Buddha, 127, 135, 161–167; *rawali*,
153–154, 156, 158; relics and idols, 16, 92,

Theravada Buddhism *(continued)*
102, 120, 122–124, 129–130, 132, 155, 183;
syncretism, 133–135, 137, 152–160, 164,
178; texts, 17, 55, 151–168
Tipu Sultan: and the Indo-Persian world, 7;
contacts with the Burmese Kingdom,
10, 65–66, 95–96; *nawab* of the Kingdom of Mysore, 10, 42, 55, 65–66, 79,
95–96, 104, 147; Seringapatam, 10,
42, 55, 60, 96; son of Haydar 'Ali,
79; wars and resistance against East
India Company, 10, 15, 42, 55, 60, 79,
95–96, 104
travel writing: genre, 53–56; Indo-Persian,
6–11, 14; *safarnama*, 6–11, 14, 53–54, 111
*Tuhfat al-'alam*, 15, 51–69, 196n6

Van Reede, Henrik, 113
*Venture of Islam*, 3–4

Vessantara jataka, 161, 163–164, 166–167
Vishnu, 125–126, 152

Wallich, Nathaniel, 124
Waq Waq, 23
Wesali Kingdom, 132
whales, 32–33, 57
white elephant, 24, 60, 62–64, 80, 108, 127,
161, 163–164, 166–167
Wood, Thomas, 86, 92, 99, 101–102

Zabaj, 23
Zadi Pyin, 181–183, 183*fig.*
Zakariya Qazvini, 58. *See also 'aja'ib u
ghara'ib*
Zayn al-Abidin Shirvani, 170
Zinat Begum Mahal, 1
*zirbad*/"lands below the winds," 14, 22, 33,
51, 59, 62, 169

THE CALIFORNIA WORLD HISTORY LIBRARY

*Edited by Edmund Burke III, Kenneth Pomeranz, and Patricia Seed*